W9-AHC-020

THE
LORD'S
WAY

THE
LORD'S
WAY

THE
LORD'S
WAY

DALLIN H. OAKS

Deseret Book Company
Salt Lake City, Utah

© 1991 Dallin H. Oaks

All rights reserved. No part of this book may be reproduced in any form or by any means without permission in writing from the publisher, Deseret Book Company, P.O. Box 30178, Salt Lake City, Utah 84130. This work is not an official publication of The Church of Jesus Christ of Latter-day Saints. The views expressed herein are the responsibility of the author and do not necessarily represent the position of the Church or of Deseret Book Company.

Deseret Book is a registered trademark of Deseret Book Company.

Library of Congress Cataloging-in-Publication Data

Oaks, Dallin H.
  The Lord's way / Dallin H. Oaks.
    p.   cm.
  Includes bibliographical references and index.
  ISBN 0-87579-578-1 (hard)
  ISBN 0-87579-960-4 (paper)
  1. Church of Jesus Christ of Latter-day Saints—Doctrines.
2. Mormon Church—Doctrines. 3. Christian life—Mormon authors.
I. Title.
BX8635.2.035   1991
230'.9332—dc20   91-30610
                                                       CIP

Printed in the United States of America

10 9   8   7   6   5   4   3   2   1

CONTENTS

Preface   vii

Introduction: God's Ways and Man's Ways   1

Chapter 1: Learning   16

Chapter 2: Reason and Revelation   45

Chapter 3: Signs and Science   77

Chapter 4: Care for the Poor   102

Chapter 5: Contention   138

Chapter 6: Litigation   153

Chapter 7: Criticism   189

Chapter 8: Church Discipline   209

Index   251

PREFACE

PREFACE

Some believe that ends justify means. If the result seems good, they have no interest in correcting (and perhaps no interest in even knowing) the means by which the result was obtained. This attitude repeats an ancient pattern. It appears in the earliest conflict described in the scriptures.

There came a time when the spirit children of God the Father needed to experience mortality in order to progress toward their ultimate destiny. The Father provided a plan. In opposition, Lucifer (Satan) proposed a radical modification. The difference between the Father's plan and Satan's modification persists in many alternatives we encounter in mortality.

The object of the Father's plan was "to bring to pass the immortality and eternal life" (sometimes called salvation) of all of his spirit children. (Moses 1:39.) He would create a world in which his children would receive mortality and exercise the agency (power of choice) he had given them. (Moses 4:3.) They would be tested "to see if they will do all

vii

things whatsoever the Lord their God shall command them."
(Abr. 3:25.)

The choices the children of God would make in the
exercise of their agency would be made in the face of opposition. (2 Ne. 2:16; D&C 29:39.) Some would make wrong
choices and be soiled by sin. The possibility of casualties
from wrong choices was the price of growth.

The Father's plan was costly and slow, but it offered a
genuine opportunity for his spirit children to achieve what
he desired for them — immortality and eternal life. To assure
immortality and to offer the opportunity of qualifying for
eternal life, the Father's plan provided a Savior, who would
redeem all from death and pay the price necessary for all
to be cleansed from sin on the conditions he prescribed.
(2 Ne. 9:19–24.)

In his proposed modification, Lucifer pretended to seek
the same outcome,* but he would use a different means.
He would save *all* the spirit children of God by eliminating
the possibility of sin. He would assure that result by re-
moving their power to choose. (Moses 4:1, 3.)

Lucifer's modification could not be accepted because his
proposed means were repugnant to the end sought to be
achieved. In the world of ends and means, ends are inex-
orably shaped by the means used to achieve them. The
objective of eternal life for the children of God could be
attained only by the methods God would approve. As he
has said in another setting, "It must needs be done in mine
own way." (D&C 104:16.)

Lucifer's methods could not achieve God's objective.
They would corrupt it. Saving everyone at the price of taking

---

* Lucifer only *pretended* to seek the same outcome. In contrast to Jesus Christ (the
premortal Beloved Son, who sought to further the work and glory of the Father),
Lucifer sought to obtain the Father's power for himself. (Moses 4:1–3; D&C 29:36.)

away everyone's agency would deny God's children the
growth toward eternal life they were intended to receive
from the creation of the world and their venture into mortality.

The adversary, Satan, is always at hand. Mirroring the
conflict in the premortal world, his opposition often pretends
to seek a desirable end, but he sponsors an alternative means
to achieve it. And most often, as in the premortal world,
Satan's method would corrupt the objective rather than attain it.

Unless we are alert, we are easily deceived by those who
praise and purport to pursue a worthy end, but who remain
obscure about the means used to achieve it. When it comes
to the work of the Lord and the attainment of his purposes,
it is not enough to obtain a good result — it must be done
in the right way.

This book discusses some instances in which the Lord's
way, as revealed in the scriptures and the teachings of the
living prophets, differs from the ways of the world, at least
as practiced in the western nations with which I am familiar.
It focuses on the ways — the procedures or methods — the
Lord has specified for us to achieve the destiny he has prescribed for his children.

A few of the ideas elaborated in chapters 1 and 2 were
briefly expressed in the last half of my general conference
address published in the May 1989 issue of the *Ensign*. The
portion of chapter 1 describing the forms and functions of
revelation was previously published in BYU's *1981–82 Fireside and Devotional Speeches of the Year*. Chapter 7, "Criticism," is an expanded version of a fireside talk published
in the February 1987 issue of the *Ensign*. I appreciate the
publishers' permissions to use those materials in this book,
and also the opportunity to quote from other authors in the

various publications cited in the endnotes. I am also grateful for the permission or indulgence of the writers of various letters I have quoted. I have chosen to omit their names, sometimes to preserve a confidence and other times to maintain consistency.

I am indebted to various friends who have examined and given valuable suggestions on drafts of different chapters of this book. I express special thanks to my secretary, Virginia Archer, who typed the seemingly endless drafts of these chapters with precision and good humor. Finally, and most importantly, I express appreciation to my eternal companion, June, for her support and patience during the long process of authorship.

While appreciative of all of the valuable assistance I have received, I must of course bear the responsibility for all that is said here. This book is a personal expression and is not an official statement of the doctrines or procedures of The Church of Jesus Christ of Latter-day Saints.

GOD'S WAYS AND MAN'S WAYS

A few years ago I heard an illuminating admission by a mission president. He was an educator by profession. When he left his professional position and took up his duties as a mission president, he brought large stacks of professional materials on training and leadership. He intended to use these materials to help his missionaries. At his first mission leadership meeting, he assigned several zone leaders to present some of these materials to the assembled missionaries.

As the meeting wore on, the mission president sensed that something important was missing. He realized, he told me later, that he was trying to accomplish his mission leadership training by following a professional model instead of by doing it in the Lord's way. He stopped a missionary in the middle of his presentation, apologized to him and to the group for making the wrong assignment, and asked a missionary to bear his testimony. As they went forward in

1

this new way, the Spirit of the Lord settled over the meeting. Testimonies and resolves were strengthened, and the necessary leadership training was given. The mission president had learned the importance of doing the Lord's work in the Lord's way. Each of us should learn that lesson.

The scriptures declare and illustrate that God's thoughts are not man's thoughts and God's ways are not man's ways. The Lord taught this principle through the prophet Isaiah: "For my thoughts are not your thoughts, neither are your ways my ways, saith the Lord. For as the heavens are higher than the earth, so are my ways higher than your ways, and my thoughts than your thoughts." (Isa. 55:8–9.)

Through the prophet/king Benjamin, the Lord told his people to believe in God and "believe that he has all wisdom, and . . . that man doth not comprehend all the things which the Lord can comprehend." (Mosiah 4:9.) In that same spirit, the apostle Paul exclaimed: "O the depth of the riches both of the wisdom and knowledge of God! how unsearchable are his judgments, and his ways past finding out!" (Romans 11:33; see also D&C 76:2.)

The Prophet Joseph Smith reminded us that "God dwells in eternity, and does not view things as we do."[1] That insight helps us understand why the Lord would refer to his great latter-day work as "bring[ing] to pass my act, my strange act, and perform[ing] my work, my strange work." (D&C 101:95.) It also helps us understand what the Lord said about the building of Zion: "Zion cannot be built up unless it is by the principles of the law of the celestial kingdom; otherwise I cannot receive her unto myself." (D&C 105:5.)

In directing how the Saints should provide for the poor, the Lord cautioned: "It must needs be done in mine own way." (D&C 104:16.) Another revelation assures us that God's promises will be fulfilled, but "it shall be in his own time, and in his own way, and according to his own will." (D&C 88:68.)

The Lord applied those principles in an instruction he gave to the Prophet after the loss of the 116 manuscript pages translated from the Book of Mormon: "The works, and the designs, and the purposes of God cannot be frustrated, neither can they come to naught. . . . Remember, remember that it is not the work of God that is frustrated, but the work of men." (D&C 3:1, 3.)

These are eternal principles, decreeing how all of God's work must be accomplished.

Those who believe in God should not find it difficult to accept these propositions — that his thoughts are higher than our thoughts, that he comprehends things we do not comprehend, that his ways are higher than our ways, and that his work "shall be in his own time, and in his own way." But in practice these are apparently difficult concessions for some to make and difficult principles for some to apply.

Many mortals have a myopic view of the power and position of God. As the brother of Jared observed, even the great power of God "looks small unto the understanding of men." (Ether 3:5.) In truth, many mortals — even some members of The Church of Jesus Christ of Latter-day Saints — are so shortsighted that they presume to judge the things of God by their own mortal reasoning. As Elder Neal A. Maxwell has observed: "Yes, we may acknowledge His overall plan but criticize His style, because He does things in His own way. . . . We would prefer that things be done in our way, even though our ways are much lower than His."[2]

I was helping my wife wash dishes on one occasion. (She would say one *rare* occasion.) She had baked nut bread. When I got to the pans, she said, "Don't try to wash those pans before you soak them in water. The residue is cooked on." Many of our erroneous ideas about the things of God and the procedures we should follow to accomplish his purposes are also "cooked on" by the heat and pressure of worldly traditions and professional practices. Those ideas will not yield to cleansing until they have been soaked in the living water of gospel principles.

Some mortals assume that God is subject to human limitations. Such an assumption limits understanding. Mortals can change their personal clock or calendar, but they cannot alter the workings of the solar system. They can change the language by which they describe or address God, but they have no power to alter the nature or purposes of God. They can try to impose their own timetable on divine actions, but to no avail. As explained to Abraham, the Lord God of Israel has his own method of reckoning time. (Abr. 3:4, 9; 5:13; see also Alma 40:8.) God's promises and words "are sure and shall not fail" (D&C 64:31), but all things must come to pass in his own due time (D&C 24:16; 64:32).

Some professionals expect that the practices and procedures of the Church will conform to the practices and procedures of their professions.[3] Others assume that the practices of the Church will follow the customs of the world. Some even seek to reconcile the Church and the world by assimilating the doctrines and practices of the Church to the beliefs and practices of the world.

The early members of the restored church received instructions on this subject. After mobs had driven the Saints from their homes in Jackson County, the Lord revealed that he had allowed these afflictions to come upon his people "in consequence of their transgressions." (D&C 101:2.) He told them through the Prophet Joseph Smith that because of these transgressions they needed to be chastened, adding, "He that exalteth himself shall be abased, and he that abaseth himself shall be exalted." (D&C 101:42.)

Then the Lord gave a parable to help them know his will "concerning the redemption of Zion." He told of a nobleman who gave his servants certain commandments and then left them in charge of a vineyard. For a time they followed his directions, but then they began to question the Lord's commandments, and eventually they substituted their own judgment on what would be best for the Lord and his vineyard. As a result, an enemy broke in and wasted the vineyard. Afterwards, the Lord of the vineyard called upon his servants and said, "Why! what is the cause of this great evil? Ought ye not to have done even as I commanded you?" The nobleman then instructed his servants on how they could have avoided the destruction of the vineyard by following his commandments. He concluded with a new command: "Go ye straightway, and do all things whatsoever I have commanded you." (D&C 101:43–60).

After giving this parable the Lord said: "Again, verily I say unto you, I will show unto you wisdom in me concerning all the churches, inasmuch as they are willing to be guided in a right and proper way for their salvation—that the work of the gathering together of my saints may continue, that I may build them up unto my name upon holy places; for the time of harvest is come, and my word must needs be fulfilled." (D&C 101:63–64.) In short, the Lord's servants must do the Lord's work in the Lord's way or their efforts will come to naught.

Just as there is a difference between mortals' ways of doing things and the Lord's way of doing things, so mortals must make significant changes in their ways of doing things when they move from worldly occupations to the perfor-

mance of Church callings. I experienced this when I was
called to full-time service in the Church.

My calling came while I was serving as a justice on the
Utah Supreme Court. As a public servant with continuing
public responsibilities, I could not appropriately leave my
judicial responsibilities immediately upon being called. Sensitive to that fact, the First Presidency said I should take the
time necessary to wind up my public responsibilities before
beginning my duties as an apostle. It required about three
weeks for me to complete the opinions I had been assigned
and to participate in decisions on other pending cases. During this time, before I assumed any church responsibilities,
I had ample time to contemplate the contrast between the
work I had been doing and the work I would be doing for
the rest of my life.

Counting my three years in law school, I had been a
member of the legal profession for thirty years. During that
time, I worked in almost every area in the profession: as
private practitioner, as government lawyer, as teacher, as
administrator, and as judge. I had extensive experience in
the learning, ways of thinking, and procedures of my profession. Along the way I also served on boards of directors of
large corporations (profit and nonprofit) and for five years
as chairman of the board of the Public Broadcasting Service.
As a result, I was familiar with the kinds of functions that
need to be performed in large organizations: financial, property management, personnel, future planning, communications, and so forth.

From my extensive contacts with General Authorities
during the nine years I served as president of Brigham Young
University, I knew that members of the Council of the Twelve
Apostles are assigned to assist in the administration of the
Church by performing many tasks with which I was already

familiar—the kinds of functions that must be performed by the leadership of any large corporation. And I knew that I might be asked to do some things of a legal nature. But I also knew that these assignments were only incidental to the calling of an apostle. The vital and unique responsibilities of that calling—to be a special witness of the Lord Jesus Christ, to hold and exercise sacred priesthood authority, and to be a leader in the ecclesiastical activities of the Church— were matters on which I had no special experience or qual- ifications.

During this period of introspection, contemplating the way I would spend the rest of my life, I asked myself what kind of apostle I would be. Would I be a lawyer who had been called to be an apostle, or would I be an apostle who used to be a lawyer? I concluded that the answer to this question depended upon whether I would try to shape my calling to my own personal qualifications and experience, or whether I would undertake the painful process of trying to shape myself to my calling.

Would I try to perform my calling in the world's ways, or would I try to determine and follow the Lord's ways?

I made up my mind that I would try to change myself to fit my calling, that I would try to measure up to the qualifications and spiritual stature of an apostle. That is a challenge for a lifetime.

This principle applies to all of us. In every area of the Church, there are wonderful men and women who are strug- gling to shape themselves to the dimensions of their callings, making the changes necessary to measure up to their as- signed responsibilities in the kingdom of our Lord and Savior, Jesus Christ.

In contrast, we have all seen examples of persons who have been unwilling to shape themselves to a new calling, but who have insisted on trying to make the calling conform to their own experience, preference, or comfort. We have seen teachers in church classes who have not taught the assigned subject, but have substituted the subject matter with which they are most familiar from their occupation or their recent reading. We have observed officers in various church organizations who have persisted in performing the duties of their callings according to the procedures of their own occupations. And we have seen speakers or others with church assignments who have used their positions as a way of serving a personal interest (such as gratifying their ego) rather than acting as servants of the Good Shepherd, who has called us to feed the flock of God.

"I won't change. You'll have to adapt to me." This is a powerful, all-purpose ideology. It is a familiar way of the world. It resists more than change. It resists learning, reformation, and repentance. It represents self-indulgence, if not self-worship. It demonstrates indifference to others, and it can lead to oppression. Indeed, it is the polar opposite of the qualities of humility, submissiveness, patience, temperance, long-suffering, brotherly kindness, faith, hope, charity, and love that qualify us for the work of God. (Alma 7:23–24; D&C 4:5–6.)

President Ezra Taft Benson gave another powerful explanation of the contrast between the Lord's way and the world's way: "The world works from the outside in. The world would take people out of the slums. Christ takes the slums out of people, and then they take themselves out of the slums. The world would mold men by changing their environment. Christ changes men, who then change their environment. The world would shape human behavior, but Christ can change human nature."[4]

Jesus taught his disciples that their ways should be different from the ways of the world. "Ye are the salt of the earth," he told them. "Ye are the light of the world." (Matt. 5:13–14.) Again and again he taught that his followers should be different.

In a vassal state held in bondage by the military power of the Roman Empire, the Lord taught that the meek should inherit the earth. (Matt. 5:5.)

To a people who were accustomed to seeing the "princes of the gentiles exercise dominion over them, and they that are great exercise authority upon them," Jesus taught: "It shall not be so among you: but whosoever will be great among you, let him be your minister; and whosoever will be chief among you, let him be your servant: even as the Son of man came not to be ministered unto, but to minister, and to give his life a ransom for many." (Matt. 20:26–28.)

To drive this lesson home, Jesus reminded them on another occasion that "he that is greatest among you shall be your servant." (Matt. 23:11; Mark 10:42–45; Luke 22:25–26.)

In the concluding days of his ministry, he told his apostles: "If ye were of the world, the world would love his own: but because ye are not of the world, but I have chosen you out of the world, therefore the world hateth you." (John 15:19.) And again: "I have given them thy word; and the world hath hated them, because they are not of the world, even as I am not of the world." (John 17:14.)

To followers who would be tempted to seek popular acclaim, Jesus declared, "Woe unto you, when all men shall speak well of you! for so did their fathers to the false prophets." (Luke 6:26.)

Less than a year after six members organized The Church of Jesus Christ, the Lord declared through his prophet: "Wherefore, I call upon the weak things of the world, those who are unlearned and despised, to thrash the nations by the power of my Spirit." (D&C 35:13.)

What a contrast to the world's way of proceeding by power, prominence, professionalism, and prestige!

There are many such contrasts between the world's ways and the directions the Lord has given to the restored church and its members.

Most Latter-day Saints live in countries whose lawmakers are popularly elected and who function by political coalitions and compromises. In contrast, the Lord instructed his church to "stand independent above all other creatures beneath the celestial world." (D&C 78:14.)

When he commanded latter-day saints to build a temple, the Lord declared that it should not be built "after the manner of the world, for I give not unto you that ye shall live after the manner of the world." (D&C 95:13.)

Just a few generations after popular sovereignty and majority rule had been established in a divinely inspired constitution of civil government, the Lord decreed that the decisions of the governing quorums of his church must be made in righteousness and must be unanimous. (D&C 107:27–30.) Church government is theocratic, not democratic. As Elder James E. Faust has explained, "This requirement of unanimity . . . ensures that God rules through the Spirit, not man through majority or compromise."[5]

To Latter-day Saints preoccupied with worldly possessions the Lord said, "Let them repent of . . . all their covetous desires, before me, saith the Lord; for what is property unto me?" (D&C 117:4.)

To a suffering Joseph Smith, held in a foul prison by the raw power of his enemies, the Lord gave these incongruous directions on the exercise of power: "No power or influence can or ought to be maintained by virtue of the priesthood, only by persuasion, by long-suffering, by gentleness and meekness, and by love unfeigned; by kindness, and pure knowledge, which shall greatly enlarge the soul without hypocrisy, and without guile." (D&C 121:41–42.)

Later, the Lord reaffirmed that his power must be obtained and exercised in different ways than earthly power: "And if any man shall seek to build up himself, and seeketh not my counsel, he shall have no power, and his folly shall be made manifest." (D&C 136:19.)

From dispensation to dispensation, the Lord has chosen his own spokesmen and designated his own methods to further his work. A scriptural commentary has noted, "The Lord prefers prophets to scholars, meekness to wealth, and simplicity to the magnificence and splendor of the world. Christ was born in a stable, not a Roman palace; his Apostles, with the exception of Judas, were unlearned fishermen of Galilee, their places of worship the hillsides and plains of Palestine."[6]

The apostle James stated the conclusion: "Know ye not that the friendship of the world is enmity with God? whosoever therefore will be a friend of the world is the enemy of God." (James 4:4.)

Contrasting ideas about power illustrate differences between the things of man and the things of God. Man tends to think of power in terms of what can affect earthly things, like transferring titles to land, toppling trees, or making tracks on the landscape. God's power can do all of that, but it also controls the often invisible but always long-lasting things of eternity. Rudyard Kipling captured the contrast between the temporary nature of mortal power and the enduring nature of God's power in these prophetic words, addressed to the British Empire:

Far-called, our navies melt away;
   On dune and headland sinks the fire.
Lo, all our pomp of yesterday
   Is one with Nineveh and Tyre!
Judge of the nations, spare us yet,
   Lest we forget, lest we forget.[7]

The chapters of this book illustrate the Lord's decree that his work must be done in his own way. They contrast the ways or methods of the Lord and his church and the ways or methods of the world.

Chapters 1 and 2 discuss learning by study (reason) and learning by faith (revelation). Both are necessary. Reason comes first, so it can serve as a threshold check on authenticity. True revelation has the last and decisive word on the things of God, for "no man knoweth of [God's] ways save it be revealed unto him." (Jacob 4:8.) Revelation has several different forms and many different functions. The principles of learning by revelation are faith, humility, seeking by prayer, obedience to the commandments, repentance, good works, and scripture study.

Chapter 3 contrasts the proofs of science with the signs the Lord has warned us not to seek. While signs or miracles should not be used to convert an unbeliever, they are appropriate to strengthen a convert. "Signs follow those that believe." (D&C 63:9.)

The Lord has commanded that we care for the poor and the needy in his own way. (D&C 104:16.) Chapter 4 explains the Lord's way of welfare and describes how these principles have been applied in the restored church since its founding.

Chapter 5 sets forth the Lord's warnings against contention. "Verily, verily I say unto you, he that hath the spirit of contention is not of me, but is of the devil, who is the father of contention." (3 Ne. 11:29.) The world's way is often contentious. Latter-day Saints should avoid contention because it separates them from the Lord and his Spirit. The Lord's way is harmony and unity and oneness.

The principles governing when a follower of Jesus Christ is justified in participating in litigation are discussed in chapter 6. These principles focus on responsibilities rather than rights. They involve forgiveness, settlement, avoiding revenge, and considering the effect of the proposed litigation upon those who might be affected by the action.

Chapter 7 reviews the gospel directions against criticism. In contrast to the relatively uninhibited adversariness that characterizes much of modern life, the Lord has commanded the faithful in all ages to refrain from faultfinding and evil-speaking. The commandment includes criticism of church leaders, but this does not mean that Latter-day Saints have no way of addressing differences with church leaders. Five appropriate methods are described.

Chapter 8 explains church discipline, contrasting its various principles and procedures with the civil or criminal rules and procedures with which it is sometimes confused. Church discipline is founded upon gospel doctrines and principles, including the fact that repentance is necessary to qualify for the mercy made possible through the atonement. Church discipline aids repentance and the change of life that is essential for salvation.

A final contrast between the ways of the Lord and the ways of the world—symbolic of all of the others—appears in an incident recorded in the Gospel of John. During his journey across Samaria, Jesus rested at Jacob's well. A Samaritan woman came to draw water, and he asked her for a drink. When she marveled that a Jew would speak to a Samaritan, he told her that if she knew who he was, she would ask him for living water. Seeing that he had no implement to draw water from the deep well, she asked him how he could obtain any water to give her.

Before reminding ourselves of Jesus' answer, we should note how this circumstance duplicates that of his faithful followers in the world. The Savior is in our midst, sometimes personally, frequently through his servants, and always by his Spirit. His power is such that he could obtain anything on this earth. He need not ask for water at the well, for tithes and offerings at the Church, or for personal service in any other work of his kingdom. He asks us for these things, just as he sought a drink from the Samaritan woman at Jacob's well, so that he can bless us with something of far greater importance to us than that which we give. That is the Lord's way.

In answer to the question how he could give the Samaritan woman living water without any way to draw it from the well, Jesus answered: "Whosoever drinketh of this water shall thirst again: but whosoever drinketh of the water that I shall give him shall never thirst; but the water that I shall give him shall be in him a well of water springing up into everlasting life." (John 4:13–14.)

We can liken the various ways of the world to implements that can draw water from a worldly well. We need such implements. We can and do use them to make our way in the world.

But while we are doing this, in our occupations, in our civic responsibilities, and in our work in other organizations, we must never forget the Savior's words, "Whosoever drinketh of this water shall thirst again." Only from Jesus Christ, the Lord and Savior of this world, can we obtain the living water whose partaker shall never thirst again, in whom it will be "a well of water springing up into everlasting life." And we do not obtain that water with worldly implements.

Jesus taught us how to obtain the living water. The teaching he gave the Samaritan woman reminds us, even as we are involved in acquiring the worldly skills and knowledge and methods to draw water from earthly wells, that what we obtain from Jacob's well gives only temporary relief. The water of Jacob's well, however significant in satisfying temporary earthly desires, is insignificant in value beside what we can obtain from Jesus' words and from his atoning sacrifice. And when we seek to obtain or share that living water, we must do it in the Lord's way.

NOTES

1. *Teachings of the Prophet Joseph Smith*, ed. Joseph Fielding Smith (Salt Lake City: Deseret News Press, 1956), 356.

2. Neal A. Maxwell, *A Wonderful Flood of Light* (Salt Lake City: Bookcraft, 1990), 67.

3. See, generally, Boyd K. Packer, "The Mantle Is Far, Far Greater Than the Intellect" in *Let Not Your Heart Be Troubled* (Salt Lake City: Bookcraft, 1991), 101–22.

4. Ezra Taft Benson, *A Witness and a Warning* (Salt Lake City: Deseret Book, 1988), 64.

5. James E. Faust, "Continuous Revelation," *Ensign* 19 (November 1989): 10.

6. Joseph Fielding McConkie and Robert L. Millett, *Doctrinal Commentary on the Book of Mormon* 1 (Salt Lake City: Bookcraft, 1987): 208.

7. Rudyard Kipling, "God of Our Fathers, Known of Old," *Hymns of The Church of Jesus Christ of Latter-day Saints* (Salt Lake City: The Church of Jesus Christ of Latter-day Saints, 1985), no. 80, verse 3.

LEARNING

The most basic example of differences between the Lord's way and man's way concerns how we learn. During mortality we must learn something of the earth and its living things and we should also learn about the things of God—his nature, his gospel, and his commandments for his children.

In modern revelation the Lord has told us to "seek learning even by study and also by faith." (D&C 109:7.) Seeking learning by study, we use the method of reason. Seeking learning by faith, we must rely on revelation. Obedient to heavenly decree, we should seek learning by reason and also by revelation.

At the outset, I should define what I mean by reason and revelation. Reason is a thinking process using facts and logic that can be communicated to another person and tested by objective (that is, measurable) criteria. Revelation is communication from God to man. It cannot be defined and tested like reason. Reason involves thinking and demonstrating. Revelation involves hearing or seeing or understanding or feeling. Reason is potentially public. Revelation is invariably personal. Reason is a process. Revelation is an experience.

As so defined, reason and revelation do not exhaust all the ways we acquire learning. For example, I know that I love my wife and I know that I prefer certain colors and certain sounds. I do not attribute such knowledge to what I define as reason or revelation.

I will not define such other means of knowing or describe their relationship to the two methods I will discuss. Some may find fault with such incomplete definitions, but they will serve my present purpose, which is not to give an exhaustive account of the various methods or processes of learning but only to contrast a familiar mortal method and a precious heavenly gift.

In this and the next chapter, I will describe the nature and relationship of reason and revelation, with emphasis on their use in learning the things of God.

Learning by Study and Reason

My familiarity with the processes of learning by study and reason comes from my personal experiences as a student in two different universities, as a professor of law in three different law schools, as director of an interdisciplinary legal research foundation, as president of Brigham Young University, and as a justice on the Utah Supreme Court.

In seeking learning by study and reason, we examine the accumulated wisdom of various fields of knowledge, we employ empirical techniques to gather new evidence, and we use the powers of reasoning placed in us by our Creator. These are the normal ways of seeking knowledge of the things of the world. Millions of men and women are involved in this kind of search for knowledge in every imaginable field of learning from the most basic practices of agriculture and personal hygiene to the currently most advanced techniques of medical science and space exploration, to cite only a few examples. Modern civilization owes an incalculable debt to the search for knowledge by study and reason.

Study and reason are also essential in the acquisition of knowledge about God and the truths of his gospel. The experience of young Joseph Smith illustrates this. Just as Joseph studied the Bible and reasoned how its promises applied to him, so each of us uses this method to begin our search for sacred knowledge. Then, like the believing boy, we must pray and seek for divine communication. (The significance of this sequence — study and reason, followed by revelation — is discussed in chapter 2.)

Another use of reason is in communicating what we have learned about the things of God. The apostle Peter taught: "Sanctify the Lord God in your hearts; and be ready always to give an answer with meekness and fear to every man that asketh of you a reason for the hope that is in you." (JST 1 Pet. 3:15.) In other words, believers should strive to give nonbelievers a reason for their faith, attempting to communicate sacred knowledge in terms understandable to those who seem to rely exclusively on reason. Perhaps this is what is meant by some of the scriptural references to reasoning with men about the things of God. (See, for example, D&C 49:4; 66:7; 68:1.)

Finally, much sacred knowledge — what we sometimes call "the truths of the gospel" — is reasonable and can be explained and understood by the techniques of reason. Thus, we read in Isaiah, "Come now, and let us reason together, saith the Lord." (Isa. 1:18.) What follows is an explanation of the effects of the Atonement. In modern revelation this same invitation to "reason together . . . even as a man reasoneth one with another" is followed by a logical explanation of the contrasting methods and effects of preaching the gospel "by the Spirit of truth or [by] some other way." (D&C 50:10–11, 17.)

Despite the importance of study and reason, if we seek to learn of the things of God solely by this method, we are certain to stop short of our goal. We may even wind up at the wrong destination. Why is this so? On this subject God has prescribed the primacy of another method. To learn the things of God, what we need is not more study and reason, not more scholarship and technology, but more faith and revelation.

Learning by Faith and Revelation

Latter-day Saints affirm the reality and effectiveness of learning by faith and revelation.

The Lord's way of revealing himself and of communicating understanding about the doctrines and ordinances of his gospel is revelation by the Holy Ghost, the Spirit of God. Indeed, the prophet Jacob declared the impossibility of uninspired man's understanding God: "No man knoweth of his ways save it be revealed unto him; wherefore, brethren, despise not the revelations of God." (Jacob 4:8.) Similarly, the apostle Paul taught, "The things of God knoweth no man, except he has the Spirit of God." (JST 1 Cor. 2:11).

President Gordon B. Hinckley explains: "Of course we believe in the cultivation of the mind, but the intellect is not the only source of knowledge. There is a promise, given under inspiration from the Almighty, set forth in these beautiful words: 'God shall give unto you knowledge by his Holy Spirit, yea, by the unspeakable gift of the Holy Ghost.' (D&C 121:26.)"[1]

Referring to revelations received in the highest councils of the Church, Elder James E. Faust speaks of the shared understanding that "this light and truth is beyond human intelligence and reasoning."[2] That same light and truth is available by right to every person who has received the gift of the Holy Ghost.

The Savior affirmed the importance of learning by revelation and described how this occurs. He asked his disciples, "Whom say ye that I am?" Simon Peter answered, "Thou art the Christ, the Son of the living God." Jesus responded, "Blessed art thou, Simon Bar-jona: for flesh and blood hath not revealed it unto thee, but my Father which is in heaven." (Matt. 16:15–17.)

The New Testament has other teachings on revelation as the means of learning about God and the truths of his gospel.

The apostle John taught the humble followers of Christ that, having "an unction from the Holy One" (the Holy Ghost), "ye need not that any man teach you," since "the same anointing [which ye have received of him] teacheth you of all things, and is truth." (1 Jn. 2:20, 27.)

The apostle Paul reminded the Corinthians that he had not taught them with "enticing words of man's wisdom." His teachings had been "in demonstration of the Spirit and of power" in order that their faith "should not stand in the wisdom of men, but in the power of God." He had taught "the wisdom of God," which God had revealed "by his Spirit." He explained that man could not know the things of God except by the Spirit of God, and he affirmed that "we have received . . . the spirit which is of God; that we might know the things that are freely given to us of God."

Concluding this teaching, Paul said that he spoke "not in the words which man's wisdom teacheth, but which the Holy Ghost teacheth." He contrasted this method of learning (which a modern apostle has called "the methodology of the Spirit"[3]) to the expectations and attitudes of the world: "But the natural man receiveth not the things of the Spirit of God: for they are foolishness unto him: neither can he know them, because they are spiritually discerned." (1 Cor. 2:4–14.)

The revelations of this dispensation contain many warnings about the importance of relying on God in seeking to learn the things of God. In his preface to these revelations, the Lord denounced those "who will not hear the voice of the Lord, neither the voice of his servants. . . . Every man walketh in his own way, and after the image of his own god, whose image is in the likeness of the world, and whose substance is that of an idol." "Wherefore," the revelation continues, the Prophet Joseph Smith has been called and the Lord has spoken from the heavens, and "the weak things of the world shall come forth and break down the mighty and strong ones, that man should not counsel his fellow man, neither trust in the arm of flesh." (D&C 1:14, 16, 19.)

This revelation echoes the Book of Mormon reference to Isaiah's caution. (Isa. 8:10.) The prophet Nephi taught the importance of trusting in revelation rather than in "the precepts of men": "Cursed is he that putteth his trust in man, or maketh flesh his arm, or shall hearken unto the precepts of men, save their precepts shall be given by the power of the Holy Ghost." (2 Ne. 28:31.)

The early leaders of the restored church had to learn that mortal reasoning was secondary to the revelations of God. On several occasions the Lord rebuked Joseph Smith, David Whitmer, and others for not having their minds on the things of God, for yielding to "the persuasions of men" (D&C 3:6; 5:21), and for being "persuaded by those whom [the Lord had] not commanded" (D&C 30:2). Like some members of today, these early leaders had to learn that the gospel includes "many great things . . . which [are] hard to be understood, save a man should inquire of the Lord." (1 Ne. 15:3.)

In the acquisition of sacred knowledge, reason must yield to revelation. I believe this is what the Savior taught when he spoke of his second coming and the fulfillment of the parable of the ten virgins: "For they that are wise and have received the truth, and *have taken the Holy Spirit for their guide,* and have not been deceived—verily I say unto you, they shall not be hewn down and cast into the fire, but shall abide the day." (D&C 45:57; emphasis added.)

Elder Bruce R. McConkie repeatedly declared the primacy of faith and revelation in gospel learning. For example: "True religion comes from God by revelation. It is manifest to and understood by those with a talent for spirituality. It is hidden, unknown, and mysterious to all others. To comprehend the things of the world, one must be intellectually enlightened; to know and understand the things of God, one must be spiritually enlightened. One of the great fallacies of modern Christendom is turning for religious guidance to those who are highly endowed intellectually, rather than to those who comprehend the things of the Spirit, to those who receive personal revelation from the Holy Ghost."[4]

I will say more on this subject in chapter 2.

Forms and Functions of Revelation

To understand how we can learn by revelation, it is necessary to understand the different forms and the various functions of revelation.

The experience we call *revelation* can occur through many different forms. Some prophets, like Moses and Joseph Smith, have talked with God face-to-face. Some persons have had face-to-face communication with angels. Other revelations have come, as Elder James E. Talmage described, "through the dreams of sleep or in the waking visions of the mind."[5]

In its most familiar forms, revelation comes by means of words or thoughts or feelings communicated to the mind. "Behold," the Lord told Oliver Cowdery, "I will tell you in your mind and in your heart, by the Holy Ghost." (D&C 8:2.) This is the experience Enos described when he said, "The voice of the Lord came into my mind." (Enos 1:10.) It is the experience Nephi described when he reminded his wayward brothers that the Lord had spoken to them in a still small voice, but they "were past feeling" and "could not feel his words." (1 Ne. 17:45.)

We often refer to these most familiar forms of revelation as *inspiration*. Inspired thoughts or promptings can take the form of enlightenment of the mind (D&C 6:15), positive or negative feelings about proposed courses of action, or even the uplifting emotions that come from inspiring performances, as in the performing arts. Elder Boyd K. Packer has explained, "Inspiration comes more as a feeling than as a sound."[6]

All of these forms of revelation are real, and all of them serve the recipient's desire for learning.

The experience of revelation is available to everyone. President Lorenzo Snow declared that it is "the grand privilege of every Latter-day Saint . . . to have the manifestations of the spirit every day of our lives."[7] President Harold B. Lee taught: "Every man has the privilege to exercise these gifts and these privileges in the conduct of his own affairs; in bringing up his children in the way they should go; in the management of his business, or whatever he does. It is his right to enjoy the spirit of revelation and of inspiration to do the right thing, to be wise and prudent, just and good, in everything that he does."[8]

Whatever its form, revelation can serve various functions. I will describe eight: to testify, to prophesy, to comfort, to uplift, to inform, to restrain, to confirm, and to impel.

1. The *testimony* or witness of the Holy Ghost that Jesus is the Christ and that the gospel is true is a revelation from God. Like the revelation to the apostle Peter (Matt. 16:17), this knowledge can be part of the personal experience of every seeker after truth. Once received, this revelation becomes a pole star to guide in all the activities of life.

2. *Prophecy* is another function of revelation. Under the influence of the Holy Ghost, a faithful member of the Church may be inspired to foresee something that will come to pass in his or her life, such as a church calling to be received. After our fifth child was born, my wife and I did not have any more children. After more than ten years, we concluded that our family would not be any larger, which grieved us. Then one day, while my wife was in the temple, the Spirit whispered to her that she would have another child. That prophetic revelation was fulfilled a year and a half later with the birth of our sixth child, for whom we had waited thirteen years.

3. Another function of revelation is to *comfort.* Such a revelation came to the Prophet Joseph Smith in Liberty Jail. After many months in deplorable conditions, he cried out in agony and loneliness, pleading with the Lord to remember the persecuted Saints. The comforting answer came: "My son, peace be unto thy soul; thine adversity and thine afflictions shall be but a small moment; And then, if thou endure it well, God shall exalt thee on high; thou shalt triumph over all thy foes." (D&C 121:7–8.) In a subsequent revelation the Lord declared that no matter what tragedies or injustices

should befall the Prophet, "Know thou, my son, that all these things shall give thee experience, and shall be for thy good." (D&C 122:7–8.)

There are many revelations of comfort to worthy persons. Some have been comforted by visions of departed loved ones or by feeling their presence. The widow of a good friend told me how she had felt the presence of her departed husband, giving her assurance of his love and concern for her. Many have been comforted as they have had to adjust to the loss of a job or a business advantage or even a marriage. A revelation of comfort can also come in connection with a blessing of the priesthood, either from the words spoken or from the feeling communicated in connection with the blessing.

Another comforting revelation is the assurance that a sin has been forgiven. After praying fervently for an entire day and night, the Book of Mormon prophet Enos recorded that he heard a voice, which said, "Thy sins are forgiven thee, and thou shalt be blessed. . . . Wherefore," Enos wrote, "my guilt was swept away." (Enos 1:5–6.) This feeling, which comes with the completion of repentance, gives assurance that the repentant sinner has been forgiven. Alma described that moment as a time when he was no longer "harrowed up by the memory" of his sins. "And oh, what joy, and what marvelous light I did behold; yea, my soul was filled with joy . . . there can be nothing so exquisite and sweet as was my joy." (Alma 36:19–21.)

4. Closely related to the feeling of comfort is the fourth function or purpose of revelation, to *uplift*. At times in our lives, each of us needs to be lifted up from a depression, from a sense of foreboding or inadequacy, or just from a plateau of spiritual mediocrity. Because it raises our spirits and helps us resist evil and seek good, the feeling of uplift

that is communicated by reading the scriptures or by enjoying wholesome music, art, or literature is a distinct function (as well as a form) of revelation.

5. Another function of revelation is to *inform*. By inspiration, persons receive the words to speak on a particular occasion, such as in the blessings pronounced by a patriarch or in sermons or other words spoken under the influence of the Holy Ghost. The Lord commanded Joseph Smith and Sidney Rigdon to lift up their voices and speak the thoughts that he would put in their hearts: "For it shall be given you in the very hour, yea, in the very moment, what ye shall say." (D&C 100:5–6; see also 84:85.)

On some sacred occasions, information has been given by face-to-face conversations with heavenly personages, such as in the visions related in ancient and modern scriptures. More often, needed information is communicated by the quiet whisperings of the Spirit. A child loses a treasured possession, prays for help, and is inspired to find it. An adult has a problem at work, at home, or in family history research, prays, and is led to the information necessary to resolve it. By faithfully following the inspired counsel of a church leader, a member experiences and learns something that answers his prayers for guidance. A church leader prays to know whom the Lord has chosen to fill a position, and the Spirit whispers a name. A member prayerfully studies the scriptures and receives new understanding of the doctrines of the everlasting gospel.

In all of these examples — familiar to each of us — the Holy Ghost acts in his office as a teacher and revelator, communicating information and truths for the edification and guidance of the recipient.

6. The sixth function of revelation is to *restrain* us from doing something. Thus, in the midst of a great sermon ex-

plaining the power of the Holy Ghost, Nephi suddenly declared, "And now I . . . cannot say more; the Spirit stoppeth mine utterance." (2 Ne. 32:7.)

Restraint is one of the most common functions of revelation. It often comes by surprise. Even though we have not asked for revelation or guidance on a particular subject, if we are keeping the commandments of God and living in tune with his Spirit, a restraining force will steer us away from things we should not do. Though not obviously related to the conventional activities of learning, this function of revelation communicates a message that must rank among the most important lessons we can learn.

One of my most formative experiences in being restrained by the Spirit came soon after I was called as a counselor in a stake presidency in Chicago. In one of our first meetings as a presidency, our stake president made a proposal that our new stake center be built in a particular location. I immediately saw four or five good reasons why that was the wrong location. When asked for my counsel, I opposed the proposal, giving each of those reasons. The stake president wisely suggested that each of us consider the matter prayerfully for another week and discuss it further in our next meeting. Almost perfunctorily I prayed about the subject and immediately received a strong impression that I was wrong, that I was standing in the way of the Lord's will, and that I should remove myself from opposition to it. Needless to say, I was restrained and promptly gave my support to the proposed construction. In a short time the wisdom of constructing the stake center in that location was evident, even to me. My reasons to the contrary turned out to be classic illustrations of the wisdom of men, and I was soon grateful to have been restrained from relying on them.

Some years later, I was editing a casebook on a legal

subject. A casebook consists of several hundred court opinions, together with explanatory material and text written by
the editor. My assistant and I had finished all the work on
the book, including the necessary research to assure that
these judicial decisions had not been reversed or overruled.
Just before sending it to the publisher, I leafed through the
manuscript and a particular court opinion caught my attention. As I looked at it, I had a profoundly uneasy feeling. I
asked my assistant to check that case again to see if everything
was in order. He did and reported that it was. In a subsequent
check of the completed manuscript, I was again stopped at
that case, again with a great feeling of uneasiness. This time
I went to the law library myself. There, in some newly received publications, I discovered that this case had just been
reversed on appeal. If that opinion had been published in
my casebook, it would have resulted in serious professional
embarrassment. I was saved by the restraining power of
revelation.

7. A common way to seek revelation is to propose a
particular course of action and then pray for inspiration to
confirm it. The Lord explained the confirming function of
revelation when Oliver Cowdery failed in his efforts to translate the Book of Mormon: "Behold, you have not understood;
you have supposed that I would give it unto you, when you
took no thought save it was to ask me. But, behold, I say
unto you, that you must study it out in your mind; then you
must ask me if it be right, and if it is right I will cause that
your bosom shall burn within you; therefore, you shall feel
that it is right." (D&C 9:7–8.)

Similarly, the prophet Alma likens the word of God to
a seed. He tells persons studying the gospel that if they will
give place for the seed to be planted in their hearts, it will
enlarge their souls and enlighten their understanding and

begin to be delicious to them. (Alma 32.) That feeling is the
Holy Ghost's confirming revelation of the truth of the
word.

In an illuminating sermon titled "Agency or Inspiration,"
Elder Bruce R. McConkie stressed our responsibility to do
all we can before we seek a revelation. He gave a very
personal example. When he set out to choose a companion
for eternity, he did not go to the Lord and ask whom he
ought to marry. "I went out and found the girl I wanted,"
he said. "She suited me; . . . it just seemed . . . as though this
ought to be. . . . [Then] all I did was pray to the Lord and ask
for some guidance and direction in connection with the
decision that I'd reached."[9]

Here is a summary of Elder McConkie's analysis of the
balance between agency and inspiration: "We're expected
to use the gifts and talents and abilities, the sense and judgment and agency with which we are endowed. . . . Implicit
in asking in faith is the precedent requirement that we do
everything in our power to accomplish the goal that we
seek. . . . We're expected to do everything in our power
that we can, and then to seek an answer from the Lord, a
confirming seal that we've reached the right conclusion."[10]

This is the method General Authorities usually follow
as they seek revelation in connection with the calling of a
stake president. They interview persons residing in the stake
who have special experience in church administration, asking them questions and hearing their counsel. As these in-
terviews are conducted, they give prayerful consideration
to each person interviewed and mentioned. They reach a
tentative decision on the new stake president and prayerfully
submit their proposed action to the Lord. If the proposal is
confirmed, the call is issued. If it is not confirmed or if they

feel restrained, that proposal is tabled and the process continues until a new proposal is formed and the confirming revelation is received.

Sometimes confirming and restraining revelations are combined. For example, during my service at BYU, I was invited to give a speech before a national association of attorneys. Because it would require many days to prepare, this was the kind of speaking invitation I had routinely declined. But as I began to dictate a letter declining this particular invitation, I felt restrained. I paused and reconsidered my action. I then considered how I might accept the invitation. As I considered it in that light, I felt the confirming assurance of the Spirit and knew that this was what I should do.

The speech I gave and the contacts I made on that occasion provided an extremely important opportunity for BYU to make friends and exert influence in opposing unlawful or unwise government regulation of higher education. As I look back on the event, I have no doubt that this was one of those occasions when a seemingly insignificant act made a great deal of difference. Those are the times when it is vital for us to receive the guidance of the Lord, and those are the times when revelation will come to aid us if we hear it and heed it.

8. The eighth function of revelation is evident in those instances when the Spirit *impels* a person to action. This is not a case in which a person proposes to take a particular action and the Spirit either restrains or confirms. This is a case in which revelation comes when it is not being sought and impels some action not being proposed. This type of revelation is obviously less common than other types, but its rarity makes it all the more significant.

A scriptural example is recorded in the first book of

Nephi. When Nephi was in Jerusalem to obtain the precious
scriptural records, the Spirit of the Lord directed him to kill
Laban as Laban lay drunk in the street. This act was so far
from Nephi's heart that he recoiled and wrestled with the
Spirit. He was again directed to slay Laban, and he finally
followed that revelation. (1 Nephi 4.)

Students of Church history will recall Wilford Woodruff's
account of an impression that came to him in the night
telling him to move his carriage and mules away from a
large tree. He did so, and his family and livestock were saved
when the tree crashed to the ground in a tornado that struck
thirty minutes later.[11]

As a young girl, my grandmother, Chasty Olsen, had a
similar experience. She was tending some children who
were playing in a dry riverbed near their home in Castle
Dale, Utah. Suddenly she heard a voice that called her by
name and directed her to get the children out of the riverbed
and up on the bank. It was a clear day, and there was no
sign of rain. She saw no reason to heed the voice and continued to play. The voice spoke to her again, urgently. This
time she heeded the warning. Quickly gathering the children, she made a run for the bank. Just as they reached it,
an enormous wall of water, originating with a cloudburst
in the mountains many miles away, swept down the canyon
and roared across where the children had played. Except
for this impelling revelation, she and the children would
have been lost.

I had a choice experience with impelling revelation a
few months after I began my service at BYU. As a new and
inexperienced president, I had many problems to analyze
and many decisions to reach. I was very dependent upon
the Lord. One day in October 1971, I drove to a secluded
area in Provo Canyon to ponder a particular problem. Al-

though alone and without any interruption, I found myself unable to think of the problem at hand. Another pending issue I was not yet ready to consider kept thrusting itself into my mind: Should we modify BYU's academic calendar to complete the fall semester before Christmas?

After ten or fifteen minutes of unsuccessful efforts to exclude thoughts of this subject, I finally realized what was happening. The issue of the calendar did not seem timely to me, and I was certainly not seeking any guidance on it, but the Spirit was trying to communicate with me on that subject. I immediately turned my full attention to that question and began to record my thoughts on a piece of paper. Within a few minutes I had recorded the details of a three-semester calendar, with all of its powerful advantages. Hurrying back to the campus, I reviewed these with my colleagues and found them enthusiastic. A few days later the board of trustees approved our proposed new calendar, and we published its dates, barely in time to make them effective in the fall of 1972.

Since that time, I have reread these words of the Prophet Joseph Smith and realized that I had the experience he described: "A person may profit by noticing the first intimation of the spirit of revelation; for instance, when you feel pure intelligence flowing into you, it may give you sudden strokes of ideas . . . and thus by learning the Spirit of God and understanding it, you may grow into the principle of revelation."[12]

In all of its forms and functions, revelation is distinct from study and reason. Revelation is an experience, most often communicated by a feeling. It is God's way of communicating to his children. It is a vital way of learning from and about God.

Requirements for Receiving Revelation

The scriptures give seven requirements for receiving revelation from God. These requirements are unique to the Lord's prescribed way of learning by revelation. They have no counterparts in the world's ways of learning by study and reason.

1. *Have faith.*

As in the gospel itself, the first principle is faith. The brother of Jared provides a model. Because of his great faith, he saw the God of Israel in person and "could not be kept from beholding within the veil." (Ether 3:9, 19.)

Nephi taught his brothers the necessity of faith, reminding them of the Lord's promise: "Do ye not remember the things which the Lord hath said? — If ye will not harden your hearts, and ask me in faith, believing that ye shall receive, with diligence in keeping my commandments, surely these things shall be made known unto you." (1 Ne. 15:11.)

In describing the many revelations received by the righteous people of his day, Jarom gave this description: "And as many as are not stiffnecked and have faith, have communion with the Holy Spirit, which maketh manifest unto the children of men, according to their faith." (Jarom 1:4.)

2. *Be humble.*

To receive revelation — to be taught by the Holy Spirit — a person must be humble. One of the best scriptural teachings on this subject appears in the only revelation given to the Prophet Brigham Young that is recorded in the Doctrine and Covenants: "Let him that is ignorant learn wisdom by humbling himself and calling upon the Lord his God, that his eyes may be opened that he may see, and his ears opened that he may hear; for my Spirit is sent forth into the world to enlighten the humble and contrite, and to the condem-

nation of the ungodly." (D&C 136:32–33; also see Ether
12:27; D&C 1:28; 112:10.)

Conversely, if we "contend against the word of the Lord,"
the Lord has warned us that he will not show us any "greater
things." (Ether 4:8.)

3. *Ask.*

As the boy Joseph Smith learned, personal guidance and
gospel knowledge come to those who pray to God for enlightenment. "Therefore," the Lord said, "if you will ask of
me you shall receive; if you will knock it shall be opened
unto you." (D&C 6:5; see also 88:63.) Seek for wisdom, the
Lord said, "and behold, the mysteries of God shall be unfolded unto you, and then shall you be made rich." (D&C
6:7.) "And if thou wilt inquire, thou shalt know mysteries
which are great and marvelous." (D&C 6:11.) (See page 42
for a discussion of what is meant by "the mysteries of God.")

President Joseph F. Smith's experience provides a model.
He read and pondered the meaning of scriptures about the
spirit world, and the Lord parted the veil for him and revealed the great truths now recorded in section 138 of the
Doctrine and Covenants. Similarly, each of us should pray
that the Lord will unfold the scriptures to our understanding.
(D&C 32:4.) God has promised that if we ask him, we will
"receive revelation upon revelation, knowledge upon
knowledge, that [we may] know the mysteries and peaceable
things—that which bringeth joy, that which bringeth life
eternal." (D&C 42:61.)

4. *Keep the commandments.*

The way to revelation is righteousness. Marveling at the
Master's teachings, his enemies asked: "How knoweth this
man letters, having never learned? Jesus answered them,
and said, My doctrine is not mine, but his that sent me. If
any man will do his will, he shall know of the doctrine,

whether it be of God, or whether I speak of myself." (John 7:15–17.)

Elsewhere, John said: "And hereby we do know that we know him, if we keep his commandments. He that saith, I know him, and keepeth not his commandments, is a liar, and the truth is not in him." (1 Jn. 2:3–4.)

After teaching that we should have virtue, temperance, patience, godliness, brotherly kindness, and charity, the apostle Peter added this promise about the consequence of such virtues: "For if these things be in you, and abound, they make you that ye shall neither be barren nor unfruitful in the knowledge of our Lord Jesus Christ." (2 Pet. 1:8.)

In our own day, the Lord has promised: "Unto him that keepeth my commandments I will give the mysteries of my kingdom, and the same shall be in him a well of living water, springing up unto everlasting life." (D&C 63:23; see also 1 Ne. 15:11; D&C 93:28.)

5, 6. *Repentance and good works.*

Two other requirements for acquiring gospel knowledge by revelation from the Holy Ghost are stated with exemplary clarity in the Book of Mormon: "He that repenteth and exerciseth faith, and bringeth forth good works, and prayeth continually without ceasing—unto such it is given to know the mysteries of God." (Alma 26:22.) Similarly, an earlier chapter of Alma teaches that "the plan of redemption" was made known to men "according to their faith and repentance and their holy works." (Alma 12:30.)

7. *Read the scriptures.*

On one occasion Elder Bruce R. McConkie said, "I sometimes think that one of the best-kept secrets of the kingdom is that the scriptures open the door to the receipt of revelation."[13] This is obviously true of the promised witness that the Book of Mormon is true, and of the help we seek and receive from the Spirit in interpreting the meaning of scriptural passages. It also extends to revelations on other subjects. Elder McConkie explained:

"All of us are entitled to the spirit of prophecy and of revelation in our lives, both for our personal affairs and in our ministry. The prayerful study and pondering of the holy scriptures will do as much, or more than any other single thing, to bring that spirit, the spirit of prophecy and the spirit of revelation, into our lives."[14]

"However talented men may be in administrative matters; however eloquent they may be in expressing their views; however learned they may be in worldly things — they will be denied the sweet whisperings of the Spirit that might have been theirs unless they pay the price of studying, pondering, and praying about the scriptures."[15]

When Revelation Is Not Received

What about those times when we seek revelation and do not receive it? We do not always receive inspiration or revelation when we request it. Sometimes we are delayed in receiving revelation, and sometimes we are left to our own judgment and understanding based on study and reason. We cannot force spiritual things. It must be so. Our life's purpose to obtain experience and to develop faith would be frustrated if our Heavenly Father enlightened us immediately on every question or directed us in every act. We must reach conclusions and make decisions and experience the consequences in order to develop self-reliance and faith.

Even in decisions we think very important, we sometimes receive no answers to our prayers. This does not mean our prayers have not been heard. It only means we have prayed about a decision that, for one cause or another, we should make without guidance by revelation.

Perhaps we have asked for guidance in choosing between alternatives that are equally acceptable or equally unacceptable. There is *not* a right and a wrong answer to every question. For many questions, there are only two wrong answers or two right answers. Thus, those who seek divine guidance on how they should retaliate against those who have wronged them are not likely to receive revelation to guide them. Neither are those who seek guidance on choices they will never have to make because some future event will intervene, such as a third alternative that is clearly preferable.

On one occasion, my wife and I prayed earnestly for guidance on a decision that seemed very important. No answer came. We were left to proceed on our own best judgment. We could not imagine why the Lord had not aided us with a confirming or restraining impression. But it was not long before we learned we did not have to make a decision on that question because something else happened that made a decision unnecessary. The Lord would not guide us in a decision that made no difference.

No answer is likely to come to a person who seeks guidance in choosing between two alternatives that are equally acceptable to the Lord. Thus, there are times when we can serve productively in two different fields of labor. Either answer is right. Similarly, the Spirit of the Lord is not likely to give us revelations on matters that are trivial. I once heard a young woman in a testimony meeting praise the spirituality of her husband, indicating that he submitted every question to the Lord. She told how he accompanied her shopping and would not even choose between different brands of canned vegetables without making his selection a matter of prayer. I think that is improper. I believe the Lord expects us to make most of our decisions by using the intelligence and experience he has given us. When someone asked the Prophet Joseph Smith for advice on a particular matter, the Prophet stated: "It is a great thing to inquire at the hands of God, or to come into His presence: and we feel fearful to approach Him on subjects that are of little or no consequence."[16]

Of course, we are not always able to judge what choices are trivial. If a matter appears of little or no consequence, we can proceed on the basis of our own judgment. If the choice is important for reasons unknown to us, such as the speaking invitation I mentioned earlier or even a choice between two cans of vegetables when one contains a hidden poison, the Lord will intervene and give us guidance. When a choice will make a real difference in our lives — obvious or not — and when we are living in tune with the Spirit and seeking divine guidance, we can be sure that we will receive the guidance we need to attain righteous goals. The Lord will not leave us unassisted when a choice is important to our eternal welfare. And when we pray for enlightenment, seeking learning by faith and revelation, he will give us knowledge by his Holy Spirit, in his own way and in his own time.

The Fruits of Revelation

At the close of his earthly ministry, the Savior promised his followers that God the Father would give them "another Comforter" who "shall teach you all things." (John 14:16, 26.) Centuries later, the prophet Moroni described that same teacher when he promised that "by the power of the Holy Ghost ye may know the truth of all things." (Moro. 10:5.) That promise of learning from the Spirit applies to all seekers after divine truth who have received the gift of the Holy Ghost and who are receptive to its ministerings.

The principle upon which that promise is based applies also to gospel teaching. President John Taylor gave this explanation of the Lord's way of gospel teaching: "There is no man living, and there never was a man living, who was capable of teaching the things of God only [except] as he was taught, instructed and directed by the spirit of revelation proceeding from the Almighty."[17]

When we attempt to teach the gospel truths that have been revealed to us by the Holy Ghost, we must teach them and others must learn them under the influence of that same Spirit.

At the beginning of the Restoration, the Lord instructed his servants, "The Spirit shall be given unto you by the prayer of faith; and if ye receive not the Spirit ye shall not teach." (D&C 42:14.) President Harold B. Lee declared that "teaching by the Spirit" is one of the four "essentials for service in the kingdom of God." In doing so, he reminded us of the scriptural principle that "when a man speaketh by the power of the Holy Ghost the power of the Holy Ghost carrieth it unto the hearts of the children of men." (2 Ne. 33:1.)[18]

Elder Bruce R. McConkie gave this memorable illustration of the importance of teaching by the Spirit. In section 50 of the Doctrine and Covenants, the Lord instructed the elders of his church that they were ordained to preach the gospel "by the Spirit, even the Comforter which was sent forth to teach the truth." (D&C 50:14.) Then he asked them whether they "preach[ed] the word of truth by the Comforter, in the Spirit of truth, . . . or [in] some other way." He added, "And if it be by some other way it is not of God." (D&C 50:14, 17–18.)

In an address to seminary and institute of religion personnel, Elder McConkie explained the significance of that revelation:

"If you teach the word of truth — now note, you are saying what is true, everything you say is accurate and right — by some other way than the Spirit, it is not of God. Now, what is the other way to teach than by the Spirit? Well, obviously, it is by the power of the intellect.

"Suppose I came here tonight and delivered a great message on teaching, and I did it by the power of the intellect without any of the Spirit of God attending. Suppose that every word that I said was true, no error whatever, but it was an intellectual presentation. This revelation says: 'If it be by some other way it is not of God' (D&C 50:18).

"That is, God did not present the message through me because I used the power of the intellect instead of the power of the Spirit. Intellectual things — reason and logic — can do some good, and they can prepare the way, and they can get the mind ready to receive the Spirit under certain circumstances. But conversion comes and the truth sinks into the hearts of people only when it is taught by the power of the Spirit."[19]

Here we learn that even though what is being taught is the truth, it is not of God unless it is being taught in the Lord's way. The great truths of the gospel must not be presented in the wrong setting, given voice by unworthy persons, accompanied by the wrong kind of music, or in other ways cheapened by association with what is not conducive to the spirit by which gospel truths must be taught. Only when "the word of truth" is taught and received "by the Spirit of truth" do we qualify for the promise that "he that preacheth and he that receiveth, understand one another, and both are edified and rejoice together." (D&C 50:19, 22.) This is the Lord's prescribed way of gospel teaching and learning.

Modern revelation promises that the Holy Ghost will

manifest "all things which are expedient." (D&C 18:18.) "Put your trust in that Spirit," the Lord said, promising, "I will impart unto you of my Spirit, which shall enlighten your mind, which shall fill your soul with joy; and then shall ye know, or by this shall you know, all things whatsoever you desire of me, which are pertaining unto things of righteousness, in faith believing in me that you shall receive." (D&C 11:12–14.)

Scriptural references to the gospel and the things of God often use the word *mysteries.* President Harold B. Lee explained that "a mystery may be defined as a truth which cannot be known except by revelation."[20] Some of these mysteries are what the scriptures call "unspeakable things, which are not lawful to be written." (3 Ne. 26:18.) But many scriptural references to mysteries concern things that are neither secret nor incomprehensible, but simply the precious doctrinal truths revealed by God to explain the gospel plan. The apostle Paul used the word in this way when he referred to his preaching "the mystery of the gospel." (Eph. 6:19.) Obedient to the Savior's command, "neither cast ye your pearls before swine" (Matthew 7:6), we do not try to explain these mysteries to those who are not spiritually ready to receive them (JST Matt. 7:9–11). But we are anxious to share these truths with all who are sincerely seeking to know the doctrines. Thus, Joseph Smith and Sidney Rigdon were commanded to expound "the mysteries [of the gospel] out of the scriptures." (D&C 71:1.) The Book of Mormon teaches that those who diligently seek shall have "the mysteries of God . . . unfolded unto them, by the power of the Holy Ghost." (1 Ne. 10:19; see also 1 Cor. 2:4–16; Alma 18:35.)

In response to a skeptic's questions about the resurrection, the prophet Alma gave this great teaching about the mysteries of God:

"It is given unto many to know the mysteries of God; nevertheless they are laid under a strict command that they shall not impart only according to the portion of his word which he doth grant unto the children of men, according to the heed and diligence which they give unto him.

"And therefore, he that will harden his heart, the same receiveth the lesser portion of the word; and he that will not harden his heart, to him is given the greater portion of the word, until it is given unto him to know the mysteries of God until he know them in full.

"And they that will harden their hearts, to them is given the lesser portion of the word until they know nothing concerning his mysteries; and then they are taken captive by the devil, and led by his will down to destruction. Now this is what is meant by the chains of hell." (Alma 12:9–11.)

We teach and learn the mysteries of God by revelation from his Holy Spirit. If we harden our hearts to revelation and limit our understanding to what we can obtain by study and reason, we are limited to what Alma called "the lesser portion of the word."

Learning the mysteries of God and attaining to what the apostle Paul called "the measure of the stature of the fulness of Christ" (Eph. 4:13) requires far more than learning a specified body of facts. It requires us *to learn* certain facts, *to practice* what we have learned, and, as a result, *to become* what we, as children of God, are destined to become. Professor Robert L. Millet explains the first part of this process:

"Surely we are put here on earth to learn as much as we can in the sciences, in the arts, in languages, in history and foreign culture, and so on. And, to the degree that we can master some of these fields, we are better able to present the gospel and its truths in a manner that would be acceptable to more and more people (see D&C 88:78–80). But there is a hierarchy of truth. Some truths matter more than others. It is valuable to know of gravity or of the laws of motion. It is vital to know of the reality of a Redeemer. It is helpful to know the laws of thermodynamics; it is essential to know how to repent and call upon God, in the name of his Son, for forgiveness."[21]

In inspired words now embodied in the scriptures of the Latter-day Saints, the Prophet Joseph Smith taught that "whatever principle of intelligence we attain unto in this life, it will rise with us in the resurrection." (D&C 130:18.) What is meant by *intelligence* is not mere *knowledge*, by whatever means it is acquired. This is evident from the following sentence: "And if a person gains more knowledge and intelligence in this life through his diligence and obedience than another, he will have so much the advantage in the world to come." (D&C 130:19.)

Note that *intelligence* is something more than *knowledge*. And note also the implication that *knowledge* is obtained by diligence and *intelligence* is obtained by obedience. Admittedly, the two methods are not mutually exclusive. But we come close to an important mystery of the gospel when we understand that the intelligence God desires us to obtain is much more than knowledge, and it cannot be obtained without obedience and revelation. That is the Lord's way, and it is far beyond the ways of the world.

NOTES

1. Gordon B. Hinckley, *Faith, the Essence of True Religion* (Salt Lake City: Deseret Book, 1989), 78.

2. James E. Faust, *Reach Up for the Light* (Salt Lake City: Deseret Book, 1990), 115.

3. Neal A. Maxwell, *A Wonderful Flood of Light* (Salt Lake City: Bookcraft, 1990), 75.

4. Bruce R. McConkie, *Doctrinal New Testament Commentary* (Salt Lake City: Bookcraft, 1973), 3:83–84.

5. James E. Talmage, *Articles of Faith* (Salt Lake City: Deseret Book, 1952), 229.

6. Boyd K. Packer, "Prayers and Answers," *Ensign* 9 (November 1979): 19.

7. Lorenzo Snow, *Conference Report* (April 1899), 52.

8. Harold B. Lee, *Stand Ye in Holy Places* (Salt Lake City: Deseret Book, 1974), 141–42.

9. Bruce R. McConkie, "Agency or Inspiration," *Speeches of the Year, 1972–73* (Provo, Utah: Brigham Young University Press, 1973), 111.

10. Ibid., 108, 110, 113.

11. Matthias F. Cowley, *Wilford Woodruff: History of His Life and Labors* (Salt Lake City: Bookcraft, 1964), 331–32.

12. *Teachings of the Prophet Joseph Smith*, ed. Joseph Fielding Smith (Salt Lake City: Deseret News Press, 1956), 151.

13. Bruce R. McConkie, *Doctrines of the Restoration*, ed. and arr. Mark L. McConkie (Salt Lake City: Bookcraft, 1989), 243.

14. Ibid., 244.

15. Ibid., 238.

16. Smith, *Teachings*, 22.

17. John Taylor, *Journal of Discourses* 17:369.

18. Lee, *Stand Ye in Holy Places*, 202.

19. McConkie, *Doctrines of the Restoration*, 332.

20. Harold B. Lee, *Ye Are the Light of the World* (Salt Lake City: Deseret Book, 1974), 211.

21. Robert L. Millet, *An Eye Single to the Glory of God* (Salt Lake City: Deseret Book, 1991), 113.

CHAPTER 2

REASON AND REVELATION

Knowledge about the earth and its various forms of life is expanding so rapidly that it can hardly be catalogued. But the world as a whole is not experiencing a comparable expansion of knowledge about God and his plan for his children. To obtain that kind of knowledge, we must understand and follow the ways God has prescribed to know the things of God. We come to know God and the truths of his gospel by study and reason and also (and always, for this kind of knowledge) by faith and revelation.

Reason and revelation are methods of learning that are available to seekers of every type of knowledge. The Church of Jesus Christ of Latter-day Saints has always encouraged its members to pursue and excel in all fields of learning, acquiring knowledge by study and reason as well as by faith and revelation. President Harold B. Lee expressed that counsel in these words: "The educational system of the Church has been established to the end that all pure knowledge must be gained by our people, handed down to our posterity, and given to all men. We charge our teachers to give constant stimulation to budding young scientists and scholars in all fields and to urge them to push further and further into the realms of the unknown."[1]

Seekers of secular knowledge who have paid the price in personal effort are often illuminated or magnified by what some call intuition and others recognize as inspiration or revelation. I believe that many great discoveries and achievements in science and the arts have resulted from such God-given illumination.

Unfortunately, some of the practitioners of study and reason are contemptuous of or hostile toward religion and revelation, maintaining that truth can only be found and learning can only occur through the methods with which they are familiar. They cannot conceive of the existence of a system of learning that assumes the existence of God and the reality of communications from his Spirit. The only ultimate authority they can conceive is reason, and the word of this god is rationality, as they define it. Such persons cannot accept the existence of a God beyond themselves and their own powers of reasoning. Brigham Young remarked that attitude when he exclaimed: "How difficult it is to teach the natural man, who comprehends nothing more than that which he sees with the natural eye!"[2]

The Book of Mormon describes that attitude among a people who depended solely "upon their own strength and upon their own wisdom" and upon what they could "witness with [their] own eyes." (Hel. 16:15, 20.) Upon the basis of reason, these persons rejected the prophecies, saying, "It is not reasonable that such a being as a Christ shall come." (Vs. 18.) Applying that same attitude, a prominent professor dismissed the Book of Mormon with the assertion, "You don't get books from angels. It is just that simple."

Those who seek gospel knowledge only by study and reason are particularly susceptible to the self-sufficiency and self-importance that sometimes characterize academic pursuits. As the apostle Paul observed in his day, "Knowledge puffeth up." He cautioned the learned: "Take heed lest by any means this liberty [knowledge] of yours become a stumblingblock to them that are weak. . . . And through thy knowledge shall the weak brother perish, for whom Christ died?" (1 Cor. 8:1, 9, 11.)

The apostle Peter foresaw that attitude in our time: "There shall come in the last days scoffers, walking after their own lusts, and saying, Where is the promise of his coming? for since the fathers fell asleep, all things continue as they were from the beginning of the creation." (2 Pet. 3:3–4.)

A Book of Mormon prophet described the origin and consequences of this attitude: "O that cunning plan of the evil one! O the vainness, and the frailties, and the foolishness of men! When they are learned they think they are wise, and they hearken not unto the counsel of God, for they set it aside, supposing they know of themselves, wherefore, their wisdom is foolishness and it profiteth them not. And they shall perish." (2 Ne. 9:28.)

The fulfillment of these prophecies is evident in our day.

Some History of Reason vs. Revelation

Many writers have analyzed what Professor Hugh Nibley calls "the age-old struggle between hard-headed realism and holy tradition." He contrasts what he calls the *sophic*, "the operations of the unaided human mind," with the *mantic*, the "prophetic or inspired, oracular, coming from the other world." He dates the rise of the sophic from the beginning of the sixth century B.C. and credits St. Augustine with "complet[ing] the process of de-Manticizing antique culture."[3]

Within a century after Christ, the confrontation with Greek philosophy brought some compromises in doctrine and practice that one scholar has characterized as "denying the principle of revelation and turning instead to human intellect."[4] Dr. Nibley quotes Leclerq's conclusion: "From the fifth century on, the church became an 'intellectual entity' and ever since one sees in 'the church a thing of reason — *un être de raîson.*' "[5]

Goethe argued that "the deepest, the only theme of human history, compared to which all others are of subordinate importance, is the conflict of skepticism with faith."[6]

For some, that conflict was resolved during the "great medieval debate" that Richard M. Weaver has called "the crucial event in the history of Western culture." This debate included a contest over whether universal truths have a real existence. Weaver explains: "The issue ultimately involved is whether there is a source of truth higher than, and independent of, man; and the answer to the question is decisive for one's view of the nature and destiny of humankind. The practical result of nominalist philosophy is to banish the reality which is perceived by the intellect [I would say, "by revelation"] and to posit as reality [only] that which is perceived by the senses. With this change in the affirmation of what is real, the whole orientation of culture takes a turn, and we are on the road to modern empiricism."[7]

In an address to a college audience, Bruce L. Christensen, president of the Public Broadcasting Service, described the consequences of this philosophy: "In other words, there was no absolute good. There was no absolute evil, or for that matter, no absolute anything. All absolutes were merely a convenience of thinking — they existed in name only (nominally) but not in reality.

"The first principle of nominalism was that there is no source of truth higher than, or independent of, man. The practical result was to deny that knowledge may be gained by any means other than that which can be perceived through man's reasoned use of his senses. Revelation was no longer an acceptable means of acquiring truth."[8]

The Nobel Prize–winning Russian novelist Aleksandr Solzhenitsyn expressed the same idea:

"The mistake [in Western thinking] must be at the root, at the very basis of human thinking in the past centuries. I refer to the prevailing Western view of the world which was first born during the Renaissance and found its political expression from the period of the Enlightenment. It became the basis for government and social science and could be defined as rationalistic humanism or humanistic autonomy: the proclaimed and enforced autonomy of man from any higher force above him. . . . This new way of thinking, which had imposed on us its guidance, did not admit the existence of intrinsic evil in man nor did it see any higher task than the attainment of happiness on earth. It based modern Western civilization on the dangerous trend to worship man and his material needs. . . . We have placed too much hope in political and social reforms, only to find out that we were being deprived of our most precious possession: our spiritual life."[9]

Despite the apparent conflict between reason and revelation, the rational and the religious views of the world are not the opposites of one another. The view of religion (at least the religion that is undiluted by apostasy) includes the methods of reason and the truths determined by them. In contrast, the *rational* view excludes what is *supernatural*. This exclusion was accomplished by merging religion and philosophy. Hugh Nibley explains that the perceived ne-

cessity for this merger was " 'to overcome the objections of
reason to revelation' — that is St. Augustine's famous reconciliation of classical and Christian learning." He continues
by describing the effects of this merger: "But how can you
call it reconciliation when it is always the church that gives
way? It is always reason that has to be satisfied and revelation
that must be manipulated in order to give that satisfaction;
this is no compromise, but complete surrender."[10]

Professor H. Curtis Wright affirms the effects of a long
interaction between religion and rational science: "The overall tendency of their interaction is always one-sided — toward
the naturalizing of religion, not toward the supernaturalizing
of science or scholarship."[11] What is here called the "naturalizing of religion" has the effect of denying the existence
of any truths or values that cannot be demonstrated by the
methods of the so-called natural or scientific order. The
ultimate and exclusive reliance upon reason that results from
this denial is at the root of many public debates. These
include the current controversy over teaching values in public schools and the earlier but continuing concern over
whether universities can simply be involved in disseminating
knowledge or whether they must share responsibility for
the probable use of that knowledge (atomic weapons, for
example).

The source of the ancient conflict between (1) reason or
intellect and (2) faith or revelation is the professor's rejection
of revelation, not the prophet's rejection of reason. The
reality of and widespread understanding of religious experience should prevent its rejection by reasonable men,
but its nature makes it difficult to accept within the categories
propounded by the practitioners of reason. Professor Obert
C. Tanner explains: "Here is a fact, yet one which defies
intellectual analysis. It is a strange thing that an experience

so decisive as to influence a person's total life and commitment should yet be described as ineffable, unutterable, indescribable, and unexpressible. It is no wonder that universities . . . are unable to deal with more than fringe religion—the ideas about religion, not the personal and private experience of religion. It is no wonder that churches and free universities are respectful but reserved toward each other."[12]

In a recent talk at Brigham Young University, Elder Boyd K. Packer gave this perceptive characterization of reason and revelation in a university environment:

"There are two opposing convictions in the university environment. On the one hand, 'seeing is believing'; on the other, 'believing is seeing.' Both are true! Each in its place. The combining of the two individually or institutionally is the challenge of life. . . .

"Each of us must accommodate the mixture of reason and revelation in our lives. The gospel not only permits but *requires* it. An individual who concentrates on either side solely and alone will lose both balance and perspective. History confirms that the university environment always favors reason, with the workings of the Spirit made to feel uncomfortable. I know of no examples to the contrary."

Elder Packer then pleaded for "the fusion of reason and revelation [which] will produce a man and a woman of imperishable worth."[13]

Reason Alone?

When persons attempt to understand or undertake to criticize the gospel of Jesus Christ or the doctrines or practices of his church by the method of reason alone, the outcome is predetermined. No one can find God or understand his doctrines or ordinances without using the means he has

prescribed for receiving the truths of his gospel. That is why
gospel truths have been corrupted and gospel ordinances
have been lost when their meaning has been left to the
interpretation and their application has been left to the sponsorship of scholars who reject the revelations and lack the
authority of God.

I believe this is why the Lord has often called his spokesmen — his prophets — from among the unlettered, those who
are unspoiled by the reasoning of men and therefore receptive to the revelations of God. President Spencer W.
Kimball explained: "The Lord seems never to have placed
a premium on ignorance and yet he has, in many cases,
found his better-trained people unresponsive to the spiritual, and has had to use spiritual giants with less training to
carry on his work."[14]

The apostle Paul explained this to the Corinthian Saints.
He told them he was not going to preach the gospel "with
wisdom of words," because "the preaching of the cross"
was "foolishness" to the sophisticated. (1 Cor. 1:17–18.) But
the sophisticated would come to naught, for, it was written,
the Lord "will destroy the wisdom of the wise, and will bring
to nothing the understanding of the prudent." (1 Cor. 1:19.)
In contrast, those who placed their faith in what Paul dryly
called "the foolishness of preaching" would be saved. (1
Cor. 1:21.) He explained:

"Because the foolishness of God is wiser than men; and
the weakness of God is stronger than men. For ye see your
calling, brethren, how that not many wise men after the flesh,
not many mighty, not many noble, are called: but God hath
chosen the foolish things of the world to confound the wise;
and God hath chosen the weak things of the world to confound the things which are mighty; and base things of the
world, and things which are despised, hath God chosen,

yea, and things which are not, to bring to nought things that are: that no flesh should glory in his presence." (1 Cor. 1:25–29; also see 1 Cor. 3:18–20.)

Those who rely exclusively on study and reason reject or remain doubtful of all absolutes that cannot be established through the five senses, including good and evil and the existence and omniscience of God. They also reject all other methods of acquiring knowledge, including revelation. They tend to be self-sufficient, self-important, and enamored of their own opinions. Reason is their god and intellectualism is their creed. They dwell in that "large and spacious building" seen in a prophet's vision of the "wisdom" and "pride of the world." (1 Ne. 11:35–36.) It may be said of them as Stephen said of the children of Israel who made a calf in the days of Aaron: they "rejoiced in the works of their own hands." (Acts 7:41.) This worldly worship of self and self-sufficiency is surely condemned by the eternal command, "Thou shalt have no other gods before me." (Ex. 20:3.)

Exclusive reliance on learning by study and reason has affected more than secular subjects. It has also affected Christian theology. Baptist educator Dr. Ben C. Fisher wrote:

"For more than a hundred years, modern theology has been marching to an increasingly secular cadence. The traditional supernatural view of man has been superseded by a completely rational outlook on his behavior and his place and activities in the world. . . . The Christ-centered gospel with its simple but uncompromising ethical demands was diluted until the very name of Christ itself, except in some oblique fashion, disappeared from the center of theological thought and writings. . . . Recovery of the authority of the Scriptures does not require repudiation of scholarship, but it does require the reaffirmation of the primacy of revelation."[15]

Those who reject revelation and approach God and a study of his gospel solely by the methods of research, deliberation, and scholarly debate are like the leaders who persecuted Jesus for healing on the Sabbath. In responding to their attack, the Savior taught this lesson about the ways of God and the ways of the world: "I am come in my Father's name, and ye receive me not: if another shall come in his own name, him ye will receive. How can ye believe, which receive honour one of another, and seek not the honour that cometh from God only?" (John 5:43–44.)

Jesus taught the same lesson to Peter. When the Savior told his followers that he must go to Jerusalem to suffer many things and be killed and raised again, the chief apostle declared that these things must not happen. Jesus rebuked him, saying, "Get thee behind me, Satan: thou art an offence unto me: for thou savourest not the things that be of God, but those that be of men." (Matt. 16:23.)

In each of these instances the Savior proclaimed the importance of the things of God above the things of man. On another occasion he applied that principle to teach his professional critics the preeminence of the prophetic over the scholarly. Jesus was confronted by a group who had hypocritically built monuments to the prophets whom their predecessors had murdered, while personally rejecting the living prophets God was sending to them. In what I understand to be a condemnation of their rejection of the fullness of gospel understanding possible through revelation, the Savior pronounced woe upon these worldly professionals: "For ye have taken away the key of knowledge, the fulness of the scriptures; ye enter not in yourselves into the kingdom; and those who were entering in, ye hindered." (JST Luke 11:47–49, 53.)

Jesus also taught the preeminence of the ways of God

over the ways of men by warning against the self-serving motives of those scholars who proclaim from their own learning: "He that speaketh of himself seeketh his own glory: but he that seeketh his glory that sent him, the same is true, and no unrighteousness is in him." (John 7:18.) This same theme recurred when Jesus explained why some converted rulers would not confess him lest they be put out of the synagogue: "They loved the praise of men more than the praise of God." (John 12:43.)

The modern manifestation of self-serving scholarship was prophesied by Nephi: "The Gentiles . . . have built up many churches; nevertheless, they put down the power and miracles of God, and preach up unto themselves their own wisdom and their own learning, that they may get gain and grind upon the face of the poor." (2 Ne. 26:20.)

Nephi's prophecy surely includes those who use the academy as their church, who pay their "religious" devotions in libraries and laboratories, and who have a natural explanation for all the miracles of God. As he explained:

"It shall come to pass in that day that the churches which are built up, and not unto the Lord, . . . shall contend one with another; and their priests shall contend one with another, and they shall teach with their learning, and deny the Holy Ghost, which giveth utterance.

"And they deny the power of God, the Holy One of Israel; and they say unto the people: Hearken unto us, and hear ye our precept; for behold there is no God today, for the Lord and the Redeemer hath done his work, and he hath given his power unto men; behold, hearken ye unto my precept; if they shall say there is a miracle wrought by the hand of the Lord, believe it not; for this day he is not a God of miracles; he hath done his work." (2 Ne. 28:3–6.)

Nephi declares that as a result of this error, "in many

instances they do err because they are taught by the precepts of men." (2 Ne. 28:14.)

Such teachings are typical of the directness and value of the Book of Mormon. Written by inspiration, it is an unfailing antidote for the doctrinal confusion and behavioral excesses of our day. Nephi explained the reason for this quality when he described the purpose for his writing what became the first part of the Book of Mormon: "Wherefore, the things which are pleasing unto the world I do not write, but the things which are pleasing unto God and unto those who are not of the world." (1 Ne. 6:5.)

The warning against trusting in the ways of man to learn the things of God was repeated in modern times: "Deny not the spirit of revelation, nor the spirit of prophecy, for wo unto him that denieth these things." (D&C 11:25; also see 1 Thes. 5:19–20.) Elder Bruce R. McConkie voiced the principle and gave illustrations: "A special standard of judgment is needed to prove anything in the spiritual realm. No scientific research, no intellectual inquiry, no investigative processes known to mortal man can prove that God is a personal being, that all men will be raised in immortality, and that repentant souls are born of the Spirit. . . . Spiritual verities can be proven only by spiritual means."[16]

The things of God cannot be learned solely by study and reason. Despite their essential and beneficial uses, the methods of study and reason are insufficient as ways of approaching God and understanding the doctrines of his gospel. We cannot come to know the things of God while rejecting or failing to use the indispensable method God has prescribed to learn these things. The things of God must be learned in his own way, through faith in God and revelation from the Holy Ghost.

Over the years, persons of scholarly inclination have

published journals and organized lectures and symposia to study the history of the Church, reason about the principles of the gospel, and share insights in the application of gospel principles to contemporary problems. I have sometimes been asked, "What is wrong with such efforts?" In my personal opinion, so long as they are private and personal and do not imply Church sponsorship or approval, there is nothing wrong with such efforts, *provided* those who participate understand and observe the limits of study and reason in such an undertaking. Unfortunately, many do not.

The problem I have observed in such activities is that for some participants, these efforts are not a prelude to or supplementary of faith and revelation, but are (or come to be) substitutes for them. That is not the Lord's way.

The danger and the principle, as I see it, can be expressed by likening revelation (which is vital to gospel knowledge and the continuation of spiritual life) to oxygen. For purposes of this analogy, we may liken reasoning to methane. In proper balance and under proper control, methane provides illumination and fuel for useful tasks. But if methane comes to dominate the atmosphere, it drives out oxygen. Those present in a room being infiltrated with methane can lose their lives for lack of oxygen, and this can happen without warning to the victims.

Like the methane in this analogy, reasoned discussions about the gospel can be useful, but they cannot sustain spiritual life by themselves. Moreover, they have a tendency, if not watched and controlled carefully, to become so dominant in the atmosphere that they can destroy spiritual life.

In short, my concern with those who patronize the journals and the lectures and the symposia is not that they will have too much discussion or too much reason, but that they

will have too little revelation because they will have (or
come to have) too little prayer, too little study of the scriptures, too little humility, and too little faith. And, as Elder
Neal A. Maxwell has observed, "Without real faith and its
attendant submissiveness, people sooner or later find one
thing or another to stumble over."[17]

Members of The Church of Jesus Christ of Latter-day
Saints should observe a respectful distinction between the
way they seek to acquire and understand (1) knowledge
that is sacred and (2) knowledge that is secular. Scholarship,
lectures, symposia, and the clash of opposing views in adversary debate are acceptable means to acquire much knowledge and understanding, but they are not suited to acquiring
and understanding the most sacred knowledge, the knowledge of God and the mysteries of his gospel. Gospel truths
and testimony are received from the Holy Ghost through
prayerful seeking, through faith, through scripture study,
through righteous living, through listening to inspired communications and counsel, through serious conversations
with persons of faith, and through reverent personal study
and quiet contemplation.

Relationships Between Reason and Revelation

Persons who pursue sacred learning through study and
reason and also through faith and revelation will always have
the problem of defining the relationship between these two
methods. This subject has intrigued people of reason and
people of faith from the earliest times. I will discuss three
of the many possible models of this relationship as applied
to obtaining knowledge of the things of God.

1. Coequal Partners

After I had given a talk on the importance of revelation
in learning the gospel, a friend wrote me his analysis of the
relationship between reason and revelation (which he called

"Spirit"). He suggested that they are coequal partners, each providing a check upon the other. I quote his letter by permission.

These two can or should act to both complement one another and be a check and balance to each other. True propositions of one are subject to examination and scrutiny by the other. Either one relied upon exclusively leads to destructive excess. Historically, relying too much on the Spirit to the exclusion of reason has often led to fanaticism, intolerance, bloodshed, and, in general, other manifestations of extreme subjectivism. Similarly, too much reliance on reason or intellect has often destroyed faith and led to a sterile cynicism. . . .

Does your thesis imply that the sort of check and balance between the Spirit and reason I have spoken of is misconceived? Can't the Spirit and reason work as co-equal partners, or at least can't they be made to work harmoniously together, and in fact should we not strive for such? And when they do not or seem not to harmonize (for me they usually do), are we not justified in withholding judgment? in *not* declaring one right and one wrong? in patiently waiting for or striving to find clearer explanations?[18]

I wrote in response:

While I believe that everyone will use reason and the Spirit (and, obviously, that some use reason better than others, and some hear [feel] the Spirit better than others), I do not believe that they are "co-equal partners" so that where they do not "harmonize," we are "justified in withholding judgment." The reason I do not believe this is that I know of no way to prove by reason some of the fundamental realities — the existence of God, and the efficacy of the Atonement, for example. Therefore, unless we are willing to give primacy to the Spirit (in the exercise of faith, which is the first principle of the gospel), we will be forever agnostic.

I have had many experiences in my life where reason has

led me to one conclusion, but the Spirit and faith have pointed the other way. In my judgment, the extent to which a person can hear [feel] the Spirit, and has the faith to follow it on the subjects I treated in my talk, is one of the best indicators of faith and spirituality. That obviously leaves plenty of room for reason to operate, but it does not give reason co-equal partnership in the areas of knowing God, learning His commandments, and understanding the doctrine of the kingdom.[19]

If I am correct in my conviction that reason and revelation are not coequal partners, then is one always dominant over the other? Some have proposed that reason is always dominant, so that we relinquish faith in whatever cannot be proven by reason. Others have urged that what is called revelation must always prevail, reason to the contrary notwithstanding. Personally, I cannot feel comfortable with either of these extremes. There must be a better, truer, explanation of the relationship between reason and revelation.

2. Division of Sovereignty

In another approach, reason is urged as the most likely way to acquire knowledge on some subjects and revelation as the most likely way on other subjects. This proposal draws a boundary line through the world of knowledge. On the one side it grants primacy to reason, and on the other side it grants primacy to revelation. This approach has been used by both religionists and philosophers, though they are not necessarily in agreement on where the boundary line should be drawn.

Philosopher Mortimer J. Adler employed this technique in a recent article. In the context of his reference to religion as "a pure act of faith, incapable of being supported or challenged by rational analysis or empirical knowledge of the world," he concluded: "In the whole range of our *currently* accepted scientific understanding of the world, I find nothing that introduces a single new difficulty into our thinking about God, or presents an intellectual obstacle to our affirming God's existence. In short, . . . nothing that I can learn from science has any bearing on the thinking that I must do when I address myself to the question whether God, as thus conceived, exists or not."[20]

Adler's faith-based definition of religion permits him to give generous tribute to religion, while rejecting as mere "superstitions" some religious beliefs and practices that run counter to what he considers scientifically proven facts. His analysis provides a penetrating challenge for those whose religious position is principally based on inheritance or cultural affinities. He explains:

"With regard to the apparent increase of secularism or irreligion in our Western society, I suggest that the men and women who have given up religion because of the impact on their minds of modern science and philosophy were never truly religious in the first place, but only superstitious. The prevalence and predominance of science in our culture has cured a great many of the superstitious beliefs that constituted their false religiosity. . . . The increase of secularism and irreligion in our society does not reflect a decrease in the number of persons who are truly religious, but a decrease in the number of those who are falsely religious; that is, merely superstitious."[21]

Many religious people also distinguish between the domain of faith and the domain of science, but some would surely disagree with where and how Adler draws the line between the two. For example, Robert J. Matthews, former dean of Religious Instruction at Brigham Young University, draws a sharp distinction "between what we call natural, or secular, truth and spiritual truth." He explains:

"Jacob stoutly denounces trusting in the wisdom and the learning of the world, especially if these prevent a person from coming to a knowledge and acceptance of the gospel, or distract those who already have the gospel. A frequent topic in the Book of Mormon is the antagonism between the learning of the world and the things of God (see, for example, 2 Nephi 26–29; Jacob 4:14). . . . Hence the Book of Mormon draws a wide distinction between the secular and the spiritual."[22]

Despite his recognition of a distinction between secular and spiritual domains, Professor Matthews surely would not agree with where philosopher Adler draws the line between them. Adler starts with what he believes science has proven, and he cedes sovereignty to religion only as to the territory that remains. Adler insists:

"The truths of religion must be compatible with the truths of science and the truths of philosophy. As scientific knowledge advances, and as philosophical analysis improves, religion is progressively purified of the superstitions that accidentally attach themselves to it as parasites. That being so, it is easier in fact to be more truly religious today than ever before, precisely because of the advances that have been made in science and philosophy. That is to say, it is easier for those who will make the effort to think clearly in and about religion, not for those whose addiction to religion is nothing more than a slavish adherence to inherited superstition. Throughout the whole of the past, only a small number of men were ever truly religious. The vast majority who gave their epochs and their societies the *appearance* of being religious were primarily and essentially superstitious."[23]

In contrast, Professor Matthews allocates primacy in
terms of subject matter: "Different truths are comprehended
by the mind of man in different ways. We perceive most
truths that we deal with in mortality through our natural
senses, but certain truths necessary to the redemption of
our souls we perceive only by revelation through the Holy
Ghost. We comprehend these truths not by intellectual activity alone but through spiritual discernment."[24]

Like Professor Matthews, I of course also reject Adler's
suggestion that every religious belief or practice that runs
counter to what he calls "the truths of science" is a superstition that must be surrendered. The world of religion
clearly has its superstitions, but, just as clearly, the world of
science has its invalid theories and its erroneous proofs. Just
as superstition can masquerade as religious truth, so can
scientific theories and erroneous proofs masquerade as scientific fact. As one Latter-day Saint commentator has noted:

"Science is wonderful—as far as it goes. But scientific
theories come and go, almost always marked by wrangling
between factions. This is the very nature of scientific theo-
rizing, an inescapable part. It seems to me critical that we
keep this limitation firmly in mind, lest science become
something that could 'deceive even the very elect.' Com-
menting on those students at BYU who lost, or abandoned,
their testimonies because of the neat 'ascent of man' sche-
matic of twenty years ago (now in complete disarray, as the
Leakey-Johanson debate shows), Nibley laments, 'It is sad to
think how many of those telling points that turned some of
our best students away from the gospel have turned out to
be dead wrong!' "[25]

Many of the casualties that occur along the contested
boundary line between science and religion result from one
or another contestant trying to occupy and control terrain

beyond the borders of his own experience — religionists who pronounce on science or scientists who pronounce on religion. In my view, both kinds of extraterritoriality are unseemly.

I remember vividly the resentment I felt when a prominent actor, invited to Brigham Young University to share insights about the arts, lectured his BYU audience on the air pollution being caused by the university's coal-fired heating plant. I feel the same way whenever anyone uses prominence acquired in one field of learning or accomplishment to magnify the volume or prominence of his pronouncements in another field.

All experts are tempted to claim expertise beyond their territory, like the legal scholar someone described as an expert on British law when he was in the United States and an expert on United States law when he was in Britain. Whoever presumes to use an expertise acquired in one field as a basis for authoritative pronouncements in another implies a unity of principles between fields that is easily assumed but rarely demonstrated.

The approach of distinguishing between secular and spiritual learning is a familiar one. It is the basis for my frequent references to revelation's being essential to learning about the things of God. It is, of course, clear that the categories are not mutually exclusive (revelation being possible for secular learning, and reason being essential for spiritual learning). Still, it is true that we comprehend secular truths predominantly by study and reason and spiritual truths finally only by revelation.

3. Sequential

Another relationship between reason and revelation in the acquisition of sacred knowledge has been described by modern revelation. That relationship is *sequential.* Study and reason come first. Revelation comes second.

We see this in Oliver Cowdery's attempt to translate ancient records. After he failed, the Lord told him this was because he "took no thought," but only asked God. He should have studied it out in his mind and then asked if it was right. Only after he applied himself to study and reason would the Lord affirm or deny the correctness of the proposed translation. And only on receiving that revelation could the text be written, because, the Lord said, "you cannot write that which is sacred save it be given you from me." (D&C 9:7–9.)

This revelation teaches that in the acquisition of knowledge about the things of God, reason is not an alternative to revelation. Study and reason can *find* the truth on many of these subjects, but only revelation can *confirm* it. Study and reason are a means to an end, and the end is revelation from God.

This sequential relationship is somewhat comparable to a science-based procedure I learned as a young man. I worked as an engineer in a small broadcasting station. I was licensed to operate the radio transmitter. I learned that the startup sequence for the final stage of the amplifiers was critical. First, we applied the power to the filaments of the vacuum tubes. These filaments, similar to the coil in an incandescent light bulb, reached their operating temperature and condition in about thirty seconds. Only then could we safely turn the switch for the high voltage supply that put the transmitter's amplified signal "on the air." Each step was essential, and each had to occur in the proper sequence. Otherwise, there would be no radio signal, and the vacuum tubes could even suffer serious damage.

This radio analogy can be applied to the receiving mechanism provided to each of us by our Creator. First we warm up the mechanism with study and reason. Then we apply

for the power of revelation in order to obtain the desired
communication.

Reason and Revelation in Sequence

In the sequential relationship between reason and revelation, it is important that reason have what we can call
"the first word" and that revelation have "the last word."

In this sequence, reason can "study it out" and formulate
a proposed solution. In addition, as we seek confirmation
or other guidance from revelation, reason can serve as a
threshold check to screen out revelation that is counterfeit
and to provide a tentative authentication of revelation that
is genuine. This is necessary because, just as there is reasoning that is faulty, so also there is revelation that is spurious.

In an important teaching about spiritual gifts, the early
members of the restored church were cautioned to beware
lest they be deceived. (D&C 46:8.) The Lord identified the
sources of deception: "That ye may not be seduced by evil
spirits, or doctrines of devils, or the commandments of men;
for some are of men, and others of devils." (D&C 46:7.)

Elder Boyd K. Packer explains: "Not all inspiration comes
from God (see D&C 46:7). The evil one has the power to
tap into those channels of revelation and send conflicting
signals which can mislead and confuse us. There are promptings from evil sources which are so carefully counterfeited
as to deceive even the very elect (see Matthew 24:24)."[26]

As a result, we need reason to authenticate revelation.
Then, once it is authenticated, true revelation can be communicated through its various forms and perform its various
functions.

By this means and in this sequence, reason screens revelation and revelation confirms or overrules reason. As con-

cerns sacred knowledge, it is just as important for reason to have the first word as it is for revelation to have the last word. I believe this is one meaning of the Lord's command for his people to "seek learning, even by study and also by faith." (D&C 88:118.)

Reason Authenticates Revelation

There are at least three tests that reason can apply as a threshold check on the authenticity of revelation. True revelation will pass all three of these tests, and spurious revelation (whose source is "of men" or "of devils") will fail at least one of them.

1. *True revelation will edify the recipient.* It must therefore be in words that are coherent or in a feeling whose message can be understood by one who is spiritually receptive.

The apostle Paul taught this principle to those who were comparing the gift of tongues and the gift of prophecy. "Forasmuch as ye are zealous of spiritual gifts," he instructed them, "seek that ye may excel to the edifying of the church. . . . Let all things be done unto edifying." (1 Cor. 14:12, 26.)

In a modern revelation given to instruct the Saints how to distinguish between the Lord's revelations and those given by the "false spirits, which have gone forth in the earth, deceiving the world" (D&C 50:2), the Lord declared: "That which doth not edify is not of God, and is darkness" (vs. 23). Similarly, the Prophet Joseph Smith taught that members should "not speak in tongues except there be an interpreter present."[27] Babblings and other incoherent communications cannot be revelations from God.

The test of edification as a way of screening out spurious and deceptive revelations from Satan was reaffirmed in a succeeding revelation to the Prophet Joseph Smith. This revelation also specifies the related tests of prayerfulness, contrite spirit, meek language, compliance with gospel ordinances, and refraining from being physically "overcome":

"And again, I will give unto you a pattern in all things, that ye may not be deceived; for Satan is abroad in the land, and he goeth forth deceiving the nations — wherefore he that prayeth, whose spirit is contrite, the same is accepted of me if he obey mine ordinances.

"He that speaketh, whose spirit is contrite, whose language is meek and edifieth, the same is of God if he obey mine ordinances. And again, he that trembleth under my power shall be made strong, and shall bring forth fruits of praise and wisdom, according to the revelations and truths which I have given you. And again, he that is overcome and bringeth not forth fruits, even according to this pattern, is not of me." (D&C 52:14–18.)

To apply these tests to evaluate and authenticate revelation or inspiration, the recipient must obviously use the techniques of study and reason.

2. *The content of a true revelation must be consistent with the position and responsibilities of the person who receives it.* The Lord taught this principle to the infant church in a revelation that explained to Oliver Cowdery that no one was appointed to receive commandments and revelations for the entire church except the Prophet Joseph Smith, "for all things must be done in order." Revelations being received by a member, Hiram Page, were the deceptions of Satan, "for, behold, these things have not been appointed unto him." (D&C 28:13, 12.)

A few months later, another revelation reaffirmed to the elders of the Church that "commandments and revelations" for the Church would be received only by the prophet the Lord had appointed, and that "none else shall be appointed unto this gift except it be through him." Those selected by the Lord to exercise this gift would "come in at the gate and be ordained as I have told you before" — thus excluding the possibility of secret callings or appointments to receive revelation. "And this shall be a law unto you, that ye receive not the teachings of any that shall come before you as revelations or commandments; and this I give unto you that you may not be deceived, that you may know they are not of me." (D&C 43:2–7.)

According to these principles, revelations for a ward come to the bishop; for the family, to its head; for the person, to him or her directly. A neighbor does not receive revelations for a neighbor, and one who has not been publicly called and set apart according to the government and procedures of the Church does not receive revelations to command or guide the Church or any group of its members. One of the surest evidences of false revelations (those based on mortal authorship or devilish intervention) is that their content, judged according to reason, is communicated through channels other than those the Lord has prescribed for that subject.

3. *True revelation must be consistent with the principles of the gospel as revealed in the scriptures and the teachings of the prophets.* The Lord will not give revelations that will contradict the principles of the gospel. His house is a house of order.

Revelations may add to the body of existing gospel knowledge ("line upon line, precept upon precept" — D&C 98:12), guide leaders in the duties of their callings, or assist individual members in applying gospel principles to particular circumstances. Personally or through his designated

spokesman, the Lord may change the ordinances and practices of his church. The Savior personally revoked the law
of offerings and sacrifices by the shedding of blood (3 Ne.
15:3–9), and commanded his people to offer the sacrifice
of a broken heart and a contrite spirit (3 Ne. 9:19–20; D&C
59:8). Peter received a revelation informing him that the
gospel should now be preached to the gentiles. (Acts 10.)
Joseph Smith and Brigham Young were directed to introduce
and practice the principle of plural marriage, and Wilford
Woodruff was directed to withdraw it. But the Lord will not
give individual members revelations that will contradict the
doctrines of his church or the instructions given through
his leaders. President Spencer W. Kimball said, "If one does
receive revelations, which one may expect if he is worthy,
they will always be in total alignment with the program of
the Church; they will never be counter."[28]

Limits on Reason's Evaluations

While reason can appropriately evaluate some aspects
of revelation, its function should be limited to the threshold
determination of the genuineness or *authenticity* (source)
of a revelation. If the test of reason goes beyond this, it can
become a check upon the *acceptability* of God's commands.
Thus, when the apostle Paul taught the Athenians about the
Resurrection, some mocked him, apparently because they
believed that the conclusions of reason were not to be challenged. (Acts 17:32.) In that view, which is common among
those who are skilled at study and reason, philosophy holds
mastery over prophecy, reason over revelation.

Just as we must put limits to the use of reason as a check
on revelation, we should also recognize the inherent limitations on the use of reason to evaluate the behavior of
persons acting in response to revelation. As Elder Boyd K.

Packer has observed, "There is no such thing as an accurate, objective history of the Church without consideration of the spiritual powers that attend this work."[29] If we try to evaluate faith-motivated behavior solely in rational terms, we distort reality. Some writings in Mormon history make that mistake.

President Gordon B. Hinckley commented on this kind of distortion in answering criticism that the Church is opposed to reason and rational thought in the writing of its history. "They have failed to realize that religion is as much concerned with the heart as it is with the intellect," he observed. "Those who criticize us have lost sight of the glory and wonder of this work. In their cultivated faultfinding, they do not see the majesty of the great onrolling of this cause. They have lost sight of the spark that was kindled in Palmyra and which is now lighting fires of faith across the earth in many lands and in many languages. Wearing the spectacles of humanism, they fail to realize that spiritual emotions, with recognition of the influence of the Holy Spirit, had as much to do with the actions of our forebears as did the processes of the mind."[30]

In short, what Church leaders have opposed in the writing of Church history is not the use of reason but the omission of revelation.

Revelation Outranks Reason

Just as reason has the first word in matters of sacred knowledge, so revelation has the last word. We cannot know the things of God without the Spirit of God. (1 Cor. 2:11.) As President Harold B. Lee said, "The revelations of God are the standards by which we measure all learning, and if anything squares not with the revelations, then we may be certain that it is not truth."[31] I believe this is what the Book of Mormon prophet meant when he said, "To be learned is good if they hearken unto the counsels of God." (2 Ne. 9:29.)

Those who apply themselves to study and reason about sacred things, but then omit or reject the outcome of the sovereign second step of revelation, can be like the priests whom the prophet Abinadi denounced for "perverting the ways of the Lord" because they had not "applied [their] hearts to understanding." (Mosiah 12:26–27.) Speaking of such persons, the Lord said, "They perceive not the light and . . . turn their hearts from me because of the precepts of men." (D&C 45:29.)

Conclusion

We are commanded to seek learning by study, the way of reason, and by faith, the way that relies on revelation. Both are pleasing to God. He uses both ways to reveal light and knowledge to his children. But when it comes to a knowledge of God and the principles of his gospel, we must give primacy to revelation because that is the Lord's way.

Latter-day Saints are fond of quoting the Prophet Joseph Smith's statement, "A man is saved no faster than he gets knowledge."[32] This is sometimes used to suggest that the pursuit of knowledge is, by itself, a saving activity, and that all men must learn all things in order to be saved. That was not what the Prophet said. In context, it is clear that his statement referred to a particular kind of knowledge, gained in a particular way.

In the last part of the sentence quoted above, the Prophet explains that without knowledge, a man "will be brought into captivity" by some evil spirit with "more knowledge, and consequently more power." The next sentence concludes the thought: "Hence it needs revelation to assist us, and give us knowledge of the things of God."[33] This statement identifies the kind of knowledge that saves and the ultimate method we must follow to obtain it.

Study and reason also have an important role in learning the things of God. Seekers begin by studying the word of God and the teachings of his servants and by trying to understand them by the techniques of reason. Reason can authenticate revelation and inspiration by measuring them against the threshold tests of edification, position, and consistency with gospel principles. But reason has no role in evaluating the content of revelation in order to accept or reject it according to some supposed standard of reasonableness. Revelation has the final word.

Unfortunately, some who are adept at acquiring knowledge by reason reject the method of revelation. As men learned that they could acquire knowledge by reason, such as by observation and experimentation, some fell into the logical fallacy of concluding that knowledge could be acquired *only* by this means. Their intellectual descendants persist to this day, rejecting the reality of whatever they cannot measure by their methods.

In contrast, the Lord has declared that "no man knoweth of [God's] ways save it be revealed unto him." (Jacob 4:8.) And he has outlined the requirements for learning by revelation: having faith, being humble, seeking by prayer, keeping the commandments, repenting of sins, doing good works, and reading the scriptures. Those who are able to learn by this method may qualify for what could be called the ultimate revelation.

In modern revelation God has promised that "the keys of the mystery of those things which have been sealed, . . . from the foundation of the world" (the fulness of the gospel) are to be "given by the Comforter, the Holy Ghost, that knoweth all things." (D&C 35:18–19). That is the ultimate revelation. It will come by the Holy Spirit, not by scholarly study or by mortal reasoning. When it comes, it will reveal to those who fear God and serve him "all mysteries, yea, all the hidden mysteries of [God's] kingdom from days of old, and for ages to come." (D&C 76:7.) "Yea, verily I say unto you, in that day when the Lord shall come, he shall reveal all things." (D&C 101:32.) In that day, as foreseen by Isaiah, "the earth shall be full of the knowledge of the Lord." (Isa. 11:9; 2 Ne. 21:9; also see D&C 84:98.)

Those who receive this revelation are described: "Their wisdom shall be great, and their understanding reach to heaven; and before them the wisdom of the wise shall perish, and the understanding of the prudent shall come to naught. For by my Spirit will I enlighten them, and by my power will I make known unto them the secrets of my will—yea, even those things which eye has not seen, nor ear heard, nor yet entered into the heart of man." (D&C 76:9–10.)

After they received the great revelation on the three degrees of glory, Joseph Smith and Sidney Rigdon wrote these inspired words: "Great and marvelous are the works of the Lord, and the mysteries of his kingdom which he showed unto us, which surpass all understanding in glory, and in might, and in dominion; which he commanded us we should not write while we were yet in the Spirit, and are not lawful for man to utter; neither is man capable to make them known, for they are only to be seen and under-stood by the power of the Holy Spirit, which God bestows on those who love him, and purify themselves before him." (D&C 76:114–16.)

In an inspired utterance, the Prophet Joseph Smith de-scribed the Lord's "pouring down knowledge from heaven upon the heads of the Latter-day Saints." (D&C 121:33.) Such is the fruit of revelation, the teaching of the Holy Spirit. Such is the heritage of the faithful who "seek learning, even by study and also by faith." (D&C 88:118.)

NOTES

1. Harold B. Lee, *Ye Are the Light of the World* (Salt Lake City: Deseret Book, 1974), 117.

2. Brigham Young, *Journal of Discourses* 1:2.

3. Hugh Nibley, "Three Shrines: Mantic, Sophic, and Sophistic," *The Ancient State* (Salt Lake City: Deseret Book and Foundation for Ancient Research and Mormon Studies, 1991), 315, 333, 354.

4. Stephen E. Robinson, "Warring Against the Saints of God," *Ensign* 18 (January 1988): 39.

5. Hugh Nibley, "Paths That Stray: Some Notes on Sophic and Mantic," *The Ancient State*, 443.

6. Quoted in H. Curtis Wright, "The Central Problem of Intellectual History," *Scholar and Educator* 12 (Fall 1988): 52.

7. Richard M. Weaver, *Ideas Have Consequences* (Chicago and London: University of Chicago Press, 1948), 3.

8. Bruce L. Christensen, "First Principles First," Forum Address at Ricks College, Rexburg, Idaho, November 19, 1987.

9. Aleksandr Solzhenitsyn, "Commencement Address," *Harvard University Gazette*, June 8, 1978.

10. Nibley, "Three Shrines," *The Ancient State*, 367.

11. Wright, "The Central Problem," 53.

12. Obert C. Tanner, *One Man's Search* (Salt Lake City: University of Utah Press, 1989), 151.

13. Boyd K. Packer, "I Say unto You, Be One," Devotional Address at Brigham Young University, February 12, 1991.

14. *The Teachings of Spencer W. Kimball*, ed. Edward L. Kimball (Salt Lake City: Bookcraft, 1982), 388–89.

15. Ben C. Fisher, *The Idea of a Christian University in Today's World* (Macon, Georgia: Mercer University Press, 1989), ix–x.

16. Bruce R. McConkie, *The Millennial Messiah* (Salt Lake City: Deseret Book, 1982), 175.

17. Neal A. Maxwell, *Not My Will, But Thine* (Salt Lake City: Bookcraft, 1988), 32.

18. Letter to author dated April 19, 1989.

19. Letter from author dated April 27, 1989.

20. Mortimer J. Adler, "Concerning God, Modern Man and Religion," *Aspen Quarterly* (Winter 1990): 100, 110.

21. Ibid., 112.

22. Robert J. Matthews, *A Bible! A Bible!* (Salt Lake City: Bookcraft, 1990), 165, 162.

23. Adler, "Concerning God," 112–13.

24. Matthews, *A Bible! A Bible!*, 162.

25. Charles L. Boyd, "Forever Tentative," *Dialogue* 22 (Winter 1989): 149, quoting Hugh Nibley, *Old Testament and Related Studies* (Salt Lake City: Deseret Book and Foundation for Ancient Research and Mormon Studies, 1986), 57.

26. Boyd K. Packer, *Let Not Your Heart Be Troubled* (Salt Lake City: Bookcraft, 1991), 212.

27. *Teachings of the Prophet Joseph Smith,* ed. Joseph Fielding Smith (Salt Lake City: Deseret News Press, 1956), 247.

28. *The Teachings of Spencer W. Kimball,* 458.

29. "The Mantle Is Far, Far Greater Than the Intellect," in Packer, *Let Not Your Heart Be Troubled,* 104.

30. Gordon B. Hinckley, *Faith, the Essence of True Religion* (Salt Lake City: Deseret Book, 1989), 76.

31. Harold B. Lee, *Stand Ye in Holy Places* (Salt Lake City: Deseret Book, 1974), 143.

32. Smith, *Teachings,* 217.

33. Ibid. Also see D&C 130:19.

CHAPTER 3

SIGNS AND SCIENCE

Science uses experiments and observation, such as watching, measuring, and analyzing, as it attempts to gain increased understanding. In contrast, the scriptures warn against seeking signs to determine religious truth. This is another illustration of the significant differences between the Lord's way and the world's way.

The kind of signs referred to in this chapter is the signs that are sought or given as proof of the existence of God, the authority of his servants, or the truths of his gospel.*

Viewed as a whole, the scriptures contain apparently conflicting teachings and examples on whether signs should be used as proof. But the instructions to modern Israel are clear. Signs are not acceptable to produce conversions, but they are acceptable — even promised — to confirm them.

---

*The scriptures also use the word *sign* to signify other meanings not discussed here. These include the sabbath as a sign of the covenant between God and Israel (Ex. 31:13, 17; Ezek. 20:12, 20), the signs of the birth and death of the Messiah (Luke 2:12; 1 Ne. 19:10; Hel. 14:20), the signs of his second coming (D&C 45:16, 39), and the signs of the times (Matt. 16:3; D&C 68:11).

Signs in the Bible

The Old Testament contains memorable examples of miracles that amounted to signs. Such were the various plagues the Lord inflicted on the Egyptians through his prophet Moses. (See Ex. 7–10.) The children of Israel were later reminded of these signs and wonders, to increase their faith. (Deut. 6:22; 26:8.) Gideon asked for and received a sign that he was chosen to deliver Israel. (Judg. 6:17.)

Another example of a highly visible miracle given as a sign was Elijah's contest with the 450 priests of Baal. The directness of this sign is clear from Elijah's challenge: "Call ye on the name of your gods, and I will call on the name of the Lord: and the God that answereth by fire, let him be God. And all the people answered and said, It is well spoken." (1 Kings 18:24.) The heavenly fire that consumed the sacrifice came in response to Elijah's prayer. The unsuccessful priests of Baal lost the contest and they also lost their lives.

The attitude toward signs seems to be different in the New Testament. Despite the many miracles Jesus performed during his ministry, in most instances the sacred accounts disclaim the use of miracles as signs to prove authority or religious truth.

At the beginning of the Savior's ministry, he was tempted. Twice Satan challenged Jesus to work a miracle to prove that he was the Son of God. Each time Jesus refused. (Matt. 4:1–11; Luke 4:1–13.)

During the Savior's ministry the scribes and Pharisees said, "Master, we would see a sign from thee." (Matt. 12:38; also see 1 Cor. 1:22.) The Pharisees and Sadducees "desired him that he would shew them a sign from heaven." (Matt. 16:1.) Each time he refused to give them a sign, declaring that it was a wicked and an adulterous generation "that seeketh after a sign." (Matt. 12:39; 16:4; also see Mark 8:11–12; Luke 11:29.)

Even as they describe the miracles Jesus performed, most of the Gospel writers report his instructions or actions that would prevent those miracles being used to prove his calling, his authority, or the truth of his message. When Jesus healed the leper, he instructed him, "See thou tell no man." (Matt. 8:4; Mark 1:44; Luke 5:14.) When he healed the multitudes from Galilee, he "charged them that they should not make him known." (Matt. 12:16; Mark 3:12.) When he raised the daughter of the ruler of the synagogue, "he suffered no man to go in, save Peter, and James, and John, and the father and the mother of the maiden," and "he charged them that they should tell no man what was done." (Luke 8:51, 56; also see Mark 5:37, 43.)

When Jesus healed the deaf man, he "took him aside from the multitude," and afterwards "he charged them that they should tell no man." (Mark 7:33, 36.) Before Jesus healed the blind man, "he led him out of the town," and after he restored the man's sight, he told him not to "go into the town, nor tell it to any in the town." (Mark 8:23, 26.)

In contrast, after Jesus cast the legion of demons out of a man in the country of the Gadarenes, he instructed him to tell his friends what great things the Lord had done for him. (Mark 5:19; Luke 8:39.) Perhaps this was a response to the multitude's request that Jesus leave their land. (Matt. 8:34; Mark 5:17; Luke 8:37.)

While the Synoptic Gospels do not portray the Master's miracles as being done to convince the unbeliever, they do note that the people who observed them "were amazed," "marvelled," or "glorified" or "gave praise" to God. (For example, Matt. 9:8, 32–33; 12:22–23; Mark 1:26–27; 2:12; Luke 4:36–37; 5:26; 7:16; 9:43; 18:43.)

In one instance, the Synoptic writers report the Savior's referring to past miracles, but he apparently did this as a sign to strengthen the wavering faith of those who already believed. The followers of John the Baptist brought the question whether Jesus was the one who should come. He told them to go back to John and tell him how they had seen the blind made to see, the lame made to walk, the lepers cleansed, the deaf made to hear, and the dead raised. (Matt. 11:2–6; Luke 7:18–23.)

As the Savior concluded his ministry, on the cross at Calvary, the chief priests and others renewed their call for a sign, mocking him with the challenge, "If he be the King of Israel, let him now come down from the cross, and we will believe him." (Matt. 27:42; see also Mark 15:29–32; Luke 23:35–37.) This mocking challenge, like many others, went unheeded.

In contrast to the Synoptic Gospels, the Gospel of John sometimes portrays Jesus' miracles as signs to the unbeliever. Perhaps this is another illustration of the different audience for which this Gospel was written. Matthew, Mark, and Luke seem to have been written for audiences of unbelievers, like a missionary tract addressed to Jews, Romans, and Greeks, respectively.[1] For that audience it would be inappropriate to portray the miracles as signs to convert the unbeliever. In contrast, the Gospel of John was written for the Saints,[2] believers whose faith could appropriately be strengthened by portraying the miracles as signs.

The book of John records more than one instance in which the Savior said that the works that he did "bear witness" of him. (John 5:36; 10:25.) On the last occasion he said, "Though ye believe not me, believe the works." (John 10:38.)

John identifies the turning of water into wine at Cana as the "beginning of miracles [that] ... manifested ... [Jesus'] glory; and his disciples believed on him." (John 2:11.) Shortly thereafter, when Jesus was in Jerusalem "at the passover, in the feast day, many believed in his name, when they saw the miracles which he did." (John 2:23.)

When he came to Jesus, Nicodemus said, "Rabbi, we know that thou art a teacher come from God: for no man can do these miracles that thou doest, except God be with him." (John 3:2.) Jesus told the nobleman who asked him to heal his sick son in Capernaum, "Except ye see signs and wonders, ye will not believe." Then he healed the son, and the nobleman and his whole house believed. (John 4:48–53.) In contrast, when Jesus healed the man born blind, the Pharisees examined the evidence and still did not believe. (John 9:1–34.)

The book of John describes one miracle the Savior did in full awareness that this would persuade the people to believe. In the presence of a large crowd, he raised Lazarus from the dead. "Then many of the Jews which came to Mary, and had seen the things which Jesus did, believed on him." (John 11:40–45.)

In concluding his record, John writes, apparently to the believers, "And many other signs truly did Jesus in the presence of his disciples, which are not written in this book: but these are written, that ye might believe that Jesus is the Christ, the Son of God; and that believing ye might have life through his name." (John 20:30–31.)

There are various instances in the rest of the New Testament in which the apostles sought to strengthen the faith of believers or to convert unbelievers by referring to previous signs and wonders done by the Savior or by his authority.

In his sermon on the day of Pentecost, Peter reminded the people that Jesus was "a man approved of God among you by miracles and wonders and signs, which God did by him in the midst of you, as ye yourselves also know." (Acts 2:22; also see John 2:19–22.) Paul reminded the Corinthians that "the signs of an apostle were wrought among you in all patience, in signs, and wonders, and mighty deeds." (2 Cor. 12:12.) The epistle to the Hebrews describes God's bearing witness "with signs and wonders, and with divers miracles, and gifts of the Holy Ghost, according to his own will." (Heb. 2:4.)

The Book of Mormon also records instances in which prophets used signs or miracles in the conversion process. In the generation preceding the birth of Christ, there were many great miracles and manifestations, and most of the Lamanites were convinced "because of the greatness of the evidences which they had received." (Hel. 5:50.) Nephi told a Nephite multitude about the murder of their chief judge and the identity of the murderer as a sign to convince them that he was "an honest man" sent "from God." (Hel. 8:27; 9:24–36.) Later, he "show[ed] signs and wonders, working miracles among the people, that they might know that the Christ must shortly come." (Hel. 16:4.)

Signs in Modern Revelation

Taken as a whole, the Bible seems somewhat ambiguous on whether signs should be used to convert the unbeliever. In contrast, modern revelations clearly forbid this because signs should not be sought or used for this purpose.

The Lord declared to the members of his restored church that "there are those among you who seek signs, and there

have been such even from the beginning." (D&C 63:8.) But
the obtaining of faith by signs was not God's way, because
"faith cometh not by signs, but signs follow those that believe." The teaching continues: "Yea, signs come by faith,
unto mighty works, for without faith no man pleaseth
God; and with whom God is angry he is not well pleased;
wherefore, unto such he showeth no signs, only in wrath
unto their condemnation. Wherefore, I, the Lord, am not
pleased with those among you who have sought after signs
and wonders for faith, and not for the good of men unto
my glory." (D&C 63:9, 11–12.)

The Book of Mormon contains many clear teachings on
the inappropriateness of seeking or using signs to obtain
faith or to secure a conversion.

While teaching the Zoramites, Alma referred to the many
who said, "If thou wilt show unto us a sign from heaven,
then we shall know of a surety; then we shall believe."
Sorrowing, he observed that this request showed a total lack
of faith. (Alma 32:17–18.)

"Dispute not because ye see not," the prophet Moroni
says in another passage, "for ye receive no witness until after
the trial of your faith." (Ether 12:6.) Speaking of this scriptural direction, President Spencer W. Kimball says: "Father
Adam understood this basic principle: 'An angel of the Lord
appeared unto Adam, saying: why dost thou offer sacrifices
unto the Lord? And Adam said unto him: I know not, save
the Lord commanded me' (Moses 5:6). . . . Men have often
misunderstood and have reversed the process. They would
have the harvest before the planting, the reward before the
service, the miracle before the faith."[3]

Jesus taught (and his prophets taught after him) that
"signs shall follow them that believe." (Mark 16:17; Mormon
9:24; D&C 84:65.) The Book of Mormon teaches the principle

in these words: "Neither at any time hath any wrought miracles until after their faith; wherefore they first believed in the Son of God." (Ether 12:18.)

Signs Impose Burdens

The Lord has given significant warnings to those who seek signs without faith. To these "he showeth no signs, only in wrath unto their condemnation." (D&C 63:11.) The Book of Mormon contains two illustrations of this principle, and a memorable explanation of how men are condemned by seeking after a sign.

Contending with Jacob, the learned Sherem said, "Show me a sign by this power of the Holy Ghost, in the which ye know so much." In this instance a sign was given. He was struck down, confessed his error, and died. (Jacob 7:13–20.)

Similarly, Korihor said to Alma, "If thou wilt show me a sign, that I may be convinced that there is a God, yea, show unto me that he hath power, and then will I be convinced of the truth of thy words." Alma refused, reminding the doubter he had adequate signs in the testimony of prophets and believers. When Korihor persisted, insisting that he would not believe "except ye show me a sign," he received a sign. He was struck dumb, cast out, and trampled to death. (Alma 30:43–59.)

In teaching the Zoramites, Alma explained how the seeking of a sign can lead to condemnation. A person who humbles himself "without being compelled to be humble" is more blessed than a person who is compelled to be humble. He likened the person who is voluntarily humble to a person who believes and is baptized "without stubbornness of heart, yea, without being brought to know the word, or even compelled to know, before they will believe." Then he gave this example:

"Yea, there are many who do say: If thou wilt show unto us a sign from heaven, then we shall know of a surety; then we shall believe. Now I ask, is this faith? Behold, I say unto you, Nay; for if a man knoweth a thing he hath no cause to believe, for he knoweth it. And now, how much more cursed is he that knoweth the will of God and doeth it not, than he that only believeth, or only hath cause to believe, and falleth into transgression?" (Alma 32:15–19.)

There are two lessons here. First, those who acquire knowledge by means of signs have no occasion to develop faith. Without that spiritual development (discussed hereafter) and without the sustaining strength of faith, they are damned in their progress and remain vulnerable to transgression and to falling away. Second, those who acquire knowledge and then fall away are more cursed than those who, following the pathway of faith, have only come so far as to believe before they fall away.

Thus, the showing of a sign can work to the condemnation of those who are brought to knowledge by that means. They miss the opportunity to develop faith, and they subject themselves to a more severe punishment for backsliding than those whose spiritual development is proceeding along the normal pathway of developing faith.

There are other "condemnations" to those who seek signs without first developing the faith God has required as a prerequisite.

One condemnation is to be misled. God warned ancient Israel against following prophets who gave signs and wonders and then sought to lead them away to the worship of strange gods. (Deut. 13:1–3.) The Savior taught his apostles that in the last days "there shall also arise false Christs, and false prophets, and shall show great signs and wonders, insomuch that, if possible, they shall deceive the very elect, who are the elect according to the covenant." (JST Matt. 24:23; also see Matt. 24:24; Mark 13:22.) The apostle Paul warned that the Savior would not come again "until after there cometh a falling away, by the working of Satan with all power, and signs and lying wonders, and with all deceivableness of unrighteousness in them that perish." (JST 2 Thes. 2:9–10.)

In the great revelation on signs, the Lord says, "He that seeketh signs shall see signs, but not unto salvation." (D&C 63:7.) President Spencer W. Kimball explained: "Certainly we should not be interested in signs. Signs are available and anyone, I believe, can have signs who wants them. I believe if one wants revelations enough to crave them beyond the rightness of it, that eventually he will get his revelations — but they may not come from God. I am sure that there can be many spectacular things performed, because the devil is very responsive. He is listening and he is eager to do it. And so he gives strange experiences."[4]

Similarly, Professor Hugh Nibley has written: "Miracles employed for purposes of demonstration never can be [infallible], for miracles are not exclusively Christian. . . . Like philosophy and mysticism, miracles — real miracles — are found throughout the whole world and are used by practitioners of religion everywhere to bedizen, amaze, and convince the doubters."[5]

Manifestly, the performance of miracles and the appearance of signs and wonders are not evidences that those who do these things are servants of God or teachers of truth. In our day, God does not use miracles or signs as a way of teaching or convincing the unbeliever. As a result, we should not ask for signs for this purpose, and we should be deeply suspicious of the so-called spiritual evidences of those who do.

Conversion by Signs

The viewing of signs or miracles is not a secure foundation for conversion. Scriptural history attests that people converted by signs and wonders soon forget them and again become susceptible to the lies and distortions of Satan and his servants. (Hel. 16:23; 3 Ne. 1:22, 2:1, 8:4.) "How long will this people provoke me?" the Lord said to Moses, "and how long will it be ere they believe me, for all the signs that I have shewed among them?" (Num. 14:11.)

Jesus made a triumphal entry into Jerusalem, but John records in sadness, "Though he had done so many miracles before them, yet they believed not on him." (John 12:37.)

In contrast to the witness of the Spirit, which can be renewed from time to time as needed by a worthy recipient, the viewing of a sign or the experiencing of a miracle is a one-time event that will fade in the memory of its witness and can dim in its impact upon him or her.[6] For example, as President Kimball observed, "Oliver Cowdery saw many signs. He handled the sacred plates; saw John the Baptist; received the higher priesthood from Peter, James, and John, and was the recipient of many great miracles, and yet they could not hold him to the faith."[7]

President George Q. Cannon summarized the experience: "I do not believe that men can be convinced as they should be convinced by such manifestations. It has been a matter of remark among those who have had experience in this Church, that where men have been brought into the Church by such manifestations, it has required a constant succession of them to keep them in the Church; their faith has had to be constantly strengthened by witnessing some such manifestations; but where they have been convinced by the outpouring of the spirit of God, where their judgment

has been convinced, where they have examined for themselves and become satisfied by the testimony of Jesus in
answer to their prayers and to their faithful seeking unto
the Lord for knowledge — where this has been the case they
have been more likely to stand, more likely to endure persecution and trial than those who have been convinced
through some supernatural manifestation of the character
to which I have alluded."[8]

The true church does not convert by signs and wonders,
but by the testimony of the Holy Ghost. The Lord's way of
teaching religious truths is not by a public miracle or sign,
but by a personal testimony.

In this way, the true church protects the integrity of
conversions to its fold. Where conversion experiences are
individual and private, potential converts have no incentive
to vie for the most significant one. The peer pressure and
group psychology that can accompany mass conversion experiences are eliminated. A true conversion is a personal
spiritual experience based on the individual communication
of the Spirit, not the witnessing of a sign or the experiencing
of a miracle.

Scientific Evidence versus Religious Faith

The methods of science, which have served mankind so
well in advancing knowledge of the things of the world, rely
heavily on observations. Scientists observe and measure
physical events, carefully designed experiments, and natural
phenomena. Their methods will differ in detail, but for all
scientists the evidence of the correctness of the answers they
are seeking lies in their detailed observations and mea-
surements. Hence, we might say that scientists seek to ad-
vance knowledge and learn truth by the physical observation
and measurement of signs. (This is not to deny that the

efforts of scientists have been directed by unmeasurables like intuition and inspiration.)

The religion of the Latter-day Saints is not hostile to any truth, however found. Latter-day Saints have been among the most effective practitioners of scientific methods, and by this means (and by revelation, when they have qualified to receive it) have contributed much to the fund of knowledge about the world in which we live. But faithful Latter-day Saints know that scientific methods are not the way to know God or to determine the truths of his gospel.

One of our most renowned scientists, Henry Eyring, was a world-class practitioner at obtaining knowledge by the scientific method, but he also knew that there are limits to that method and that there is another way to find answers to the questions that matter most. His attitude was described by his son, Bishop Henry B. Eyring:

"Now, when someone tells you the questions that matter yield only to some rational analysis, remember that the stunning achievements of reason over the past three hundred years have sprung from what is called the 'scientific method.' I hope you'll also remember, as I always will, the scientist Henry Eyring on his knees, when the questions that really mattered yielded to the method for finding truth he'd learned as a little boy at his mother's knee in Old Mexico. This was long before he took the train to Tucson, and Berkeley, and Madison, and then on to Berlin and Princeton to use the scientific method to create theories that changed the scientific world. What he learned on his knees brought him peace and changed my life."[9]

A premier Catholic theologian, Joseph Cardinal Ratzinger, gives this description of the relationship between the differing methods of science and religion:

"Theology—the study of God and God's relationship

with humanity—cannot be confused with the natural sciences. This is because in its own terms theology observes that God is supernatural. It is fundamental to all human knowledge to recognize that the object of study indicates and determines the proper method to be followed to understanding. One does not approach surgery like politics or art, or art like chemistry. . . . We, because we believe in God, already recognize that natural science is not adequate to study the divine. The real natural scientist who is a believer knows enough about the limits of his own scientific methodology to know that with it alone one cannot see God. . . . We cannot deny to humanity the ability to be responsive beyond the boundaries of pure reason."[10]

Professor Joseph F. McConkie explains the relationship in this way: "All true religion must be premised on the supernatural or miraculous. Of necessity, true religion requires faith in its acceptance and faith in its observance. Without an omnipotent God, a God beyond the reasoning and powers of man, there can be no true religion. True religion finds answers in the omnipotence of God. It is not earthbound, nor does it seek verification at the hands of mortal men. True religion will not seek answers in science or any other man-made discipline. Its principles and practices must profess to be rooted in heaven."[11]

The scriptures clearly reject the approach by which men would use scientific methods or signs to acquire faith: an experiment staged or invited by the will of man and at the time pleasing to him. The Lord decrees that when signs are given, they will be given on his terms: by the will of God and in the time and under the circumstances he chooses. "Yea, signs come by faith, not by the will of men, nor as they please, but by the will of God." (D&C 63:10.)

Why is this so? The answer lies in the purpose of life.

We mortals are not placed on earth to prove the existence of God. We are here to prove ourselves. To realize our eternal destiny, we must develop faith.

As the apostle Paul taught, "Without faith it is impossible to please [God]: for he that cometh to God must believe that he is." (Heb. 11:6.) To allow us to develop that faith, the conditions of mortality were, as Bruce C. Hafen has said, "carefully and deliberately designed *not* to *compel* belief."[12] For example, after the text of the Book of Mormon was made available, the gold plates were taken away so they were not available to prove the Book of Mormon. Faith does not come from scientific evidence or miraculous signs. That would reverse the order prescribed by God and prevent the spiritual growth that comes from developing and exercising faith.[13]

Faith comes in the Lord's way: by desire, by groping and trusting, by praying and serving. God has placed us in a mortal habitat where we can acquire faith in the way he has prescribed. In his way, the proofs and the signs come later. As President George Q. Cannon said, "The reliable testimony must come from within—that is, the Saint should have the testimony of the Holy Ghost within. Outward signs and evidences go to corroborate and strengthen the inward testimony."[14]

This helps us understand why the methods of science are not applicable to establishing the truthfulness of the gospel, the fact of the Restoration, or the origin and truth of the Book of Mormon. President Ezra Taft Benson has declared: "It never has been the case, nor is it so now, that the studies of the learned will prove the Book of Mormon true or false. The origin, preparation, translation, and verification of the truth of the Book of Mormon have all been retained in the hands of the Lord."[15]

Some Latter-day Saints have not accepted this reality and are preoccupied with evidences to prove the Book of Mormon. On this subject I agree with BYU religion professors Joseph Fielding McConkie and Robert L. Millet: "In such evidences we may find fuel for testimony, but only if the fire of testimony already burns brightly. Such things can add to the burning fire but have no power in themselves to kindle that fire. They are not the source of testimony and thus have no profitable place in proselyting efforts. Evidences, be they external or internal, convert neither Jew nor Gentile. Such things may anchor the converted but they do not convert. It is the order of heaven that signs follow belief; they do not precede it."[16]

The lack of decisive scientific proofs of scriptural truths does not preclude gospel defenders from counter-arguments of that nature. When opponents attack the Church or its doctrines with so-called proofs, loyal defenders will counter with material of a comparable nature to defend. As Elder Neal A. Maxwell has said, "We can be assured that enough plausible, supporting data and external evidence will come forth to prevent scoffers from having a field day with the scriptures, but not enough to remove the requirement of faith."[17]

Just as science will not *prove* religious truth, neither will science *disprove* it. The eternal verities of religion will not be disproven by even the latest proofs or the firmest laws of science. Science is too tentative.

During the past century, great strides have been made in human understanding of the nature of the physical universe and the living things within it. Friends who are scientists tell me that Newton's laws are now seen to be applicable only to a restricted set of conditions; they do not fit the behavior of tiny particles at high speeds. The atomic nature of matter was far from being universally accepted a century ago, and now the most accurate description of an atom is a complex mathematical equation. Comparable strides have been made in our understanding of photosynthesis, a basic process in the plants that sustain all life on this planet. Just a few decades ago scientists believed that the oxygen produced in this process came from carbon dioxide; today they are sure that it comes from water. Less than a half century ago scientists believed that the proteins in the cell were the genetic material of the cell. When DNA manipulations became possible, scientists quickly became convinced that the genetic material of cells was DNA, not protein.

In the exciting efforts of scientists, old explanations are shown to be less accurate than newer ones. Old and respected explanations of relationships are found to be wrong or of limited applicability. The dynamic process continues, and, as we say, knowledge expands. But the knowledge obtained by the scientific method is forever tentative, and surely provides no basis for disproving the existence or work of God. Professor Hugh Nibley gives this conclusion:

"The words of the prophets cannot be held to the tentative and defective tests that men have devised for them. Science, philosophy, and common sense all have a right to their day in court. But the last word does not lie with them: Every time men in their wisdom have come forth with the last word, other words have promptly followed. The last word is a testimony of the gospel that comes only by direct revelation. Our Father in heaven speaks it, and if it were in perfect agreement with the science of today, it would surely be out of line with the science of tomorrow. Let us not, therefore, seek to hold God to the learned opinions of the moment when he speaks the language of eternity."[18]

The Role and Sharing of Signs

What, then, is the legitimate role of signs and miracles? It is surely not in preaching the gospel. As Elder George Q. Cannon observed:

"The Gospel of Jesus was not and is not dependent on miracles alone for the evidence necessary to support its truthfulness. . . . By a careful perusal of the Scriptures we find that Jesus did not work miracles to convince the people of the truth of His system, neither did His Apostles. If they had recognized this as being the correct way of converting men, they certainly would have adopted it; and no man could have been condemned for not embracing their doctrines who had not beheld a supernatural (as we have it) exhibition of power. He, however, before His ascension into heaven, in speaking to His disciples, plainly and pointedly said that these signs or exhibitions of power should follow them that believed—they were to be the consequences of faith and not the only foundation for faith to be based upon."[19]

Signs are a means of strengthening the faith and blessing the lives of believers. The New Testament records the Savior's promise that "signs shall follow them that believe." (Mark 16:17.) It further records that when his servants went forth preaching, the Lord "confirm[ed] the word with signs following." (Mark 16:20.)

The promise that signs shall follow and confirm the word has been reaffirmed by the prophets in many other scriptures. (See, for example, Morm. 9:24; Ether 4:18; D&C 58:64; 68:10; 84:65.) Nephi taught that the gentiles must be convinced that Jesus Christ "manifesteth himself unto all those who believe in him, by the power of the Holy Ghost; . . . working mighty miracles, signs, and wonders, among the children of men according to their faith." (2 Ne. 26:13.)

Those who chronicled the history of the early church noted that the apostles performed many "signs and wonders." (Acts 2:43; 5:11–14; 9:33–35, 40–42; 13:9–12.) Similarly, in modern times the Lord has promised, "I will show miracles, signs, and wonders, unto all those who believe on my name." (D&C 35:8.) At the same time, he has cautioned the holders of his priesthood that they should "require not miracles, except [he] shall command [them]." (D&C 24:13.)

The principle that signs are shown to those who already believe is clearly illustrated in Nephi's experience. He desired that he might see and know the things his father had seen in a vision. (1 Ne. 10:17.) After he had diligently and prayerfully sought this manifestation, and after he had demonstrated his faith, he was shown a vision. (1 Ne. 11:1.) The Spirit explained that this vision was given to him as a sign, because of his faith: "Blessed art thou, Nephi, because thou believest in the Son of the most high God; wherefore, thou shalt behold the things which thou hast desired. And behold this thing shall be given unto thee for a sign, that after thou hast beheld . . . ye shall bear record." (1 Ne. 11:6–7.)

Similarly, in modern revelation the Lord has reaffirmed that spiritual gifts are given not as a sign for the unbeliever but as a help to the believer: "For verily I say unto you, they are given for the benefit of those who love me and keep all my commandments, and him that seeketh so to do; that all may be benefited that seek or that ask of me, that ask and not for a sign that they may consume it upon their lusts." (D&C 46:9.)

There is another contrast between scientific evidence and the signs or miracles God gives to confirm the word to the faithful. It concerns the extent to which such experiences are shared with others. To fulfill its function, scientific evi-

dence must be made public. In contrast, signs and miracles
are not to be shown before the world.

While renewing his promise of the signs that would
follow those who believed, the Lord commanded the members of his church that "they shall not boast themselves of
these things, neither speak them before the world; for these
things are given unto you for your profit and for salvation."
(D&C 84:73.) Two years later he repeated that direction to
the erring Saints in Missouri, cautioning them that they
should not "boast of faith nor of mighty works." (D&C
105:24.) Later the Prophet Joseph Smith cautioned, "Let us
be faithful and silent, brethren, and if God gives you a manifestation, keep it to yourselves."[20]

By and large, Latter-day Saints observe this direction.
They do not speak publicly of their most sacred experiences.
They seldom mention miracles in bearing their testimonies,
and they rarely preach from the pulpit about signs that the
gospel is true. They usually affirm their testimony of the
truthfulness of the restored gospel by asserting the conclusion, not by giving details on how it was obtained.

This reluctance to speak of miracles or sacred experiences is sometimes misunderstood by those who do not
understand Latter-day Saints, even by other devout Christians. Some years ago I lectured on a legal subject at a
prominent Protestant university. Afterwards, several faculty
members in the divinity school took me to lunch. They said,
"We know about the Mormons' great emphasis on family
life. We respect the way faithful Mormons pay a tenth of
their income in tithing. We are aware of the many successful
Mormons in various fields. But we don't know anything
about your private religious lives. We have never heard our
Mormon friends speak of this. Do Mormons have any religious experiences?"

I understood these devout ministers to be saying, "How can you be saved if you have not had a witness of the Spirit?" And "If Mormons have such experiences, why don't they speak about them, as we do in describing the occasion when we were 'saved'?" I assured them that Mormons do have religious experiences, but I explained that we hold such experiences so sacred that we rarely speak of them.

Privately, I thought to myself that we Latter-day Saints may go beyond the intent of the command not to boast of miracles or show them before the world. By failing to communicate the richness of our religious life in private conversations with receptive persons of other faiths, we lose opportunities to glorify God and testify of Christ and the blessings of his gospel. We may even mislead some when we say so much about the visible fruits of Mormonism and the commendable accomplishments of prominent Latter-day Saints and so little (even in general terms) about the rich, private spiritual experiences of the rank and file of Latter-day Saints.

Conclusion

The Lord has commanded that signs not be used for converting the unbeliever. Signs follow those who believe and have faith, as a confirmation and strength to them. In this matter, the Lord's way differs sharply from the methods of science, which have led to so many advances in worldly knowledge.

Some confuse the methods of science and the methods of the Lord (including the proper and improper use of signs) and fail to understand the acceptable application of each. Perhaps some of this misunderstanding is attributable to the use of the word *proof* in connection with spiritual things.

The apostle Paul said, "Prove all things; hold fast that

which is good." (1 Thes. 5:21.) Similarly, in reaffirming the commandment of tithing, through the prophet Malachi, the Lord said: "Prove me now herewith, saith the Lord of hosts, if I will not open you the windows of heaven, and pour you out a blessing, that there shall not be room enough to receive it." (Mal. 3:10.)

Speaking for the Lord, Malachi gave specific promises to those who would bring their tithes into the storehouse (for example, "I will rebuke the devourer for your sakes"). These scriptural passages invite the faithful to prove the Lord by keeping the commandments and then looking for the promised blessing. But this "experiment" is not the kind of sign we are commanded to avoid.

Since the kind of proof that comes from keeping the commandments and then looking for the promised blessing is the result of an exercise of faith on the part of the actor, the signs that follow those who believe are not forbidden signs but appropriate ones. This is evident in what is perhaps the most powerful invitation to proof in all of the scriptures: "And when ye shall receive these things, I would exhort you that ye would ask God, the Eternal Father, in the name of Christ, if these things are not true; and if ye shall ask with a sincere heart, with real intent, having faith in Christ, he will manifest the truth of it unto you, by the power of the Holy Ghost." (Moro. 10:4.)

Moroni makes an explicit promise of a spiritual manifestation to one who seeks to know the truthfulness of the Book of Mormon. But, it must be noted, this promise is only extended to the person who will "ask with a sincere heart, with real intent, having faith in Christ." The manifestation that is given in response to this promise, therefore, is not a sign given to convert an unbeliever. It is a sign that follows individual faith and commitment.

In a recent general conference address, President Howard W. Hunter reaffirmed Elder James E. Talmage's caution against the arrogance of those who reject the reality of miracles and signs they have not experienced and cannot understand: "Science and the unaided human mind . . . have not advanced far enough to analyze and explain these wonders. But, [Elder Talmage] cautioned, to deny the reality of miracles on the ground that the results and manifestations *must* be fictitious simply because we cannot comprehend the means by which they have happened is arrogant on the face of it. . . . Indeed, those who have been the beneficiaries of such miracles are the most compelling witnesses of all."[21] This counsel applies specially to the sacred witness that the Holy Ghost bears to a seeking heart. Those who are not spiritually attuned to receive this witness should beware against asserting that it does not exist because they have not experienced it.

Writing in a journal of modern culture, a Latter-day Saint scholar gives this analysis of the Mormon belief in miracles and the witness of the Spirit:

"The most anachronistic feature of Mormonism may be its continuing openness to the miraculous. [Richard] Bushman makes the point that since the 18th century most Christian denominations have rejected the possibility of supernatural events not recorded in the Bible. Mormons offend fundamentalists and agnostics alike by violating this Enlightenment-Christian synthesis with their talk of angels, healings, prophecy, and revelation in our time. Caring little for the contemporary 'authenticity' of existential doubt, Mormons individually affirm that their faith has been miraculously confirmed by a witness from the Holy Ghost received in answer to prayer. Even professional Mormon scholars such as Bushman and [Leonard J.] Arrington would explain that such revelatory experiences are as essential to their faith as documentary research, empirical evidence, or hermeneutical logic. . . . Short of the Judgment, public agreement seems possible only on the undeniable proposition that Mormons are set against the spirit of the age."[22]

Professor Hugh Nibley has noted a mortal tendency for religious things "to gravitate to two opposite poles — a purely intellectual on the one hand, and a vulgar and superstitious on the other."[23] In other words, religious things are susceptible to corruption at one extreme by intellectualism and at the opposite extreme by superstition. That tendency is evident in the contrast between signs and science.

The purely intellectual approach to religion rejects modern miracles and suspects any religious verity that cannot be proven by the methods of science. At the opposite extreme are the superstitious, those who reject the possibility of knowing God by any means, scientific or religious. Science considers itself the master of signs. Superstition shows itself the servant of signs.

True religion is neither intellectual nor superstitious. The true role of signs illustrates the middle ground of truth. Signs are not to prove religious truth, as some people believe the methods of science can do. Neither are signs a substitute for knowledge, as superstition would have it. The truth about God and his commandments for his children comes by faith and revelation from the Holy Ghost, a method unacceptable to superstition and unprovable by science. Then, when faith is gained and exercised, signs follow those who believe.

NOTES

1. C. Wilfred Griggs, "The Testimony of John," in *Studies in Scripture,* ed. Kent P. Jackson and Robert L. Millet, 5 (Salt Lake City: Deseret Book, 1986): 111; Bruce R. McConkie, *Doctrinal New Testament Commentary* 1 (Salt Lake City: Bookcraft, 1973): 65.

2. Ibid.

3. Spencer W. Kimball, *Faith Precedes the Miracle* (Salt Lake City: Deseret Book, 1972), 4.

4. *The Teachings of Spencer W. Kimball*, ed. Edward L. Kimball (Salt Lake City: Bookcraft, 1982), 458.

5. Hugh Nibley, *The World and the Prophets* (Salt Lake City: Deseret Book and Foundation for Ancient Research and Mormon Studies, 1987), 139.

6. See Joseph Fielding Smith, *Doctrines of Salvation* 1 (Salt Lake City: Bookcraft, 1954): 44.

7. Kimball, *Faith Precedes the Miracle*, 5.

8. George Q. Cannon, *Journal of Discourses* 22:361–62.

9. Henry B. Eyring, "Going Home," in *Brigham Young University 1986–87 Devotional and Fireside Speeches* (Provo, Utah: University Publications, 1987), 76–77.

10. Quoted in Paul T. Stallsworth, "The Story of an Encounter," in *Biblical Interpretation in Crisis: The Ratzinger Conference on Bible and Church*, ed. Richard J. Neuhaus (Grand Rapids, Mich.: Wm. B. Eerdmans, 1989), 106–7.

11 Joseph Fielding McConkie, *Prophets and Prophecy* (Salt Lake City: Bookcraft, 1988), 156.

12. Bruce C. Hafen, *The Believing Heart* (Salt Lake City: Deseret Book, 1986), 6.

13. Ibid., 46–48.

14. George Q. Cannon, *Gospel Truth*, ed. Jerreld L. Newquist (Salt Lake City: Deseret Book, 1987), 152.

15. Ezra Taft Benson, *A Witness and a Warning* (Salt Lake City: Deseret Book, 1988), 31.

16. Joseph Fielding McConkie and Robert L. Millet, *Doctrinal Commentary on the Book of Mormon* 2 (Salt Lake City: Bookcraft, 1987): xiii.

17. Neal A. Maxwell, *But for a Small Moment* (Salt Lake City: Bookcraft, 1986), 35.

18. Nibley, *The World and the Prophets*, 134.

19. Cannon, *Gospel Truth*, 151–52. One scripture notes that *tongues* are a sign to the unbeliever. (1 Cor. 14:22.) Perhaps this merely describes the function the gift of tongues has in preaching to unbelievers.

20. *Teachings of the Prophet Joseph Smith*, ed. Joseph Fielding Smith (Salt Lake City: Deseret News Press, 1956), 91.

21. Howard W. Hunter, "The God That Doest Wonders," *Ensign* 19 (May 1989): 16.

22. Bryce Christensen, "Mormons and Modernism," *Chronicles of Culture*, July 1985, 10.

23. Nibley, *The World and the Prophets*, 142.

CHAPTER 4

CARE FOR THE POOR

No illustration of the contrast between the Lord's way and man's way is more vivid than the way The Church of Jesus Christ of Latter-day Saints and its members seek to resolve the age-old problem and the eternal commandment to care for the poor.

The Commandment to Care for the Poor

Ancient and modern scriptures are clear in their commands to care for the poor and the needy. Their passages on these subjects are too numerous to permit extensive quotation and too well-known to require it. Several illustrations will suffice.

Elder Russell M. Nelson has observed that "when the Lord sent prophets to call Israel back from apostasy, in almost every instance, one of the first charges made was that the poor had been neglected."[1] Thus, part of John the Baptist's message of repentance was, "He that hath two coats, let him impart to him that hath none; and he that hath meat, let him do likewise." (Luke 3:11.)

The prophets of the Book of Mormon taught that the care of the poor was the only way we could obtain essential blessings. The prophet/king Benjamin declared that we must impart of our substance to the poor, "such as feeding the hungry, clothing the naked, visiting the sick and administering to their relief" for the sake of "retaining a remission of [our] sins from day to day, that [we] may walk guiltless before God." (Mosiah 4:26.)

After teaching the fundamental principles of the gospel (including the Atonement and the necessity for faith, repentance, and prayer), Amulek continued: "And now . . . do not suppose that this is all; for after ye have done all these things, if ye turn away the needy, and the naked, and visit not the sick and afflicted, and impart of your substance, if ye have, to those who stand in need—I say unto you, if ye do not any of these things, behold, your prayer is vain, and availeth you nothing, and ye are as hypocrites who do deny the faith." (Alma 34:28.)

In modern times the Lord told his people they "must visit the poor and the needy and administer to their relief" (D&C 44:6), and "he that doeth not these things, the same is not my disciple" (D&C 52:40). The Lord commanded his saints to "learn to impart one to another as the gospel requires." (D&C 88:123.) President Marion G. Romney explained the importance of these commandments by relating them to the Savior's statement that when he comes in his glory, he will divide his people "as a shepherd divideth his sheep from the goats." (Matt. 25:32.) He said, "The test on which the division [will] be made on that great day [will] be the care given to the poor and the needy."[2]

Notwithstanding the importance of this duty toward the poor, it comes second to another duty. The Lord's plan for the care of the poor and the needy commands and then presupposes that each of us will provide for ourselves and our families, as far as we are able. This includes caring for the members of our own households — parents caring for children, and children caring for parents.[3] Thereafter, we care for the poor members of the Church, and then extend our assistance to others as far as our means permit.[4] We do this first by paying tithing; second, by donating liberally to the fast offering funds; and then by making other contributions of labor and money as our means permit.[5] That is the duty the Lord has put upon each member of his church.

Traditionally, religions have taught men and women to worship a God who commands them to love one another and to serve one another. But today there are a host of pseudoreligions that teach men and women to worship themselves and to celebrate their worship with the sacrament of self-indulgence. True religion preaches responsibilities, teaching us to give. Modern counterfeits preach rights, teaching us to take. True religion produces a citizenry educated to serve; modern counterfeits produce a citizenry educated to demand service.

Government Efforts

This is not the place for an extensive description or evaluation of government efforts to care for the poor. A brief summary will suffice as a basis for comparison between man's way and the Lord's way.

There is widespread dissatisfaction with government welfare programs. Critics include not only the taxpayers who finance the assistance and resent the fact that it seems to fall far short of its stated aims, but also the persons who receive assistance and who resent the extent and nature of the aid and the administrative controls that accompany it. Some scholars and some politicians complete the chorus of opposition.

The most severe critics contend that government welfare programs have failed to reduce poverty; they have probably increased it, while contributing to a host of associated social evils.[6] John Goodman, president of the National Center for Political Analysis, has said: "The USA's welfare system is a disaster. It is creating poverty, not destroying it. It subsidizes divorce, unwed teenage pregnancy, the abandonment of elderly parents by their children, and the wholesale dissolution of the family. The reason? We pay people to be poor. Private charities have always been better at providing relief where it is truly needed."[7]

What has happened to the massive public funds devoted to the relief of the poor? Robert L. Woodson, president of the National Center for Neighborhood Enterprise and chairman of the Council for Black Economic Agenda, has written: "Since 1964, the federal government has poured billions of dollars into employment, housing, public welfare, and economic development programs designed to help the poor. The main beneficiary of this massive effort, it has now become clear, was the 'social service industry' parachuted in from outside the community to administer aid programs at salaries and fees that consumed the lion's share of allocated monies."[8]

Some would, of course, disagree with these serious charges. For present purposes it is sufficient to confirm that there is widespread dissatisfaction with government assistance to the poor. It is also appropriate to observe that the administration of this assistance involves large numbers of compensated personnel and other expenses (such as for administrative offices and supplies) that make relief of the poor a big business from which many non-poor derive significant financial gain.

The business of obtaining personal profit by promoting

the use of tax revenues to help the poor, which someone
has called "doing well by doing good," has an ancient history.
In the meridian of time, Judas complained that the ointment
used to anoint the feet of Jesus had not been sold for the
benefit of the poor. The Gospel of John explains Judas's real
motive: "This he said, not that he cared for the poor; but
because he was a thief, and had the bag, and bare what was
put therein." (John 12:6.)

There are modern manifestations of this same motive
in the promotion and administration of government assistance for the poor. Some poverty programs are promoted
not out of concern for the poor but because the promoters
"have the bag," and the proposed programs will promote
their own acquisition of property, prominence, or power.

Another characteristic of the current administration of
government assistance to the poor is criticized by Robert L.
Woodson: "These vast bureaucratic and professional em-
pires, with a state-enforced monopoly over social services,
also exacted social and human costs. Those who receive
services lose their autonomy as human beings by being
converted into 'clients' (which, in Latin legal terminology,
means a dependent individual). This psychological depen-
dency has perverted both public and private morality, fos-
tering a climate of powerlessness, irresponsibility, and
resentment. As passive 'clients,' the poor and disadvantaged
have been led by the hand into a limbo where a bare min-
imum cash payment subsidizes their poverty and saps individual initiative, making their dependence addictive."[9] In
short, though the intentions may have been good, the means
were counterproductive.

In contrast, President Spencer W. Kimball observed:
"Teach them truth and give them the gospel and ambition
is born, pride is nurtured, independence replaces slothful-

ness and men learn how to build their own homes and to furnish them and paint them, and then to build for others."[10]

God's Way of Welfare

A key scripture on the Lord's way to provide for the poor and needy is this revelation from the Doctrine and Covenants:

"It is my purpose to provide for my saints, for all things are mine. *But it must needs be done in mine own way;* and behold this is the way that I, the Lord, have decreed to provide for my saints, that the poor shall be exalted, in that the rich are made low.

"For the earth is full, and there is enough and to spare; yea, I prepared all things, and have given unto the children of men to be agents unto themselves. Therefore, if any man shall take of the abundance which I have made, and impart not his portion, according to the law of my gospel, unto the poor and the needy, he shall, with the wicked, lift up his eyes in hell, being in torment." (D&C 104:15–18; emphasis added.)

To summarize: (1) The Lord desires to provide for the temporal as well as the spiritual needs of his Saints. (2) However, it must be done in the way he directs. (3) His way will exalt the poor (that is, help the poor spiritually as well as temporally and thus move them toward exaltation). (4) His way will also make the rich low (that is, humble the rich and thus also move them toward greater spirituality and exaltation). (5) The earth contains more than enough to support everyone. (6) Men are morally responsible to use their abundance to provide for the poor and the needy. (7) Those who do not will be punished with the wicked in hell.

The Lord's way of providing for the poor and the needy

was revealed to Adam and his posterity, along with the other principles of the gospel. These principles were taught and exemplified by the prophets in Old Testament and Book of Mormon times and by the Savior and his apostles in their day. They were revealed to the Prophet Joseph Smith in the earliest days of the restored church.

The Lord's way of caring for the poor was practiced in the move across the plains. In a revelation given to the prophet Brigham Young, the Lord commanded: "Let each company bear an equal proportion, according to the dividend of their property, in taking the poor, the widows, the fatherless, and the families of those who have gone into the army, that the cries of the widow and the fatherless come not up into the ears of the Lord against this people." (D&C 136:8.) These same principles were practiced in the Saints' settlement of the Mountain West. Then, as conditions changed, some of the means of implementing these principles fell into disuse and some of the underlying principles were even forgotten or neglected.

To meet the grievous economic challenges of the Great Depression, leaders of the Church reemphasized the basic principles of caring for the poor and the needy and established what some saw as a new means of implementing them. Some, including most non–Latter-day Saints, even thought that what we now call the Church welfare program originated in 1936. But that was only the latest manifestation of principles as old as the gospel itself.

The First Presidency's explanation of why they established the modern welfare program contains two stated purposes, one described as the "announced objective" and the other identified as "our primary purpose."

"The *announced objective* set for the Church under this Program was to provide by October 1, 1936, by a wholly voluntary system of gifts in cash or in kind, sufficient food, fuel, clothing, and bedding to supply through the coming winter, every needy and worthy Church family unable to furnish these for itself, in order that no member of the Church should suffer in these times of stress and emergency.

"Our *primary purpose* was to set up, in so far as it might be possible, a system under which the curse of idleness would be done away with, the evils of a dole abolished, and independence, industry, thrift and self respect be once more established amongst our people. The aim of the Church is to help the people to help themselves. Work is to be re-enthroned as the ruling principle of the lives of our Church membership."[11] (Emphasis added.)

The announced objective was to provide for the poor so they would not suffer for lack of food, clothing, and shelter. But the primary purpose, expressive of eternal principles in caring for the poor, was to provide needed assistance in such a way as to correct spiritual deficiencies: doing away with idleness and the evils of a dole, and helping members with opportunities to work in order to enjoy independence and self-respect.

In describing the reason for the concentrated effort launched in 1936, the First Presidency explained that "the real purpose of the Church [Welfare] Plan is to assist each individual to secure independence, to help make him self-supporting, to replace idleness with thrift and productivity."[12] Similarly, almost a century ago, President Joseph F. Smith said: "It is the purpose of God in restoring the gospel and the holy Priesthood not only to benefit mankind spiritually, but also to benefit them temporally."[13]

As used in this setting, the words *temporal* and *spiritual* require clarification. *Temporal* signifies what pertains to mortal life, including food, shelter, employment, and property. *Spiritual* signifies what pertains to eternity, including faith, repentance, sanctification, covenants, and ordinances. Since temporal choices have spiritual consequences, and vice versa, temporal and spiritual are inseparable in the long run. To God, all things are spiritual, and none of his commands are temporal. (D&C 29:34–35.) Still, in the short run of mortality, it is sometimes useful to identify temporary and worldly things as *temporal* and less worldly and more heavenly things (the things of eternity) as *spiritual*. That is the sense in which President Joseph F. Smith used those words, and that is the sense in which they are used in the remainder of this chapter.

Temporal and spiritual objectives always go hand in hand in the Lord's plan, but the spiritual should always be primary in church-administered programs. Individual charitable acts and various charitable organizations can administer to the temporal needs of the poor, but only priesthood-directed and church-sponsored welfare activities can administer to the spiritual needs of those who are assisted and of those who assist them. President Marion G. Romney taught this principle succinctly when he said, "The prime duty of help to the poor by the Church is not to bring temporal relief to their needs, but salvation to their souls."[14]

The Savior taught the preeminence of the spiritual over the temporal. When Mary anointed Jesus' feet with costly ointment, Judas asked, "Why was not this ointment sold for three hundred pence, and given to the poor?" Jesus' reply taught a great principle to his followers: "Let her alone: against the day of my burying hath she kept this. For the poor always ye have with you; but me ye have not always." (John 12:5, 7–8.) Thus, while the care of the poor was important, its importance should be seen in a spiritual context. In this instance, there was something more important to do with this ointment than to give its value to the poor. The things of eternity, including what Jesus could teach his followers concerning the salvation of their souls and what he could do for them by his death and resurrection, were more important than the temporal care of the poor. Indeed, one reason we have the poor "always . . . with [us]" is to give the rest of us the spiritual testing and growth that come when we minister to their needs.

The preeminence of the spiritual over the temporal, which Jesus taught, has many applications in our own day. For example, it explains why our church spends great sums preaching the restored gospel and building temples to perform the ordinances of eternity rather than (as some advocate) devoting these same resources to temporal concerns already being pursued by others, such as preserving the environment, researching cures for diseases, or administering to other physical needs that can be accomplished without priesthood power or direction.

All of the modern prophets who have carried the major responsibility of explaining the Lord's way in the relief of the poor have stressed the predominance of spiritual over temporal goals. This includes Presidents David O. McKay, Spencer W. Kimball, Ezra Taft Benson, J. Reuben Clark, Henry D. Moyle, Marion G. Romney, Gordon B. Hinckley, and Thomas S. Monson. All have stressed the importance of methods that build the spirit as well as nourish the body.

In a notable message on welfare, delivered while he was president of the Church, Spencer W. Kimball listed the six "specific principles that undergird this work." He declared: "Only as we apply these truths can we approach the ideal of Zion. . . . This highest order of priesthood society is founded on the doctrines of [1] love, [2] service, [3] work, [4] self-reliance, and [5] stewardship, all of which are circumscribed by [6] the covenant of consecration."[15] Note that most of these are spiritual principles whose temporal or material significance is only indirect.

Other teachings stress that the Lord's way of caring for the poor and needy hallows those who give, because they act voluntarily, and exalts those who receive by teaching them the privilege of participating in a heavenly venture by contributing whatever their abilities permit. (D&C 104:16.) "The Lord's way builds individual self-esteem and develops and heals the dignity of the individual, whereas the world's way depresses the individual's view of himself and causes deep resentment," President Kimball explained.[16] "When viewed in this light, we can see that Welfare Services is not a program, but the essence of the gospel. *It is the gospel in action.* It is the crowning principle of a Christian life."[17]

When the First Presidency instituted what we call the Church Welfare Program in the 1930s, they stressed three principles of administration.

1. *The plan is based upon religious principles.* These principles are the ones discussed above, plus the principle of self-reliance (see p. 115).

2. *The plan is carried out entirely by Church agencies and principally by unpaid personnel who have no personal interest in the administration of assistance.*

The most important church officer in the Lord's program to care for the poor is the bishop. He is assigned this responsibility in modern revelation (for example, D&C 38:34–36; 42:30–31; 72:9–10, 12). His responsibility was reaffirmed when the welfare program was reinstituted. The First Presidency said: "The responsibility of seeing that no one is hungry or cold or insufficiently clad rests upon the bishops, each one for the members of his own ward."[18]

Bishops perform the duty of "searching after the poor

to administer to their wants by humbling the rich and the proud." (D&C 84:112.) President J. Reuben Clark, Jr., described that responsibility: "By the word of the Lord the sole mandate to care for and the sole discretion in caring for, the poor of the Church is lodged in the bishop. . . . It is his duty and his only to determine to whom, when, how, and how much shall be given to any member of his ward from Church funds and as ward help."[19]

Priesthood quorums have an important but different responsibility in the administration of church welfare. Theirs is the task of getting their quorum members into a position where they can be permanently self-sustaining. In a notable address given at the outset of the program, President J. Reuben Clark explained this responsibility: "This assistance may take the form of helping the needy brother in his actual need and problem, to build a home, or to start in a small business, or, if he be an artisan, to get him a kit of tools, or, if he is a farmer, to get him seeds, or to help him plant or harvest a crop, or to meet some urgent credit need he has."[20]

The Relief Society also has its essential role in the administration of welfare assistance. President Clark described it as follows:

"In all that relates to the supplying of clothing, the preparation and preservation of foodstuffs, the nursing of the sick, the burial of the dead, in all that relates to the infinities of kindly attention and sympathy, in all that relates even remotely to the love and ritual of motherhood, [members of] the Women's Relief Society carry the burden. The bishop is the father of his ward; the Relief Society is the mother. The Church Welfare Plan could not be carried on without them; it serves in greatest measure where they are most active. They establish sewing and cooking centers, they help with making budgets, they encourage the heavily burdened and despondent, they hold up the hands of the faint-hearted, they sweep despair out of the hearts of the distressed, they plant hope and faith and righteousness in every household. Womanhood, ripened into righteous motherhood, is the nearest approach to the divine, which mortals know. Mothers make the great membership of the Relief Society."[21]

Like the priesthood quorums, Relief Societies assist in the administration of welfare by helping their members acquire the knowledge and skills they need to fulfill their family and community responsibilities. The knowledge and skills their members will need differ from time to time and from place to place. Thus, homemaking skills that might have been taken for granted fifty years ago may need to be specially taught to some today. To cite another example, the greatest temporal training need for some members in a worldwide church is basic literacy. Relief Societies can assist in these and many other ways.

3. *The plan's measures seek to afford temporary relief, such as food, shelter, and clothing, to maintain individual life and well-being, rather than to cure the overall social and financial disorders that have caused individual needs.*[22]

The primary focus of church assistance for the poor and the needy has always been to alleviate distress on a temporary basis. Consistent with that mission, the assistance given to each recipient is tailored to the needs of that particular individual. Unlike most public assistance programs, there is no standardized amount or entitlement and no fixed duration for assistance.

In summary, in furtherance of religious principles the bishop gives individually tailored help for immediate physical needs, such as food, clothing, and fuel. The Relief Society assists in a variety of ways in compassionate service and sisterhood. And the priesthood quorums look after the more permanent needs, such as the education or other resources needed to help quorum members become self-supporting.

The Principle and Practice of Self-Reliance

In order to achieve its spiritual goals, the temporal aid given under church welfare must be subject to the fundamental gospel principle of self-reliance. No pair of ideas better express the contrast between government and church in the care of the poor than the words *work* and *self-reliance.*

Self-reliance means to work to provide for oneself to the maximum extent of one's ability. "In the sweat of *thy* face shalt thou eat bread," the Lord told Adam. (Gen. 3:19; emphasis added.) Our responsibility to provide for ourselves and our families is a vital principle in our relationship to God, to one another, and to civil government. Latter-day Saints expect to work for what they receive, whether it be salvation or sustenance. The only handout they desire is opportunity.

In our relationship with God, this principle is expressed in the familiar aphorism, "The Lord helps those who help themselves." Knute Rockne applied that principle to football when he said, "Prayers work best when players are big."[23] Carl Sandburg's biography of Lincoln gives a nineteenth-century illustration of this attitude when it tells of a New England farmer who asked his minister to pray that his farm would produce better crops. After looking over the stony, barren soil, the minister said, "This farm doesn't need prayer—what this farm needs is manure!"[24]

Some might find this attitude sacrilegious; others deem it outdated. To Latter-day Saints it exemplifies a law of life. It also shows the goodness of God, who expects us not only to have faith in him but also to have faith in ourselves, and to show our faith and appreciation by strenuous personal efforts to magnify the talents and opportunities he has given us. In short, we seek to apply the old aphorism: to pray as if everything depended on the Lord and then to work as if everything depended on us.

Work and self-reliance are ancient principles in the Christian faith. The apostle Paul taught that "if any would not work, neither should he eat." (2 Thes. 3:10.) He also wrote: "But if any provide not for his own, and specially for those of his own house, he hath denied the faith, and is worse than an infidel." (1 Tim. 5:8.)

These same principles were reaffirmed by revelation in the last dispensation: "Thou shalt not be idle; for he that is idle shall not eat the bread nor wear the garments of the laborer." (D&C 42:42.) "Every man who is obliged to provide for his own family, let him provide, and he shall in nowise lose his crown; and let him labor in the church. Let every man be diligent in all things. And the idler shall not have place in the church, except he repent and mend his ways." (D&C 75:28–29.)

President Brigham Young explained: "My experience has taught me, and it has become a principle with me, that it is never any benefit to give, out and out, to man or woman, money, food, clothing, or anything else, if they are able-bodied, and can work and earn what they need. . . . This is my principle, and I try to act upon it. To pursue a contrary course would ruin any community in the world and make them idlers."[25]

President Joseph F. Smith taught the same thing as a principle of individual behavior: "Men and women ought not to be willing to receive charity unless they are compelled to do so to keep them from suffering. Every man and woman ought to possess the spirit of independence, a self-sustaining spirit, that would prompt him or her to say, when they are in need, 'I am willing to give my labor in exchange for that which you give me.' No man ought to be satisfied to receive, and to do nothing for it."[26]

The doctrine of self-reliance, of course, imposes no obligation of work on the aged, the incapacitated, the sick, or others who are unable to work to support themselves.[27]

Work and self-reliance have an obvious application to our relationship to civil governments. For example, work and self-reliance were inherent in the most important United States government distribution of the nineteenth century. Under the Homestead Act of 1862, the United States government offered a deed to 160 acres of public land to "the head of a family, or [other person] who has arrived at the age of twenty-one years," who improved that land by residing upon it and cultivating it for a term of five years.[28] Settlers who obtained title to public lands by this means, including many Mormon pioneers, worked for what they received. Their government gave them an opportunity, not a handout. They made the nation stronger by subduing its frontiers, settling its public lands, paying its taxes, and producing food for its people.

A more recent example is the G.I. Bill, by which a grateful government gave educational benefits to members of its armed forces who had interrupted their other activities to serve their country.

In contrast to the traditional ideal of self-reliance, government welfare programs of this century have rarely included any requirement that the recipient work for what he or she receives.

The passage of the Social Security Act in 1935 marked a turning point in modern social welfare development in the United States. The benefits granted under that legislation had little or no relation to the contributions recipients had made to what was called the insurance fund. So far as individual workers were concerned, they had no interest in a segregated fund.

That is still true after more than a half-century. The huge sums that potential recipients and their employers pay as social security taxes are hardly distinguishable from income taxes, and the amounts received as social security payments bear little relationship to the amounts the recipient has paid into the fund. Some pay much more than their expected return; some pay much less. It can therefore be said that in economic effect, social security disbursements are difficult to distinguish from welfare payments.[29]

However, there is a great difference in terms of motive. Since all social security recipients have paid something for the assistance they are receiving (and some have even contributed more than they will receive), for purposes of the recipient's motive it is possible to liken social security to the purchase of an annuity for life. In any event, it is virtually impossible for employees or employers to avoid the taxes that are labeled for the support of social security payments. In those circumstances, church members and church corporations (as employers) have no practical alternative other than to participate, even though the social security system leaves much to be desired when measured against the principles of self-reliance.

No leader has spoken more frequently on the importance of self-reliance than President Marion G. Romney. His conference address of October 1982 was typical of his advocacy on this vital subject:

"Many programs have been set up by well-meaning individuals to aid those who are in need. However, many of

these programs are designed with the shortsighted objective
of 'helping people,' as opposed to 'helping people help
themselves.' Our efforts must always be directed toward
making able-bodied people self-reliant. . . .

"The practice of coveting and receiving unearned benefits has now become so fixed in our society that even men
of wealth, possessing the means to produce more wealth,
are expecting the government to guarantee them a profit. . . .

"All of our Church and family actions should be directed
toward making our children and members self-reliant. We
can't always control government programs, but we can control our own homes and congregations. If we will teach
these principles and live them, we can do much to counter
the negative effects which may exist in government programs
in any country."[30]

Many scholars, lawmakers, and administrators of government welfare have advocated a work requirement for
those who receive public assistance. The theory is popular,
but the goal has usually proven unattainable in practice. It
probably costs more to administer a work program (through
salaried supervisors) than to forgo it. Since total cost is the
most important criterion applied to public assistance, work
requirements have been abortive or short-lived.

President Ezra Taft Benson has defined the evil that self-
reliance seeks to counter. His words explain why the Church
has persisted in the work requirement that government programs have forgone as impractical and/or unnecessary: "Welfare recipients should work to the extent of their ability to
earn commodity or fast offering assistance. When meaningful
jobs are not provided, when people are not encouraged to
work, a demoralizing Church dole would develop, and the
purpose for which the welfare program was established
would be undermined. It is a law of heaven, and one we

haven't learned fully here on earth, that you cannot help people permanently by doing for them what they can do, and should do, for themselves."[31]

There is an ancient conflict between individual self-reliance on the one hand and group responsibility and co-operative efforts to care for the poor on the other. How do we promote the one without weakening the other?

An informed observer paid tribute to the LDS resolution of this conflict. William Rees-Mogg, editor of the *London Times*, observed:

"Sometimes in the United States one feels that the conservative attitude in politics is pushed to that extreme point at which individualism becomes anti-social. . . .

"In Utah the results of extreme individualism, which has permitted the disfigurement of some American states, do not follow. I think it is because Utah balances the pioneer principles of independence and self-reliance with those of voluntary social responsibility, derived from both the religious teachings and from the historic experience of the Mormons. Like all pioneers, the Mormons had to depend on themselves; like all pioneers they also had to depend on each other. Brigham Young, one of the greatest of American pioneer leaders, chose the beehive as the symbol of the new state, and a beehive is a symbol both of work and of cooperation. . . .

"Utah has therefore a conservatism in which the libertarian elements are balanced with elements of social co-operation and with the stability that comes from a communal religious faith and a strong family life."[32]

The Purpose and Method of Giving

President Marion G. Romney explained the eternal purpose of the commandment to help the poor and the needy: "In this modern world plagued with counterfeits for the

Lord's plan, we must not be misled into supposing that we can discharge our obligations to the poor and the needy by shifting the responsibility to some governmental or other public agency. Only by voluntarily giving out of an abundant love for our neighbors can we develop that charity characterized by Mormon as 'the pure love of Christ.' (Moro. 7:47.) This we must develop if we would obtain eternal life."[33]

Does the individual's obligation to help the poor and needy include an obligation to help persons who can support themselves but refuse or neglect to do so? This is an ancient problem in the Christian faith.

How do we reconcile the individual's obligation to care for him- or herself with other individuals' (and congregations') obligations to care for the poor? Alfred P. Doolittle, the lovable rogue in *My Fair Lady,* gives voice to that problem when he declares: "I am a member of the undeserving poor. That means I'm up against middle-class morality all my days."[34] Part of the middle-class morality Doolittle laments is working people's unwillingness to support able-bodied persons who could work to support themselves.

Under the Lord's plan for the relief of the poor and needy, Latter-day Saints escape that problem as to donations made through the Church. They pay their fast offering, and the Lord, through his servant, the bishop, decides who should receive them and upon what conditions.

Welfare Principles in Practice

Those who act upon the principle that relief of the poor and the needy should be administered in the Lord's way encounter many challenges. The contrary philosophies and methods of various government welfare programs are pervasive and highly visible, and they exert a constant influence upon the procedures of church workers who administer assistance and upon the expectations of the needy who receive it.

At the doctrinal or theoretical level, there is a rich opportunity for confusion over the principle of self-reliance. For example, some have experienced confusion in how the principle of self-reliance applies to the twin goals of temporal well-being and spiritual salvation. The true principle is self-reliance in temporal matters and ultimate total dependence on our Savior, Jesus Christ, in spiritual matters. As Nephi taught, "It is by grace that we are saved, after all we can do." (2 Ne. 25:23.)

In common with C. S. Lewis, the perceptive author of *The Screwtape Letters,* I believe that one of Satan's most effective techniques is to pretend to accept a true principle and then act so as to corrupt it. Thus, Satan would surely like to corrupt the practice of self-reliance in order to make us self-reliant in spiritual things (thinking we can "work out our own salvation") and largely dependent on others in temporal things. He desires this corruption since misunderstanding of either role of self-reliance forestalls an important part of the personal growth that the Father's plan seeks to afford us. A misunderstanding of both relationships is doubly devastating.

There are powerful forces at work to beguile us into self-sufficiency in spiritual things and to lure us into some degree of dependence in temporal things. It is easy for Latter-day Saints to fall prey to those forces.

For example, since most government programs have no counterpart to the requirement that needy persons who receive church assistance should work to the extent of their ability, it is easy for recipients and tempting for bishops to consider this requirement an unwelcome imposition. In ministering to the needs of their flocks, church leaders are perhaps more effective at providing the assistance necessary to meet temporal needs than in administering the work requirement necessary to serve spiritual needs. To a busy bishop or other leader it is sometimes awkward to require and often difficult to administer the work requirement in an urban environment where there are fewer opportunities for manual labor than in an agrarian society. But if a bishop is not careful in administering the work requirement, he may dispense temporary assistance in such a way as to encourage permanent dependence.

Experience teaches that the larger an organization becomes, the more difficult it is to administer a requirement that must be individualized for each person. Thus, it is often much easier to produce and deliver a sack of potatoes to each of many needy persons than it is to devise and administer an individualized work program for each recipient. That is one reason why government assistance tends to settle into cash payments computed from prescribed formulas, without individualized work requirements.

Another challenge in administering assistance in the Lord's way rather than in the highly visible government way concerns the nature and amount of aid given. Church welfare has always preferred the distribution of commodities produced by other members on church welfare properties. But this is obviously much more difficult and sometimes even more expensive than the government way of distributing cash. And many recipients prefer cash.

Finally, church assistance is intended to sustain life rather than to maintain a recipient's current standard of living. This limitation can be painfully difficult to administer when it requires that the bishop be a close observer while a previously self-sufficient but presently needy member suffers the pains of decompression in his or her standard of living.

Transients who seek to soak up as much assistance as possible before moving on to a new location also put pressure on a program that seeks to trust and help needy people but also desires to protect its resources from predators.

If not thoroughly taught and properly led, Latter-day Saints in any nation can slip into depending on the Church to provide for their temporal needs. This dependence can go well beyond the temporary provision of food and shelter for the poor and the needy. Most General Authorities have received letters from Saints in various places asking, "Why doesn't the Church do something about . . . ?" According to the conditions in a particular area, this question may refer to unemployment or other economic conditions, to the extent or nature of educational alternatives, or even to political conditions.

An attitude of dependence by Latter-day Saints upon church initiatives or financing is hard to combat in many countries because it is so pervasive in the government system and social welfare environment. But dependence on the Church in temporal things cannot be encouraged or even acquiesced in because it is counter to the Lord's way. His way teaches us to support the Lord's church, not to expect to be supported by it. He teaches us to look on the gospel as a command for us to help others, not as a command for others to help us.

Methods Change

The *principles* God has revealed for caring for the poor are eternal and will not change. The *methods* used to carry those principles into action will differ from time to time, and even from nation to nation.

President Spencer W. Kimball stressed the differences between principles and methods in a definitive address titled

"Welfare Services: The Gospel in Action." First he reviewed what he called the "foundational truths" or "welfare principles" governing the Lord's way of caring for the poor: love, service, work, self-reliance, consecration, and stewardship. Second, he discussed what he called "some of the activities and programs that represent ways to live these principles."[35] This contrast reminds us that as laws and social conditions change in a particular nation, inspired leaders will change welfare activities and programs. Revelation is required not only to teach the eternal principles, but also to direct how those principles will be applied in a particular time and place.

Storehouses

When the Lord's way of caring for the poor and the needy was made known during the restoration of the gospel, the revelations directed the establishment of a storehouse. (D&C 51:13; 72:10, 12; 78:3.) Most of the early revelations link the storehouse to the law of consecration. Faithful members consecrated and conveyed all their property to the Church. They received back sufficient for their own needs, and the residue was taken into the storehouse for the bishop to administer to the poor and needy. (D&C 42:33–34; 51:1–13; 78:1–14; 83:5–6.)

When the conveyance of all property to the Church was discontinued after a few years, the bishop's storehouse continued to perform the key function in the collection of tithes (the Lord's law of finance following initial consecration–D&C 119) and in the care of the poor. The storehouse was essential in the administration of tithing when most tithing was paid in kind. When a money economy became dominant in the areas where most members lived, so that tithing was rarely paid in kind, the bishop's storehouses fell into disuse.

When the cooperative effort that came to be known as the Church Welfare Program was launched during the Great Depression of the 1930s, the Church restored the old system of bishop's storehouses. They served as the collection, storage, and dissemination points for the food, fuel, and clothing produced and donated by members for the relief of the poor and needy.[36]

Welfare Projects

Consistent with the underlying principle of self-reliance, the reinstituted welfare plan presupposed and provided that persons would work for what they received. Indeed, recipient work was securely linked to the nature of the assistance provided. Local church units were encouraged to develop work projects that had two functions: "to produce commodities and to provide work for those who are unemployed."[37] Pursuant to the overriding spiritual goals of the welfare program, these projects also provided opportunities for the general membership to work together to help others.

In a society where almost all members lived on farms or in an urban area with relatively close access to farmland, this arrangement worked well. A needy person could be fed with commodities and work on a farm that produced them. Different projects could produce different commodities, and the storehouse could provide the necessary functions of storage and exchange. The prototype of this approach was Welfare Square in Salt Lake City, a facility whose main building was constructed largely by the labor of Latter-day Saints who were being assisted by commodities such as those to be stored and processed there.[38]

The Project and Storehouse Program in Action

Productive projects and well-stocked storehouses made possible the Church's remarkable effort to relieve the suffering of its European members immediately after World

War II. On relatively short notice, 133 carloads of relief supplies were dispatched to Europe. The temporal blessings realized by this timely relief were significant, but just as important were the spiritual blessings that came to both donors and recipients.[39]

The mature operation of the commodity and storehouse method of caring for the poor appears in the nature and extent of welfare operations in the published reports for the year 1955. There were 689 welfare production projects (largely in agriculture, but some in manufacturing) and 140 bishop's storehouse units. About 50,000 people were assisted with cash or commodities, and more than 92,000 people donated approximately 790,000 hours of labor on welfare projects.[40] Members donated labor on such projects as beef ranches, dairy farms, or citrus acreage so needy members could receive such commodities as beef, milk, and oranges. In 1975, twenty years later, 73 percent of the wards and stakes in the United States and Canada were involved in welfare production projects, and the rest were still being urged to do likewise.[41]

Recent Changes

As the fiftieth anniversary of the reestablishment of the welfare plan approached, it was apparent that conditions were changing and that the Church's cooperative efforts to care for the poor and needy would have to change with them. The membership was no longer concentrated in a few western states, but included large numbers in urban centers across the nation and in many parts of the world. In 1935, The Church of Jesus Christ of Latter-day Saints had 746,000 members, two-thirds of whom lived in Utah, Idaho, and Arizona. In 1983, the membership was 5.3 million, with fewer than one-third living in those three states. In 1983, 1.6 million members were living outside the United States.

By the 1980s Latter-day Saints lived under many different government systems. Even in the United States, the laws and environment of what had come to be called "the welfare state" impinged on every private effort of a charitable nature (including schools and hospitals as well as the care of the poor), and the tax laws of counties, states, and the nation created major problems for a cooperative and commodity-based program of church care for the poor.

At a leadership meeting during general conference in April 1983, the Church announced what its leaders called "the most significant and far-reaching" modifications in welfare since President Grant defined its purposes in 1936.[42] Speaking for the First Presidency, President Gordon B. Hinckley "reaffirm[ed] the basic principles of the welfare program" and gave assurance that "there will be no departure from those foundation principles."[43]

Speaking in that same meeting, Elder Thomas S. Monson stressed the difference between the unchangeable basic principles of caring for the poor and the changeable methods by which those principles are to be achieved. He quoted President Harold B. Lee's statement that "nobody changes the principles and doctrines of the Church except the Lord by revelation. But methods change as the inspired direction comes to those who preside at a given time."[44] As he reviewed the history of the welfare program, Elder Monson observed that "the procedures were revealed to fit a particular time," and he affirmed that these newly announced changes are "part of a continuing chain."[45]

Elder Monson summarized the changed conditions that required modifications in the Church's methods of caring for the poor and the needy:

"Today, we have become an urban society. Final 1980 census figures show the nation's farm population has dropped to 2.5 percent in the United States. With 97.5 percent of the population living in an urban setting, it has become increasingly difficult to obtain production projects which meet the objectives for which they are intended. Farms are being located further and further from the members who own them. In addition, with improved technology, farming has become a capital intensive business, as opposed to one which is labor intensive. Also, the international growth of the Church has caused no small amount of thought as to how the Welfare Program should be modified to meet international demands. These are but a few of the current conditions taken into consideration."[46]

The changes of program or method were extensive. The annual storehouse commodity budget cash assessments (paid by each stake through production projects or cash payments) were discontinued. The commodity program would now be funded by voluntary fast offering (cash) contributions. The financing of storehouses and production projects would now be provided by general church funds, without local contributions. Existing production projects would be evaluated with a view to combining, trading, or reassigning them to provide greater efficiency. Only those properties that would produce welfare goods needed within the system would be retained as welfare projects. Others would be sold or managed as taxpaying investment properties.[47]

Under this major change of method, the number of production projects was significantly reduced, most notably in areas without large concentrations of membership. Many production projects and most storehouses remained, but their functions were rolled back to the original purposes of producing and distributing commodities directly for the relief of the poor and providing work opportunities for those assisted and for significant numbers of the general membership. When these objectives could not be served by a project, assistance of the poor and needy was to be administered on a cash basis.

These changes reduced or eliminated the welfare projects' market competition with the farmers or businessmen who made their living by producing comparable products. It also eliminated much controversy over real estate and income tax exemptions for welfare properties.

In 1989 the Church published a booklet titled *Basic Self-Reliance*. In a letter to Church leaders dated November 16, 1989, President Howard W. Hunter explained that this booklet was to be used "to help improve the health and well-being of Church members in developing areas of the world." The booklet has basic training materials on disease prevention, nutrition, hygiene and sanitation, home health care, and gardening. These materials are to be taught under the direction of the ward welfare committee, according to the needs of ward members. Area presidencies were given the responsibility "to administer training in basic self-reliance."

The impact of the changes announced in 1983 is evident from a public report given just four years later. In testimony before the House Ways and Means Subcommittee on Public Assistance, Keith B. McMullin, managing director of Welfare Services for the Church, gave a comprehensive description of the Church's program and hardly mentioned production projects. Some production projects remained, but they were the exception rather than the rule.

After reviewing the underlying religious principles of church welfare, Director McMullin described the methods: "We seek first and foremost to foster self-reliance and provident living," including the acquisition of needed skills and suitable employment, living within one's income, and avoiding unnecessary debt. Latter-day Saints are encouraged to provide "appropriate reserves of food [and] clothing," to follow "sound health practices," and to cultivate "habits that ensure social, emotional and spiritual well-being." He explained that when individuals have done all they can do to care for themselves, the immediate and extended family are expected to help; and when family resources are no longer sufficient, the Church supplies needed assistance. This assistance "may consist of food or clothing, counseling, adoption services, job training, the payment of bills, or the compassionate service of neighbors and friends."[48]

In short, in the 1980s the principles of church welfare remained, but the methods had undergone significant changes. There was a new emphasis on prevention, as in the booklet *Basic Self-Reliance.* There was continued focus on temporary assistance, but the type of assistance had now been expanded well beyond the food, fuel, clothing, and bedding of the 1930s. Production projects were deemphasized, and bishops were empowered to give a wider variety of assistance than could be held in a storehouse building. The concept of the storehouse was enlarged to include the family's inventory of food, clothing, and talent, and the similar resources of nearby members. This modified definition appears in *Providing in the Lord's Way, A Leader's Guide to Welfare,* published in 1990:

"The Lord's storehouse receives, holds in trust, and dispenses consecrated offerings of the Saints. In form and operation, the storehouse is as simple or sophisticated as circumstances require. It may be a list of available services, money in an account, food in a pantry, or commodities in a building. A storehouse is established the moment faithful members give to the bishop of their time, talents, skills, compassion, materials, and financial means in caring for the poor and in building up the kingdom of God on the earth."[49]

These new methods were obviously better suited to current laws and living patterns in the United States and in other parts of the world.

Government Assistance

With these changes in the methods by which the Church administers assistance to the poor and needy came other changes in the recipient's relationship to government assistance.

In its inception, church welfare was an alternative to government welfare, and members were encouraged to avoid all assistance from government. That method was feasible in the United States in the 1930s and 1940s, but it was difficult to apply in the various socialist countries where membership expanded significantly in the 1950s or even in the social welfare environment in the United States of the 1970s.

In 1977 President Ezra Taft Benson explained the basic principles governing whether Latter-day Saints should accept government assistance: "Occasionally, we receive questions as to the propriety of Church members receiving government assistance instead of Church assistance. Let me restate what is a fundamental principle. Individuals, to the extent possible, should provide for their own needs. Where the individual is unable to care for himself, his family should assist. Where the family is not able to provide, the Church should render assistance, not the government. We accept the basic principle that 'though the people support the government, the government should not support the people.' "[50]

He then voiced an important distinction between "earned" and "unearned" assistance, explaining its importance in terms of its spiritual impact on the recipient: "Latter-day Saints should not receive *unearned* welfare assistance from local or national agencies. This includes food stamps. Priesthood and Relief Society leaders should urge members to accept the Church welfare program and earn through the program that which they need, even though they may receive less food and money. By doing so, members will be spiritually strengthened, and they will maintain their dignity and self-respect."[51]

By the 1980s, Latter-day Saints all over the world were being taxed to support a variety of government services not limited to the poor—free hot lunches in grade schools, low tuition in colleges, and counseling services in between, to cite only a few examples. Should they forgo access to such generally available government programs—which they were taxed to support—and turn only to the Church for aid?

As in President Benson's message quoted above, the Church has continued to counsel its members not to accept traditional government support of the poor, such as food stamps. But where a government-supported program is generally available to all citizens and where it can be squared with self-reliance and the other principles of church welfare, church leaders now raise no objection to their members' participation. For example, no objection is raised when a member makes a significant personal contribution in order to realize the benefits of a program (such as a student who must study in order to realize the benefit of the tax subsidy inherent in a low-tuition college education).

The principle of self-reliance and its relationship to government assistance is described in this key passage in the *Leader's Guide to Welfare:*

"Latter-day Saints have the responsibility to provide for themselves and their families. Individual members, however, may find it necessary to receive assistance beyond that which the family can provide, in which case they may turn to the Church for help. In some instances, individual members may decide to receive assistance from other sources, including government. In all such cases, members should avoid becoming dependent upon these sources and strive to become self-reliant. Where possible, they should work in return for assistance rendered."[52]

In his testimony before the House Committee, Welfare Managing Director McMullin gave public expression to the new approach: "Where community resources are available that are compatible with our approach, we are happy to use them. Our overarching aim, however, is always to help people help themselves."[53]

There is a large and perhaps widening gap between government's way and the Church's way of caring for the poor and the needy. The gap is inevitable because the Church's purposes, dictated by the commandments of God, are to serve spiritual as well as temporal goals.

Increasing urbanization and the diversities encountered in a worldwide church pose many challenges for those who are responsible to use the Lord's resources to help the poor and the needy. Recent changes in church organization and procedures facilitate this sacred mission, but the most important variables are still the attitude of the potential recipient and the inspired direction of the bishop. Neither of those fundamentals has changed. The Lord's way of welfare will continue unchanged, so long as the members are determined to support themselves to the best of their ability and then to participate in assisting others less fortunate, and so long as bishops continue to administer assistance in the Lord's way.

NOTES

1. Russell M. Nelson, "In the Lord's Own Way," *Ensign* 16 (May 1986): 25.

2. Marion G. Romney, "Caring for the Poor and Needy," *Ensign* 3 (January 1973): 97.

3. Nelson, "In the Lord's Own Way," 27.

4. Joseph F. Smith, *Gospel Doctrine* (Salt Lake City: Deseret Book, 1986), 308.

5. Romney, "Caring for the Poor," 99.

6. See, for example, Charles Murray, *Losing Ground* (New York City: Basic Books Inc., 1984).

7. Quoted in Thomas S. Monson, "A Provident Plan—A Precious Promise," *Ensign* 16 (May 1986): 64.

8. Robert L. Woodson, "Race and Economic Opportunity," *Vanderbilt Law Review* 42 (May 1989): 1025.

9. Ibid., 1026.

10. *The Teachings of Spencer W. Kimball,* ed. Edward L. Kimball (Salt Lake City: Bookcraft, 1982), 370.

11. *Conference Report,* October 1936, 2–3.

12. "Greetings of the First Presidency," *Improvement Era* 41 (January 1938): 7.

13. Smith, *Gospel Doctrine,* 209.

14. Marion G. Romney, "The Role of Bishops in Welfare Services," *Ensign* 7 (November 1977): 81.

15. Spencer W. Kimball, "Welfare Services: The Gospel in Action," *Ensign* 7 (November 1977): 78.

16. *Teachings of Spencer W. Kimball,* 369.

17. Ibid., 365.

18. "The First Presidency Speaks on Church Security," *Improvement Era* 40 (January 1937): 3; reprinted in *Messages of the First Presidency,* James R. Clark, comp., 6 (Salt Lake City: Bookcraft, 1975): 22, 24.

19. Quoted by Marion G. Romney in "Church Welfare—Some Fundamentals," *Ensign* 4 (January 1974): 91–92.

20. Clark, *Messages of the First Presidency* 6:76. Also see Gordon B. Hinckley, "Welfare Responsibilities of the Priesthood Quorums," *Ensign* 7 (November 1977): 85.

21. Clark, *Messages of the First Presidency* 6:77.

22. See "The Message of the First Presidency to the Church," *Conference Report,* October 1936, 2–6; J. Reuben Clark, Jr., "Church Welfare Plan," in *Messages of the First Presidency,* 6:63–88 (address at a conference in Estes Park, Colorado, 1939).

23. Andrew J. Maikovich, ed., *Sports Quotations* (Jefferson, N.C.: McFarland & Co., 1984), 90.

24. Carl Sandburg, *Abraham Lincoln: The Prairie Years,* 1 (New York: Harcourt, Brace & World, 1926): 125.

25. Quoted in Romney, "Church Welfare—Some Fundamentals," 89.

26. Smith, *Gospel Doctrine,* 234.

27. Marion G. Romney, "The Celestial Nature of Self-reliance," *Ensign* 12 (November 1982): 92.

28. *United States Statutes at Large* 12 (1862): 392.

29. Louis Kohlmeier, "Social Security and Welfare on an Historic Convergence Course," *Financier* 1 (September 1977): 6.

30. Romney, "The Celestial Nature of Self-reliance," 91–92.

31. Ezra Taft Benson, "Ministering to Needs Through the Lord's Storehouse System," *Ensign* 7 (May 1977): 83.

32. William Rees-Mogg, "Conservatism Shines Its Brightest in Utah," *Deseret News,* March 31, 1980, pp. A1, A3.

33. Romney, "Caring for the Poor," 98.

34. *My Fair Lady,* act 1, sc. 5.

35. Kimball, "Welfare Services," 78.

36. Clark, "Church Welfare Plan," *Messages of the First Presidency* 6:74.

37. *Priesthood and Church Welfare* (Salt Lake City: Deseret Book, 1938), 33.

38. Henry D. Taylor, "The Church Welfare Plan," 1984, bound manuscript in History Library–Archives, The Church of Jesus Christ of Latter-day Saints, Salt Lake City, Utah, p. 57.

39. See, generally, Ezra Taft Benson, *Conference Report,* April 1947, 152; Alfred W. Uhrhan, "Welfare in the Church," *Improvement Era* 59 (November 1956): 852; Taylor, "The Church Welfare Plan," 58–59; Ezra Taft Benson, *A Labor of Love* (Salt Lake City: Deseret Book, 1989).

40. Taylor, "The Church Welfare Plan," 59.

41. Marion G. Romney, "Welfare Services," *Ensign* 5 (November 1975): 127.

42. "News of the Church," *Ensign* 13 (May 1983): 84.

43. Quoted in Taylor, "The Church Welfare Plan," 122.

44. Harold B. Lee, "God's Kingdom—A Kingdom of Order," *Ensign* 1 (January 1971): 10.

45. Thomas S. Monson, quoted in Taylor, "The Church Welfare Plan," 124–25.

46. Ibid., 125.

47. "News of the Church," *Ensign* 13 (May 1983): 83; Taylor, "The Church Welfare Plan," 123.

48. Keith B. McMullin, prepared testimony before the House Ways and Means Subcommittee on Public Assistance, as quoted in a press release of The Church of Jesus Christ of Latter-day Saints, March 11, 1987.

49. *Providing in the Lord's Way, A Leader's Guide to Welfare* (Salt Lake City: The Church of Jesus Christ of Latter-day Saints, 1990), 11.

50. Ezra Taft Benson, "Ministering to Needs Through the Lord's Storehouse System," 84.

51. Ibid.

52. *Providing in the Lord's Way,* 15.

53. McMullin, press release, March 11, 1987.

CHAPTER 5

CONTENTION

Another subject on which the Lord has specified a special "way" concerns what the scriptures call *contention*. Since this word and its variations (such as *contend*) have several meanings in the scriptures, it is necessary to emphasize that the kind of *contention* discussed in this chapter is synonymous with wrath, strife, angry disputes, and quarreling.* This is the meaning expressed in the adjective *contentious*. (For examples, see Alma 9:1–4; 19:25–28; 21:5–6.) Holding different views or conversing about points of disagreement does not constitute this kind of contention. Neither does an argument or a debate, if (a big *if*) it can be done with a peaceful spirit and method. In short, the kind of contention

---

* In contrast, *contend* sometimes signifies physical conflict, as in "the Nephites were obliged to contend with their brethren, even unto bloodshed." (Alma 43:14.) *Contend* and *contention* are also used to signify a vigorous, reasoned explanation of a point, such as the apostle Paul's statement that "we were bold . . . to speak unto you the gospel of God with much contention." (1 Thes. 2:2.) Similarly, Jude counseled that we should "earnestly contend for the faith." (Jude 1:3; also see D&C 18:20; 112:5.)

treated here consists of disagreement *plus* a wrathful spirit or a quarrelsome method.

Examples of Contention

As a lawyer with experience in civil litigation and criminal prosecutions, in legal scholarship, and in judicial service, I have had considerable personal exposure to the controversies that are inherent in the adversary process. In their most aggressive manifestations, such professional disputes can constitute contention. My experience in the legal profession has also made me familiar with the reality that adversaries can communicate about disagreements without contention.

In my personal life and even in my church work, I have sometimes been guilty of crossing over the boundary between the permissible range of reasoned discussion and the forbidden arena of contention. For example, as a law student, newly schooled in the adversary system of the courtroom, I sought to use adversary techniques to present the gospel subjects I was teaching an elders group. I sometimes encouraged debate and controversy, and I occasionally played the role of the devil's advocate (justly so named). Each of these techniques verged on or invited contention. I recall these immature mistakes whenever I observe others using the techniques of controversy to attempt to teach gospel subjects. This is not the Lord's way.

Joseph Smith observed such an effort in the early days of the Church, and used it to give some corrective counsel. In Kirtland, Ohio, on November 18, 1835, a weekday evening, he called at the home of a family and found that "some of the young Elders, were about engaging in a debate" on the question of whether Christ intended to establish his gospel by miracles. The Prophet's journal continues:

"After an interesting debate of three hours or more, during which time much talent was displayed, it was desided by the presidents of the debate in the negative; which was a righteous descision I discovered in this debate, much warmth displayed, to much zeal for mastery, to much of that enthusiam that characterizes a lawyer at the bar, who is determined to defend his cause right or wrong. I therefore availed myself of this favorable opportunity, to drop a few words upon this subject by way of advise, that they might improve their minds and cultivate their powers of intellect in a proper manner, that they might not incur the displeasure of heaven, that they should handle sacred things verry sacredly, and with due deference to the opinions of others and with an eye single to the glory of God."[1]

Here the Prophet counsels us how to avoid the "displeasure of heaven" when discussing sacred things. We should handle them "very sacredly, and with due deference to the opinions of others." And the purpose of our discussion should be appropriate, not characterized by the familiar "zeal for mastery," but "with an eye single to the glory of God."

A half century later, President George Q. Cannon expressed the same counsel about adversary discussions: "Is it right for Latter-day Saints to contend and to have arguments? It is not right; it is not according to the mind and will of God. Whenever two Elders contend and argue, they may know and everyone may know that the Spirit of God is not there to the extent that it should be, because where the Spirit of God reigns there is no contention, no controversy. Men may differ in their views, but after they have expressed these differences then contention should cease; in fact, it should never exist."[2]

He also explained why Latter-day Saints should avoid

contention: "All our ideas of heaven cause us to feel that dissension and division, strife and factional differences and contention concerning any important point are effectually excluded from that blest abode. . . . Therefore, inasmuch as religion is given for the purpose of preparing us to dwell eternally with God our Eternal Father, it is natural that we should expect that religion would have the effect upon mankind to give them a foretaste of that bliss and union and love and peace, the full realization of which is expected to be enjoyed in heaven."[3]

Confrontation and other adversary techniques are accepted ways of pursuing knowledge in many fields. In contrast, in ancient and modern scriptures the Lord instructs his followers to refrain from contending over the points of his doctrine and to avoid disputes and contention in personal relationships.

Scriptural Teachings Against Contention

The Savior's most explicit teaching on the evils of contention is recorded in the Book of Mormon. When the risen Lord gave his disciples power to baptize his followers on the American continent, he observed that there had previously been disputes among them on the manner of baptism. After giving specific directions on how this ordinance should be performed, the Savior added this great teaching on disputation and contention:

"And there shall be no disputations among you, as there have hitherto been; neither shall there be disputations among you concerning the points of my doctrine, as there have hitherto been. For verily, verily I say unto you, he that hath the spirit of contention is not of me, but is of the devil, who is the father of contention, and he stirreth up the hearts of men to contend with anger, one with another. Behold, this is not my doctrine, to stir up the hearts of men with anger, one against another; but this is my doctrine, that such things should be done away." (3 Ne. 11:28–30.)

It is noteworthy that the Savior did not limit his teaching about disputations and contention to those who had *wrong* ideas about doctrine or procedure. He forbade disputations and contention by *everyone,* saying, "He that hath the spirit of contention is not of me." Men should not be stirred up "with anger, one against another."

The commandment to avoid contention applies to those who are right as well as to those who are wrong. It is not enough for the Savior's followers to have a correct understanding of doctrine and procedure. They must also be harmonious in their personal relationships and in the way they seek to serve him.

In the years following the Savior's personal ministry to his followers on the American continent, all were converted and enjoyed a golden age of righteousness, peace, and prosperity. I find it significant that the scriptural description of this period stresses that "there were no contentions and disputations among them" (4 Ne. 1:2; also see verse 15), suggesting that the absence of contention is a most significant bellwether of righteousness.

In the Sermon on the Mount, the Savior taught another facet of this principle: the need for reconciliation of personal differences before we approach God to offer our gifts. "Therefore if thou bring thy gift to the altar, and there rememberest that thy brother hath ought against thee; leave there thy gift before the altar, and go thy way; first be reconciled to thy brother, and then come and offer thy gift." (Matt. 5:23–24.) This command apparently takes no account of the cause of the difference—who is right and who is wrong. We are obliged to "be reconciled to [our] brother" even when he is wrong and we are only the victim of the grievance. For purposes of the commandment of reconciliation, fault is unimportant. The object is reconciliation, not adjudication; peace, not justice. Reconciliation seeks the restoration of relationships, not the adjudication of differences.

If we can avoid rehashing and attempting to adjudicate the causes, and just work at restoring the relationship, we can be reconciled to our brothers and sisters. How many marriages could be saved, how many families could be united, how many friendships could be restored, if persons could only abandon contention and apply this principle of reconciliation!

Throughout the Sermon on the Mount, the Savior emphasized and reemphasized the avoidance of contention: "Ye have heard that it hath been said, An eye for an eye, and a tooth for a tooth; but I say unto you, That ye resist not evil: but whosoever shall smite thee on thy right cheek, turn to him the other also." (Matt. 5:38–39.)

In a stimulating analysis of the application of this commandment in the circumstances of our day, Leonard E. Read, the long-time editor of *The Freeman,* concluded that it meant "not to argue with anyone. . . . In a word, away with confrontation!" He gave this illustration: "Now and then we experience shysterism: a broken promise, overcharge, underquality, an attempt to 'get the best' of one. Resist not this evil; that is, pay no heed; not a scolding word; simply walk away and fail to return. While resistance will harden the malefactor in his sins as he rises to his own defense, nonresistance leaves him alone with his soul, his shop, and his jobbery, a plight even a malefactor will ponder and understand."[4]

Contention is also avoided by adherence to another teaching in the Sermon on the Mount: "Ye have heard that it hath been said, Thou shalt love thy neighbour, and hate thine enemy. But I say unto you, Love your enemies, bless them that curse you, do good to them that hate you, and pray for them which despitefully use you, and persecute you." (Matt. 5:43–44.) This great command is thought by many to be the supreme test of Christian behavior.

In the Sermon on the Plain (recorded in the sixth chapter of Luke), the Savior elaborated his instruction to love our enemies by relating this to the avoidance of contention:

"And unto him who smiteth thee on the cheek, offer also the other; or, in other words, it is better to offer the other, than to revile again. And him who taketh away thy cloak, forbid not to take thy coat also. For it is better that thou suffer thine enemy to take these things, than to contend with him. Verily, I say unto you, your Heavenly Father who seeth in secret, shall bring that wicked one into judgment." (JST Luke 6:29–30.)

Speaking of these verses, President George Q. Cannon wrote: "When we are sued at law, we should not indulge in the same spirit. We should not revile if we are reviled. We should not render evil for evil. But we should constantly strive to render good for evil. . . . We should love our enemies. . . . Until we all overcome the disposition that prompts men to take this evil course ['cursing for cursing'], we cannot claim the blessings that the Lord has promised."[5]

The New Testament contains many other teachings on the avoidance of contention.

No writer in all of holy writ gave more frequent warnings against contention than the apostle Paul. His most detailed teaching on this subject is in his letter to the Romans. He introduces his concern over contention by stating that in "the judgment of God," which will "render to every man

according to his deeds," persons who are contentious shall
have "tribulation and anguish." (Rom. 2:2, 6, 8–9.)

Later in his letter, Paul gives a vivid illustration of why
we should avoid contention and how this can be done. He
expresses concern for "him that is weak in the faith" and
directs that such a person shall be received, "but not to
doubtful disputations." (Rom. 14:1.) By way of illustration,
he reminds the Romans of the differing opinions about what
a Christian could properly eat, which was apparently a fertile
source of contention among them. He then pleads that those
who pursue different dietary choices not "despise" or
"judge" one another: "Let not him that eateth despise him
that eateth not; and let not him which eateth not judge him
that eateth: for God hath received him." (Rom. 14:3.)

In short, we should love one another and leave the
judging to God. "Let us not therefore judge one another any
more: but judge this rather, that no man put a stumblingblock
or an occasion to fall in his brother's way." (Rom. 14:13.)

Paul then gives this memorable example. Referring to
dietary choices, he said he was "persuaded . . . that there is
nothing unclean of itself." Nevertheless, there was something much more important than his own opinion on this
subject: other members considered certain food to be unclean. In that circumstance, the overriding principle of love
and concern for others required Paul to refrain from conduct
that would destroy, weaken, or offend others.

"But if thy brother be grieved with thy meat, now walkest
thou not charitably. Destroy not him with thy meat, for whom
Christ died. . . . *Let us therefore follow after the things which
make for peace,* and things wherewith one may edify another. For meat destroy not the work of God. All things
indeed are pure; but it is evil for that man who eateth with
offence. It is good neither to eat flesh, nor to drink wine, nor

any thing whereby thy brother stumbleth, or is offended, or is made weak." (Rom 14:14–21; emphasis added.)

Later, as he concluded this letter to the Romans, Paul made a final plea to avoid divisions among the Saints:

"Now I beseech you, brethren, mark them which cause divisions and offences contrary to the doctrine which ye have learned; and avoid them. For they that are such serve not our Lord Jesus Christ, but their own belly; and by good words and fair speeches deceive the hearts of the simple." (Rom. 16:17–18.)

In brief, don't create divisions among the Saints by behavior that some consider to be evil. Don't put a stumbling block in the way of a brother or sister. Serve the Lord by "follow[ing] after the things which make for peace." (Rom. 14:19.)

The Acts of the Apostles record that Paul "disputed" in the synagogue. (See Acts 17:17; 19:8.) In light of his own teachings on contention, those accounts surely describe reasoned discussions, not angry confrontations.

In Paul's first letter to the Corinthians, he gave them the same advice: "If any man seem to be contentious, we have no such custom, neither the churches of God." (1 Cor. 11:16.) In his second letter, he expressed the fear that when he came to them he would find "debates, envyings, wraths, strifes, backbitings, whisperings, swellings, tumults." (2 Cor. 12:20.)

Similarly, Paul advised Titus to "avoid foolish questions, . . . and contentions, and strivings about the law; for they are unprofitable and vain." (Titus 3:9.) He instructed Timothy, "Foolish and unlearned questions avoid," because "they do gender strifes." He continues: "And the servant of the Lord must not strive; but be gentle unto all men, apt to teach, patient, in meekness instructing those that oppose themselves." (2 Tim. 2:24–25.)

The apostle James also taught the avoidance of contention and its causes: "Wherefore, my beloved brethren, let every man be swift to hear, slow to speak, slow to wrath: for the wrath of man worketh not the righteousness of God." (James 1:19–20.) Later, he elaborated that teaching in vivid terms: "For where envying and strife is, there is confusion and every evil work. But the wisdom that is from above is first pure, then peaceable, gentle, and easy to be intreated, full of mercy and good fruits, without partiality, and without hypocrisy." (James 3:16–17.)

The Book of Mormon prophets also warned against contention. King Benjamin taught: "O, my people, beware lest there shall rise contentions among you, and ye list to obey the evil spirit." (Mosiah 2:32.) Alma commanded his people that "there should be no contention one with another." (Mosiah 18:21; see also 23:15.) Earlier, Nephi had prophesied that those who would build up false churches and "teach with their learning, and deny the Holy Ghost, which giveth utterance" would "contend one with another." (2 Ne. 28:4.)

As quoted earlier, the risen Lord commanded his Nephite followers, "There shall be no disputations among you." (3 Ne. 11:28; also see 11:22.) Later he said, "And blessed are ye if ye have no disputations among you." (3 Ne. 18:34.)

Modern Warnings Against Contention

The revelations given to the Prophet Joseph Smith to instruct the leaders of the restored church and to establish procedures for its administration contain many warnings against contention.

After the manuscript pages of the Book of Mormon were lost from the possession of Martin Harris, the Lord gave a revelation stating that he was "bring[ing] to light the true points of my doctrine," explaining that he was doing this to "establish my gospel, that there may not be so much contention." The teaching continues: "Yea, Satan doth stir up the hearts of the people to contention concerning the points of my doctrine; and in these things they do err, for they do wrest the scriptures and do not understand them." (D&C 10:62–63.)

In subsequent revelations the Lord emphasized and re-emphasized that the gospel should not be preached with contention. In publishing their glad tidings, the elders were instructed to "do it with all humility, trusting in me, reviling not against revilers." (D&C 19:30; also see 31:9.) "Let your preaching be the warning voice, every man to his neighbor, in mildness and in meekness." (D&C 38:41.) They were not to preach the gospel "in wrath nor with strife." (D&C 60:14.) Consistent with these directions, the Prophet Joseph Smith instructed the elders to "avoid contentions and vain disputes with men of corrupt minds, who do not desire to know the truth."[6]

At some time or another, most Latter-day Saints have been involved in an argument over a gospel subject. But, as Professor Richard Lloyd Anderson has said, "Argument is a poor tool for discovering truth because it defends a narrow position but usually lacks breadth. Anyone can make a 'case' for or against anything."[7]

Argument is never an appropriate way to resolve differences about the content or application of gospel principles. It is Satan who stirs up the hearts of people to contend over points of doctrine. (D&C 10:63.) Elder Russell M. Nelson has taught, "Divine doctrine of the Church is the prime target of attack by the spiritually contentious. . . . Dissecting doctrine in a controversial way in order to draw attention to oneself is not pleasing to the Lord."[8]

The seriousness of the Lord's command to avoid contention was stressed in the revelation in which the Lord instructed his people on why he had suffered persecution and other afflictions to come upon them in Missouri: "Behold, I say unto you, there were jarrings, and contentions, and envyings, and strifes, and lustful and covetous desires among them; therefore by these things they polluted their inheritances." (D&C 101:6.) Fourteen years later, as the Latter-day Saints were preparing for the trek west, the Lord spoke to them through another prophet, commanding them to "cease to contend one with another." (D&C 136:23.)

Elder Bruce R. McConkie explained how Latter-day Saints should apply the principle of noncontention to the false claims of critics of the Church:

"Our divine commission is to declare glad tidings to the world, not to quarrel with others about the meaning of texts. There are, of course, answers to all of the false claims of those who array themselves against us — I do not believe the devil has had a new idea for a hundred years — but conversion is not found in the dens of debate. It comes rather to those who read the Book of Mormon in the way Moroni counseled. Most members of the Church would be better off if they simply ignored the specious claims of the professional anti-Mormons."[9]

Latter-day Saints should not allow themselves to be drawn into becoming what Elder Marvin J. Ashton has called "anti-anti-Mormon." He explains:

"Whether accusations, innuendoes, aspersions, or falsehoods are whispered or blatantly shouted, the gospel of Jesus Christ reminds us that we are not to retaliate nor contend. . . .

"Never will peace and hatred be able to abide in the same soul. Permanent peace will elude those individuals or groups whose objective is to condemn, discredit, rail at, or tear down those whose beliefs are different from their own. These people live by hatred and would destroy others insofar as it is in their power to do so. True Christians have no time for contention. Lasting peace cannot be built while we are reviling or hating others. Those who preach hate, ridicule, and untruths cannot be classified as peacemakers. Until they repent they will reap the harvest to which those engaged in the business of hatred are entitled. Feelings of enmity and malice can never be compatible with feelings of peace."[10]

During the twenty years I have been intimately acquainted with the leaders of The Church of Jesus Christ of Latter-day Saints, I have marveled at how effectively they live the commandment to avoid disputation and contention. They are not always in agreement, but they are always in harmony. They are not uniform in opinions, but they are united in effort. They are many, but they are one.

These assertions are impossible to prove without violating the confidences that surround the work of General Authorities. However, careful observers of the day-to-day conduct of church business can see proof of this absence of contention, and thoughtful readers of the biographies of church leaders can find ample written evidence that the leaders manage their differences of opinion in the Lord's way, with mutual respect and without contention.[11]

The command to avoid contention is still current. The conditions of our day make it more needful than ever.

In a recent conference message, Elder Russell M. Nelson expressed concern "that contention is becoming accepted as a way of life." In the press, on television, and in various aspects of political and public affairs, the *modus operandi* is contention. We live in an environment of contention. But, as Elder Nelson reminds us, contention is not the Lord's way: "How easy it is, yet how wrong it is, to allow habits of contention to pervade matters of spiritual significance, because contention is forbidden by divine decree: 'The Lord God hath commanded that men should not . . . envy; that they should not have malice; that they should not contend one with another." (2 Ne. 26:32.)[12]

The Savior is the "Prince of Peace," and the devil is the "father of contention." (3 Ne. 11:29.) In the language of Elder Bruce R. McConkie, "The Spirit of the Lord leads to harmony and unity and agreement and oneness. The spirit of the devil champions division and debate and contention and disunity."[13]

This is the heart of the matter. The Lord has commanded us to avoid contention because contention separates us from the Lord and his Spirit. This is why Latter-day Saints are directed to govern their families "in meekness" (D&C 31:9) and to "live together in love" (D&C 42:45). This is why the Lord reminded the Latter-day Saints that they must have unity: "I say unto you, be one; and if ye are not one ye are not mine." (D&C 38:27.)

NOTES

1. Dean C. Jessee, comp.-ed., *The Personal Writings of Joseph Smith* (Salt Lake City: Deseret Book, 1984), 90.

2. George Q. Cannon, *Gospel Truth*, ed. Jerreld L. Newquist (Salt Lake City: Deseret Book, 1987), 160 (sermon delivered August 3, 1890).

3. Ibid., 159.

4. Leonard E. Read, "Resist Not Evil," *The Freeman* (September 1970): 530–34.

5. George Q. Cannon, "Editorial Thoughts," *Juvenile Instructor* 26 (1891): 572–73.

6. *Teachings of the Prophet Joseph Smith*, ed. Joseph Fielding Smith (Salt Lake City: Deseret News Press, 1956), 43.

7. Richard Lloyd Anderson, *Investigating the Book of Mormon Witnesses* (Salt Lake City: Deseret Book, 1989), 151.

8. Russell M. Nelson, "The Canker of Contention," *Ensign* 19 (May 1989): 70.

9. Bruce R. McConkie, *Doctrines of the Restoration*, ed. Mark L. McConkie (Salt Lake City: Bookcraft, 1989), 233.

10. Marvin J. Ashton, *Be of Good Cheer* (Salt Lake City: Deseret Book, 1987), 88.

11. L. Brent Goates, *Harold B. Lee, Prophet and Seer* (Salt Lake City: Bookcraft, 1985), 222, 327–30, 336, 366–67, 382–84; D. Michael Quinn, *J. Reuben Clark: The Church Years* (Provo: Brigham Young University Press, 1983), 113–44, 197–219, 251–78; Edward L. Kimball and Andrew E. Kimball, Jr., *Spencer W. Kimball* (Salt Lake City: Bookcraft, 1977), 228, 344, 357.

12. Nelson, "The Canker of Contention," 68.

13. McConkie, *Doctrines of the Restoration*, 231.

CHAPTER 6

LITIGATION

One of the most common manifestations of controversy in the United States is the lawsuit. As this country has grown in population and complexity, it has experienced commensurate or greater growth in government regulatory and private controversies that are resolved through litigation in the courts. This familiar feature of American life provides another illustration of the many contrasts between the Lord's way and the world's way.

Some Latter-day Saints mirror the typical American acceptance of an increasing use of civil courts to resolve public and private disputes. Others, sensitive to scriptural and prophetic cautions on this subject, are bewildered or uneasy about whether or when the Lord would justify us in participating in litigation to resolve disputes. A letter I received from a BYU student over fifteen years ago is illustrative of that uneasiness. He wrote:

> How does a "good" Latter-day Saint (that is, one who is honestly striving to live the commandments and implement

153

the scriptures into his or her daily life) reconcile the legal
processes of our society with the statements in the New
Testament and Doctrine and Covenants about forgiving your
neighbor and not taking him to court?[1]

After giving some examples from his personal experiences with motor vehicle accidents and landlord-tenant controversies, this conscientious student asked if he should have
forgotten the wrongs he received or if he should have pursued his legal rights, either for his own benefit or to prevent
a guilty party from victimizing others. He concluded as follows:

> In my mind it seems that laws are made to be a peaceable
> way to right wrongs without having to resort to violence —
> that they are there to use to protect ourselves and our neigh-
> bors from unethical practices. Yet when it comes to taking
> a brother in the gospel to court (or a fellow child of our
> Father in Heaven, whether he's a Mormon or not) I don't
> feel quite so sure about the matter. If we don't use courts,
> how do we stop injustice — legally speaking? Yet don't Paul
> and modern-day revelation tell us not to take people to court,
> and doesn't the Sermon on the Mount tell us to even pay
> double if we are taken to court? I don't know the answers
> to this question, and don't know if anyone does.[2]

Because of my experience as a lawyer, law professor,
educator, and judge, I have received many such questions
about when it is appropriate for a faithful Latter-day Saint
to be involved in litigation. I have always felt inadequate in
responding to such inquiries. Though sometimes able to
answer a question about one specific circumstance, I have
never been able to outline comprehensive principles to use
as a guide in the multitude of circumstances in which such
questions arise.

The preparation of this book has given me the opportunity and the incentive for research and prayerful consideration of this question. What follows is my personal summary and interpretation of what the scriptures and the modern prophets have taught on this subject and how those teachings apply in the circumstances of our day.

Two Extreme Positions

At the outset, I reject two extremes.

1. Some have asserted that a conscientious Christian can *never use the courts to resolve disputes.* A few illustrations will suffice to indicate that this extreme is unrealistic and even at odds with the scriptures themselves.

Modern revelation directs that a person who has killed, robbed, stolen, or lied "shall be delivered up and dealt with according to the laws of the land." (D&C 42:79, 84–86.) Those laws are, of course, administered in the civil and criminal courts.

The Church's "declaration of belief," published in 1835, states: "We believe that men should appeal to the civil law for redress of all wrongs and grievances, where personal abuse is inflicted or the right of property or character infringed, where such laws exist as will protect the same." (D&C 134:11.) This declaration obviously contemplates that there will be some circumstances in which a Latter-day Saint will appropriately use the courts, since that is the usual way of appealing to the civil law for the redress of wrongs and grievances.

In addition, there are a multitude of circumstances in which a person cannot avoid being involved in litigation. This is almost always true of persons who have been sued by someone else and have to go to court to defend themselves. There are also circumstances in which a person is compelled to initiate action in a court because a judicial decree, order, or judgment is the only way our laws provide to achieve a result that is desirable and, in many circumstances, perfectly righteous. Examples include decrees of probate, adoption, or divorce, and a court order declaring the meaning of a contract or clarifying the ownership of property. Persons who are public officials, trustees, or officers of a corporation have fiduciary responsibilities that sometimes require them to initiate litigation. These individuals do not have the freedom to forgo litigation even if they have personal preferences against it.

These examples do not exhaust the circumstances in which one can appropriately be involved in litigation, but they are surely sufficient to require us to reject the extreme position that a Latter-day Saint is never justified in going to court.

2. At the opposite extreme, some Latter-day Saints have apparently assumed that there are *no religious restraints on participating in litigation,* thus succumbing to the popular notion that every wrong must have a legal remedy, properly enforceable in court.

This attitude has contributed to an expensive public problem. Any conscientious reader of the public press over the past few decades has seen many reports of lawsuits that can fairly be characterized as abusive or frivolous. A nine-year-old girl sued the makers of Crackerjack because the toy was missing from the box she purchased. A Chicago Bears fan sued his team for consumer fraud because the Bears had a losing record. A frustrated man brought suit for being stood up on a date. The list of similar examples is distressingly long.

In a recent conference address, Elder Boyd K. Packer cited an example that is less extreme, but more common:

"Self-justification leads one to blame another for his mistakes.

"For example, when you seek financial gain, you may be tempted by others to miscalculate, even ignore, risks. When things go wrong—and they can go wrong even in carefully managed affairs—some look for others to blame. They want some 'deep pocket' to make them whole. . . .

"They have little difficulty finding some attorney willing to act as high priest in transferring their responsibility to someone else. They file suit with little or no merit, intending to force others to settle in order to avoid the unconscionable cost of defending themselves in court.

"There is no dishonor in appealing to a court of law for either justice or protection. I refer to those who do so to justify themselves and shift their own responsibility to someone else."[3]

It is common knowledge that our courts are overloaded and that the number of lawsuits has increased in recent years at a rate far greater than the growth of population.[4] Experts disagree on the reasons for these increases. One legal scholar declared that "we are the most litigious people in the world." He coined the term *hyperlexis* to describe our current circumstances.[5] In contrast, another scholar suggests that the so-called litigation explosion might be nothing more than a natural consequence of the increase of injuries produced by a highly industrialized and organized society (when the environment is more crowded, we inevitably bump or jostle one another more often), an educated citizenry's greater awareness of the causes of injuries, and the increased use of government processes to regulate relationships in a complex society.[6]

Whatever the merit of those opposing evaluations, there is no dispute over the proposition that the increasing use

of civil courts to resolve private disputes is exceedingly costly
to the private disputants and to the public purse. Other
costs — harder to measure but nonetheless real — include the
effects on society of millions of private acts by persons seeking to protect themselves from a lawsuit rather than pursuing
what is best for their patient, their partner, and so forth.
This category includes medical practitioners who abandon
the healing arts because of the cost of malpractice insurance
or who prescribe marginally necessary but highly expensive
diagnostic techniques in the practice of what is called de-
fensive medicine. It also includes the plight of potential
employers who cannot rely upon the letters of recommen-
dation they receive because so many are written by persons
who must be more concerned with avoiding legal liability
than with giving honest but negative judgments about a
candidate.

In his State of the Judiciary Address in 1984, U.S. Chief
Justice Warren E. Burger summarized official discontent with
the current dimensions of litigation. He characterized our
current reliance on "the adversary process as the principal
means of resolving conflicting claims" as "a mistake that must
be corrected." He explained: "For some disputes, trials will
be the only means, but for many, trials by the adversary
contest must in time go the way of the ancient trial by battle
and blood. Our system is too costly, too painful, too destructive, too inefficient for a truly civilized people."[7]

As I will discuss hereafter, there are religious as well as
ethical restraints on the use of courts to resolve disputes
that can be resolved in other ways.

In summary, one extreme maintains that a good Latter-
day Saint should *never be involved in litigation*. The other
extreme recognizes *no religious restraints on litigation*.
Both of these extremes are in error. As is often the case,

the correct position lies between the two extremes. But where?

Litigation by Church Leaders

There are scriptural teachings that seem to forbid participating in any civil litigation. Some of the confusion resulting from these scriptures has come from failing to recognize that some of these directions were given to church leaders rather than to the general multitude of members and believers. Modern prophets have clarified this point, but some conscientious members have still considered themselves bound by scriptural directions that were not addressed to them.

In the Sermon on the Mount, the Savior taught that we should not resist evil, but should turn the other cheek, "and if any man will sue thee at the law, and take away thy coat, let him have thy cloke also." (Matt. 5:39–40.) Elder James E. Talmage explains: "These instructions were directed primarily to the apostles, who would be professedly devoted to the work of the kingdom to the exclusion of all other interests. In their ministry it would be better to suffer material loss or personal indignity and imposition at the hands of wicked oppressors, than to bring about an impairment of efficiency and a hindrance in work through resistance and contention."[8]

Elder Bruce R. McConkie agrees: "It was more important, in the social and political circumstances then prevailing, for the Lord's servants to suffer legal wrongs than that their ministries be hindered or halted by legal processes. . . . Nothing is so important as the spread of truth and the establishment of the cause of righteousness. The petty legal processes of that day must not be permitted to impede the setting up of the new kingdom."[9]

The Book of Mormon casts a slightly different light on
this subject. When the Savior gave these teachings to the
Nephites, they were not included in the separate instructions
given to the twelve who were specially called. (3 Ne. 11:22–
12:1.) They were part of a sermon given to a multitude at
the temple. (3 Ne. 11:1, 12:1, 39–40.) One writer has suggested that this multitude was a very select group of temple
worshipers,[10] but it was clearly not limited to leaders who
were specially called. Consequently, these teachings against
litigation cannot be said to be entirely limited to the leaders
of the Church. As will be discussed more fully hereafter, the
principle of noncontention and the commandment to love
and reach out to our neighbors make these Book of Mormon
teachings applicable to all of us.

Some Directions Are Temporary

During some periods in recorded history, the prophets
of God have directed the faithful not to take their disputes
to the civil courts. Some have considered these directions
binding upon all believers in all times and circumstances.
Others consider these directions to have been temporary
for their time.

Studying the commandments and counsel the Lord has
given through his prophets in different ages, I am convinced
that the directions to avoid taking any disputes to civil courts
were temporary. These directions were responsive to the
unique circumstances of believers and civil courts in the
day in which they were given, but they were superseded
when the motivating circumstances changed. (Other directions relevant to resolving disputes through the civil courts
represent eternal principles, binding at all times and all
places. These will be discussed later.)

The most direct scriptural teaching against the faithful

taking their disputes to civil courts is in Paul's first letter to the Corinthians:

"Dare any of you, having a matter against another, go to law before the unjust, and not before the saints?

"Do ye not know that the saints shall judge the world? and if the world shall be judged by you, are ye unworthy to judge the smallest matters?

"Know ye not that we shall judge angels? how much more things that pertain to this life?

"If then ye have judgments of things pertaining to this life, set them to judge who are least esteemed in the church.

"I speak to your shame. Is it so, that there is not a wise man among you? no, not one that shall be able to judge between his brethren?

"But brother goeth to law with brother, and that before the unbelievers.

"Now therefore there is utterly a fault among you, because ye go to law one with another. Why do ye not rather take wrong? why do ye not rather suffer yourselves to be defrauded?" (1 Cor. 6:1–7.)

The New English Bible (1970) translates the first and last of these verses as follows:

"If one of your number has a dispute with another, has he the face to take it to pagan law-courts instead of to the community of God's people? . . .

"Indeed, you already fall below your standard in going to law with one another at all. Why not rather suffer injury? Why not rather let yourself be robbed?"

In counseling the Corinthian saints not to take their disputes to the pagan law courts, Paul explains that the saints, who are in preparation to judge the world in eternal things, should have someone among themselves wise enough to judge their earthly disputes.

We would understand both the reason for and the temporary nature of this counsel if we knew more about the civil courts to which the Corinthian saints had been referring their disputes.* If these courts followed Roman procedures, as seems probable, then a criminal proceeding could be initiated only by the accuser's taking an oath. In order for his testimony to be heard in civil or criminal cases, a witness would also have to take an oath.[11] In these pagan courts, such oaths might have required sacrifices to pagan gods. They would at least have involved swearing by—or other ritual obeisance to—pagan gods or others such as the Roman Emperor. Consequently, to worshipers of the one true God (Jews or Christians), the formalities required to participate in a pagan court were idolatrous. (Matt. 5:33–37.) That is a sufficient reason for Paul's counsel not to go to law "before the unbelievers." (1 Cor. 6:6.)

Another possible reason for Paul's counsel is found in the comparable counsel of Jewish leaders, which comes to light about two generations after Paul wrote. Soon after the destruction of the temple in A.D. 70, when Roman law restricted Jewish judicial autonomy for a short period, faithful Jews were told that it was wrong to participate in gentile courts. A scholarly commentator has noted two reasons for this direction. Resort to a gentile court was blasphemous because it amounted to denial of the Divine Presence and a profaning of the Divine Name. Thus, a rabbi from the end of the first century is quoted as saying, "Whoever leaves a judge of Israel and goes before a foreigner has first denied God and then has denied the law."[12] Using a gentile court was also disloyal, because it undermined the Jewish courts,

---

*I am indebted to Professor John W. Welch of the J. Reuben Clark Law School at Brigham Young University for the insights and sources set out in this paragraph and the next.

whose separateness and vitality were essential to Jewish autonomy.[13]

A second example of temporary directions against going to a civil court came from Presidents Brigham Young and John Taylor during the early history of the Church in the Intermountain West.

Most Latter-day Saints are aware of the highly critical remarks Brigham Young made about lawyers during this period. LDS lawyers, who have felt the lash of those comments, feel more keenly than most that they do not apply with the same force in our day.

The temporary character of President Young's comments is evident from the circumstances in which he spoke them. His criticisms of lawyers were given in the context of his directions that Latter-day Saints not take their private disputes to the civil courts. These directions were given in circumstances analogous to those in which the apostle Paul gave similar directions to the Corinthian saints.

During nearly all of their forty-six-year duration, the civil courts of the Utah Territory were administered by judges, prosecutors, and attorneys who were predominantly hostile to the Church and its members. Like the apostle Paul, church leaders in that circumstance directed the Saints not to "go to law . . . before the unbelievers."

In an address given on April 7, 1852, President Young said: "For those who bear the name of Saints to go into a Gentile court to settle their differences is a stink in the nostrils of the Almighty."[14]

In 1856 President Young denounced the loss of time involved in settling disputes in the civil courts. He ordered the faithful to "keep away from court houses; no decent man will go there unless he goes as a witness, or is in some manner compelled to," explaining: "There is not a righteous person, in this community, who will have difficulties that cannot be settled by arbitrators, the Bishops Court, the High Council, or by the 12 Referees (as provided in Resolution No. 4, page 390 of Utah Laws), far better and more satisfactorily than to contend with each other in law courts, which directly tends to destroy the best interests of the community, and to lead scores of men away from their duties, as good and industrious citizens."[15]

Warming to his subject, Brother Brigham became even more direct: "Does the Lord love your conduct when you drag each other before the ungodly? When you run after difficulties, contentions, broils, and strifes? . . . There is not a man or woman in this house, whether Saint or sinner, Jew or Gentile, bond or free, black or white, that can so believe for a moment."[16]

We can understand President Young's directions only when we understand the circumstances in which they were given. The leading scholarly study of this subject concludes: "For Latter-day Saints in the nineteenth century, the civil courts, lawyers, and law represented an inadequate and frequently corrupt system that worked against the establishment of Zion."[17] The use of civil courts worked against the Saints' interests because a critical part of their effort to establish Zion as an alternative to pluralistic America was the establishment of their own ecclesiastical courts, whose existence "enhanced the independence of the church from the state."[18]

From the arrival of the pioneers until about the turn of the century, church courts resolved private disputes for members in matters of "real property, natural resources, domestic relationships, contractual arrangements, and tort claims."[19] For most of that period, members were subject to church discipline if they used the civil courts in those areas where the church courts were considered, by church law, to have exclusive jurisdiction.[20] The prominent role of church courts was relatively easy to maintain, since most disputes in that period were within local communities where the church leaders were also the community leaders.[21]

The counsel to avoid the civil ("gentile") courts was intensified by President John Taylor, who succeeded Brigham Young in 1877 and was president of the Church during the strenuous persecutions of the 1880s. President Taylor acquiesced in the use of civil courts to settle grievances with nonmembers,[22] but he strongly emphasized the importance of using church courts for settling grievances among members.

In a sermon given in 1878, President Taylor explained the duty of a faithful Latter-day Saint involved in a controversy with another Latter-day Saint. He should first go to his adversary and attempt to settle the matter privately. If unsuccessful, he should again wait upon his adversary, "taking with [him] another brother." If that did not work, he should bring the matter to the notice of "the Teachers or the Priests." If that failed, a charge could be preferred before the bishop and his counselors. If either party was dissatisfied with their decision, an appeal could be taken to the high council. If the losing party would not accept the decision of that tribunal, he would be "severed from the Church." Then, a member would finally be justified in pursuing a remedy against him through the civil courts, since he was no longer a member of the Church.[23]

What should a faithful member do if another member proceeded against him in the civil courts? President Taylor gave this instruction: "I tell you what you should do, whenever a man would attempt to 'pop' you through the courts of the law of the land, you should 'pop' him through the courts of our Church; you should bring him up for violating the laws of the Church, for going to law before the ungodly, instead of using the means that God has appointed."[24] President Taylor explained that "as Saints of God we should be governed by [God's] laws, and not by the laws of the world." Consequently, he counseled stake presidents that when they found one of their members "going to law with his brother before the ungodly," they should "bring him up and deal with him for his fellowship."[25]

Following Utah's statehood in 1896, and during the ensuing period of reconciliation between the Church and national authority, church leaders receded from their position that members who used the civil courts to resolve disputes against each other would be subject to church discipline. "The gradual acceptance of American political pluralism in place of the Mormon concept of [independent] Zion marked the end of an era for the Mormon ecclesiastical court system."[26]

In this period, church leaders withdrew their strong opposition to their members' use of civil courts, but the role of church courts as the preferred method of settling disputes among members continued for another generation.

In 1903, President Joseph F. Smith and his counselors declared: "The courts of the Church are entirely ecclesiastical. They adjudicate between Church members in matters of dispute and in the promotion of Church discipline. Litigation among them is deprecated, and it is deemed wrong for brother to go to law against brother. But no penalty is enforced other than disfellowshipment, or excommunication, as the extreme punishment. The courts of law are recognized in their secular capacity and their decisions are honored and observed."[27]

An important trend was evident in 1908, when a committee of the Council of the Twelve Apostles recommended "that church courts be not used as agencies for the collection of ordinary debts."[28]

A 1919 article by Elder James E. Talmage explains the Church's continuing counsel that disputes among members should first be settled by brotherly mediation. If that failed, members disputing one another should go to the bishop's court, then to the high council, and only then to the Council of the Twelve Apostles. The article continues with what now seems to be the Church's last statement of counsel that members should not take their disputes to the civil courts. "The courts of the Church in no sense assume to oppose or supersede the secular law," the article states. However, it continues, "We hold that in matters of difference between brethren, in which no specific infraction of the secular law is involved, and in offenses called 'civil' as distinguished from 'criminal,' it is as truly unworthy of members of the Church today as it was in Paul's time that 'brother goeth to law with brother'; and that it stands to our shame if righteous judgment cannot be rendered among ourselves. (1 Cor. 6:5–7.)"[29]

In an address in the general conference of April 1923, President Anthony W. Ivins of the First Presidency gave the Church's first expression of the current definition of the relationship between the Church and its laws and the state and its laws: "Render allegiance and submission to the laws of men in civil government, and to the laws of God in that which pertains to the Kingdom of Heaven."[30]

President Ivins said there was no conflict between civil and ecclesiastical law, except that which resulted from "ignorance, or wilful misinterpretation of both."[31] His definition of the function of church courts included settling differences between church members, but he made no mention of any

duty or counsel for members to use church courts in preference to civil courts, or even to make efforts to settle disputes through church mediation before taking them to litigation. His main theme in all of this discussion was the
contrast between the compulsory methods of the civil law
and the "entirely voluntary" methods of the priesthood.[32]

He advised the members and leaders of these conclusions: "That it is the duty of each member of the Church to
honor and obey the law of the land, and sustain the men
who are chosen to administer it, in so far as they do so in
righteousness and justice. That the Priesthood is conferred
upon us for the development and control of the Church of
Christ, and that it cannot be legitimately used for any other
purpose."[33]

President Ivins's statement marks the end of the compelled or preferred use of church courts in the resolution
of private disputes among church members.

The Church's continued recognition of its members'
freedom to use the civil courts to resolve disputes with other
members without fear of church discipline or disapproval
is evident in Elder Bruce R. McConkie's commentary on First
Corinthians, chapter 6: "If the saints go to law with each
other, they may choose to do so under either state or church
jurisdiction. Paul is here counseling them to handle their
own affairs in their own courts, and his counsel is good and
might well be followed by church members today. Manifestly
where grievances involve nonmembers of the church, redress must be sought before civil tribunals (see D&C
134:11)."[34]

In summary, some scriptural and prophetic directions
against *any* recourse to the civil courts are temporary. So
it was with Paul's counsel to the Corinthians and with President Young's and President Taylor's counsel to the Latter-

day Saints in the Utah Territory. With the removal of the impediments that blocked the civil courts (or required favoring the church courts), this prophetic counsel became inapplicable.

Today the number of members of the Church and the extent of long-distance contacts among them means that most disputes among members will involve persons who reside in different stakes. In that circumstance, the resolution of personal disputes by a bishop's court or a high council court is impractical and inadvisable because there is no local church council that has jurisdiction over all the parties.

Does the Church's relinquishment of any function in the adjudication of disputes among members mean that members have no moral impediments to their use of civil courts to resolve disputes with other members? Of course not. The restored church has a long history of encouraging its members to resolve their disputes without using the civil courts. The counsel of President Young and President Taylor on that subject remains in force, even though the procedures they recommended (such as using the ward teachers) have fallen into disuse. The metes and bounds of this counsel to resolve disputes without using the civil courts will be discussed below.

Eternal Principles Governing the Use of Civil Courts to Resolve Disputes

Although there is no absolute prohibition against members of The Church of Jesus Christ of Latter-day Saints going to court to resolve disputes — even with other members — there are eternal principles that forbid such action in some circumstances and impose significant conditions in others. Persons who desire to engage in litigation should measure their proposed action against some tests (based on these principles) that will show whether they are conducting their legal affairs in the Lord's way or in the way of the world. These principles and their related tests are defined in the scriptures and in the teachings of modern prophets.

1. *Forgive.*

The first test is whether the potential litigant can forgive his or her adversary. This test is imposed by the Lord's command: "When ye stand praying, forgive, if ye have ought against any: that your Father also which is in heaven may forgive you your trespasses. But if ye do not forgive, neither will your Father which is in heaven forgive your trespasses." (Mark 11:25–26.)

In a modern revelation the Lord commanded: "Ye ought to forgive one another. . . . Of you it is required to forgive all men. And ye ought to say in your hearts — let God judge between me and thee, and reward thee according to thy deeds." (D&C 64:9–11.)

The importance of forgiving one another was given spectacular illustration and emphasis two years after the above revelation. In 1833 the Missouri Saints had been driven from their homes in Jackson County. Their possessions were scattered, their printing press was smashed, and individuals were whipped and otherwise abused. Without an effective remedy from the state or the federal government, these victims of persecution had two alternatives: armed resistance or peaceful submission. That was the setting in which the Lord gave the revelation in section 98 of the Doctrine and Covenants.

After comforting the Saints, this revelation instructed them on the importance of civil law and of seeking good and wise men for public office. It cautioned them to "forsake all evil" and declared that the Lord would "chasten them" if they did not repent of their "wicked ways." In contrast, it promised that if they would keep the commandments, the Lord would "turn away all wrath and indignation" from them. (Vss. 5–11, 20–22.)

As to the choice before them, the Lord directed them to "renounce war and proclaim peace." (Vs. 16.) He then gave these specific directions on the Saints' behavior toward those who had wronged them: "Now, I speak unto you concerning your families — if men will smite you, or your families, once, and ye bear it patiently and revile not against them, neither seek revenge, ye shall be rewarded." (Vs. 23.) Further, if an enemy smote them a second time and a third time and they bore it patiently and did not revile against their enemy, their reward would be greatly magnified. (Vss. 25–26.) Even if their enemy did not repent of wronging them, they should forgive him three times. (Vss. 41–43.) Next, if the enemy escaped the vengeance of God, they should "warn him in [the Lord's] name, that he come no more" upon them. Then, if he does, the Lord says, "I have delivered thine enemy into thine hands." But even then, "If thou wilt spare him, thou shalt be rewarded for thy righteousness." (Vss. 28–30.)

These verses provide a pointed application of the Savior's great teaching, "Love your enemies, bless them that curse you, do good to them that hate you, and pray for them which despitefully use you, and persecute you." (Matt. 5:44.) They teach that if we bear injustice and persecution patiently, our reward will be great. The succeeding verses even apply this principle to armed conflict among nations or peoples, directing that the faithful seek peace three times and bring these efforts before the Lord, and go out to battle against their adversary only when the Lord commands it. Then, the Lord promises, "I, the Lord, [will] fight their battles." (D&C 98:33–37.)

It should be remembered that this revelation was given after a large body of Latter-day Saints had been driven out of Jackson County, Missouri, by an armed mob. It was given to guide a group for whom there was no remedy in the courts or in other government authority, and who were considering the possibility of organized force to combat their persecutors. At the same time, these directions to forgive a wrongdoer, even in such extreme circumstances, seem to have continuing application to one who considers using the civil courts to remedy a wrong or resolve a dispute.

Elder Boyd K. Packer spoke of this subject in the October general conference, 1987:

"If you have a festering grudge, if you are involved in an acrimonious dispute, 'Behold what the scripture says [and it says it fifty times and more] — man shall not smite, neither shall he judge; for judgment is mine, saith the Lord, and vengeance is mine also, and I will repay' (Morm. 8:20).

"I say therefore, 'John, leave it alone. Mary, leave it alone.'

"If you need a transfusion of spiritual strength, then just ask for it. We call that prayer. . . . If you resent someone for something he has done — or failed to do — forget it. . . . We call that forgiveness. Forgiveness is powerful spiritual medicine. To extend forgiveness, that soothing balm, to those who have offended you is to heal."[35]

President Gordon B. Hinckley has also given inspired counsel on the importance of forgiveness:

"We see the need for it in the homes of the people, where tiny molehills of misunderstanding are fanned into mountains of argument. We see it among neighbors, where insignificant differences lead to undying bitterness. We see it in business associates who quarrel and refuse to compromise and forgive when, in most instances, if there were a willingness to sit down together and speak quietly one to another, the matter could be resolved to the blessing of all. Rather, they spend their days nurturing grudges and planning retribution. . . .

"Is there a virtue more in need of application in our time than the virtue of forgiving and forgetting? There are those who would look upon this as a sign of weakness. Is it? I submit that it takes neither strength nor intelligence to brood in anger over wrongs suffered, to go through life with a spirit of vindictiveness, to dissipate one's abilities in planning retribution. There is no peace in the nursing of a grudge. There is no happiness in living for the day when you can 'get even.' "[36]

One of the noblest acts of the human soul is the act of forgiveness. It can be exquisitely difficult when the wrong has been grievous, but the healing and joy that come in its wake arc wonderful.

Among my prized possessions are two letters from a woman who described the effects of her forgiving her older brother, who had abused her sexually when she was a child.

> The day before [regional] conference (when I was in pain from injuries received from the abuse), I had told my husband how angry I sometimes became and how sometimes I wanted to hurt my brother back for all the pain he had inflicted on me. I have tried to forgive him, but my heart wasn't totally committed to that yet.
>
> Then Sunday morning I went to conference. It seemed as if you were ready to end your talk, but the Lord prompted you to say one more thing. You said we should forgive those who had wronged us. What a witness I felt. I knew I had to forgive and LOVE my brother. And I know that only with the Lord's help can I do it, for without Him, I am nothing.
>
> The price for that sin has already been paid by Him in Gethsemane. I have no right to hold on to it and demand justice, so I gladly hand it back to Him and rejoice in His

love and mercy.... My heart is so full of joy, peace and gratitude and love! Isn't His work glorious? How I do love Him! Words cannot express my feelings.[37]

I replied, and a week later I received a second letter, describing what followed her change of heart.

"The day I received your letter I felt the healing process was completed for me," she wrote, "and I was filled with charity for my brother." The next day she received word that her brother, a less-active member of the Church who lived in another state, had been hospitalized with a serious injury. She immediately phoned and asked a friend to give him a priesthood blessing. In that blessing he was told that his sister loved him. The next night, while he was on support systems, hovering between life and death, she felt his spirit in her home and was able to feel his realization of the horror of what he had done to her and to others. She felt his remorse and his desire to repent, and she felt that she was able to communicate with him. The next day he died. She wrote me: "I feel such mercy from the Lord, realizing that [my brother] just wasn't quite strong enough to right his life here. And I plead for mercy that the price he has to pay will not be too harsh.... I love the Lord so much. Being a convert to the Church, it is so sweet to feel His love. I can never express my gratitude to Him adequately. I marvel at His ways and His love and mercy."[38]

There is nobility in this example. It can serve as a model for all of us.

Before initiating litigation, Latter-day Saints should consider the Lord's command: "Wherefore, I say unto you, that ye ought to forgive one another; for he that forgiveth not his brother his trespasses standeth condemned before the Lord; for there remaineth in him the greater sin. I, the Lord, will forgive whom I will forgive, but of you it is required to forgive all men." (D&C 64:9–10.)

We note that this commandment refers to forgiveness, not to litigation. In the world's way of thinking, an injured party's question is usually whether or not to litigate. According to the Lord's way, the question is not whether or not to litigate, but how the injured party feels toward the aggressor. In many instances, an attitude and feeling of forgiveness will preclude litigation. In some instances it will not. Whatever its effect on litigation, forgiveness is always necessary because it is required of a believer.

2. *Pursue private settlement.*

As we have noted in the earlier quotes from Presidents Brigham Young and John Taylor, before Latter-day Saints initiate litigation they have a duty to pursue the settlement of grievances personally or with the aid of a mediator. This duty is grounded in the same eternal principles used to counsel the Saints against conflict and controversy.

Why should Saints seek to avoid litigation by prior settlement or even by suffering injury without recompense? Speaking of the Savior's teaching on this subject, Elder Bruce R. McConkie explained: "Contention leads to bitterness and smallness of soul; persons who contend with each other shrivel up spiritually and are in danger of losing their salvation. So important is it to avoid this evil that Jesus expects his Saints to suffer oppression and wrong rather than lose their inner peace and serenity through contention. 'He that hath the spirit of contention is not of me,' he told the Nephites, 'but is of the devil, who is the father of contention, and he stirreth up the hearts of men to contend with anger, one with another' (3 Ne. 11:29)."[39]

Since litigation almost inevitably involves contention and is prevented by reconciliation and forgiveness, these teach-

ings stand as a strong direction for Latter-day Saints to use
every reasonable means to compose their differences and
avoid litigation with their fellow members or others.

The Savior taught that we should be reconciled to our
brother before we make a gift at the altar, and that we should
turn the other cheek when we are wronged. (See 3 Ne.
12:23–24, 39.) He also taught that we should settle our grievances directly: "Moreover if thy brother shall trespass against
thee, go and tell him his fault between thee and him alone:
if he shall hear thee, thou hast gained thy brother." (Matt.
18:15.)

In modern times, the Lord has again commanded that
his people seek reconciliation with one another: "If thy
brother or sister offend thee, thou shalt take him or her
between him or her and thee alone; and if he or she confess
thou shalt be reconciled." (D&C 42:88.)

The early leaders of the restored church were strong in
teaching the need for private settlement of disputes. In an
address given in 1852, Brigham Young said: "I have no
fellowship for men who are guilty of . . . contending with
each other, and going to law before Gentile or Bishops'
courts to settle their difficulties. There is a better way of
settling difficulties than either of these. . . . When a difference
of judgment exists between two parties, let them come together and lay their difficulties at each other's feet, laying
themselves down in the cradle of humility, and say 'Brother,
(or sister,) I want to do right; yea, I will even wrong myself,
to make you right.' . . . After taking this course, if you cannot
come together, then call in a third person and settle it."[40]

President Young was still giving this direction in 1871:
"Do not go to law at all; it does you no good, and only
wastes your substance. . . . If you have difficulties that you

cannot settle among yourselves, have recourse to arbitration."[41]

On this subject, Brigham Young's counsel sounds as modern as the latest conference on judicial administration. Experts in what is now called "alternative dispute resolution" say that private settlement, arbitration before persons experienced in the area of dispute, and mediation before a neutral third party are most appropriate for disputes between persons whose relationship should survive the resolution of their dispute. This includes such commercial relationships as suppliers and customers of goods or services, a landlord and his tenants, neighboring property owners, and even a student and his or her educational institution. The same principle obviously applies to family members (even in divorces, where children are involved) and to members of the Church. In all of these instances, it is better to resolve the dispute by private settlement, mediation, or arbitration, rather than by adversary litigation.

President John Taylor also counseled church members to settle controversies privately and not bring them before church tribunals. In a sermon given in 1877, he complained that "very trivial affairs" (involving no more than ten to twenty dollars) were being brought before high councils for trial. He said, "The High Council would prefer to put their hands in their pockets and pay the amount in dispute rather than listen to their nonsense."[42]

President Joseph F. Smith repeated this counsel in 1916: "Be reconciled with each other. Do not go to the courts of the Church nor to the courts of the land for litigation. Settle your own troubles, and difficulties; . . . there is only one way in which a difficulty existing between man and man can be truly settled, and that is when they get together and settle it between them. The courts cannot settle troubles between me and my brother."[43]

The counsel to settle differences privately without litigation continues with great force in our day. In a recent general conference address, President Gordon B. Hinckley said:

"We live in an environment where there is much of litigation and conflict, of suing and countersuing. Even here the powers of healing may be invoked. As a young man I worked with Elder Stephen L Richards, then of the Council of the Twelve. When he came into the First Presidency of the Church, he asked me to assist him with a very delicate and sensitive matter. It was fraught with most grave and serious consequences. After listening to him discuss it, I said, 'President Richards, you don't want me; you want a lawyer.' He said, 'I am a lawyer. I don't want to litigate this. I want to compose it.'

"We directed our efforts to that end, and wonderful results followed. Money was saved, much of it. Embarrassment was avoided. The work was moved forward without fanfare or headlines. Wounds were closed. The healing powers of the Master, the principles of the gospel of Jesus Christ, were invoked in a delicate and difficult situation to compose what otherwise could have become a catastrophe.

"It is not always easy to live by these doctrines when our very natures impel us to fight back. . . .

"Most of us have not reached that stage of compassion and love and forgiveness. It is not easy. It requires a self-discipline almost greater than we are capable of. But as we try, we come to know that there is a resource of healing, that there is a mighty power of healing in Christ, and that if we are to be His true servants we must not only exercise that healing power in behalf of others, but, perhaps more important, inwardly."[44]

Why are we given such urgent counsel to settle our disputes rather than take them to court?

There are, of course, good practical reasons for this advice. Abraham Lincoln is quoted as saying: "Discourage litigation. Persuade your neighbors to compromise whenever you can. Point out to them how the nominal winner is often a real loser—in fees, expenses, and waste of time."[45]

Professor Roger Fisher of Harvard Law School agrees: "Like warfare, litigation should be avoided. Let's candidly admit that from the client's point of view virtually every litigated case is a mistake. Unless one client or both had made a mistake, the case could have been settled and both would have been better off. They might have been able to craft an outcome reconciling their differing interests far better than a court could later. At the worst, they could have saved and divided between them the impressive legal fees that litigators earn."[46]

There are even more important reasons—spiritual reasons—for seeking private settlement of disputes. As Elder Packer observed in a recent conference address, lawsuits often involve a "long trail of acrimony with brother against brother over property or money." He cautioned: "Be careful lest you yourself become the [scape]goat [of Old Testament times] and carry unseen spiritual burdens into the wilderness. More serious by far than the loss of property or money are the unseen spiritual penalties which accrue like interest on a debt which one day, in the eternal scheme of things, must surely be paid." His message emphasized the wisdom of those litigants who settled lawsuits because they could see "that what they might gain materially was not worth the cost spiritually."[47]

A friend wrote me this description of the spiritual penalty
he felt through being a party to litigation:

> As a patriarch in our stake I was giving one or two blessings
> each week and trying, as every patriarch does, to stay worthy
> and be ready. I then entered into a joint lawsuit against a
> man who had, by fraud and falsehood, taken a significant
> amount of money from us.
>
> At the first I pursued the lawsuit with vigor and with
> righteous indignation. After about three weeks I found my
> feelings changing and I had a hard time feeling good about
> what I was doing. After six weeks I told my wife I would
> like to drop the suit but I didn't know how to do it without
> hurting the case for the others who were involved. I also
> mentioned to her that it seemed like it had been awhile
> since I had given a patriarchal blessing.
>
> After ten weeks my feelings were completely reversed; I
> had started the litigation enthused and anxious to recover
> my financial loss, and now I was carrying a burden of misery
> and unhappiness that I needed to unload. After a good talk
> with my wife I notified our lawyer that I was dropping all
> charges and withdrawing from the suit. This decision felt
> right to both of us and almost immediately the feelings of
> misery and unhappiness left me.
>
> The very next day a young lady in the stake called to make
> an appointment for a patriarchal blessing, and as I looked
> at my appointment calendar it came to my attention that the
> last blessing I had given was on the Sunday before we filed
> the lawsuit. As I sat there looking at the appointment book,
> a personal testimony came into my heart and mind that the
> spirit of suing and the spirit of blessing are opposites. Bless-
> ing is the spirit of love and agency. Suing is the spirit of
> force and compulsion. I saw that I personally, as a stake
> patriarch, could not bless if my life was dominated by feelings
> of suing.[48]

For practical and spiritual reasons, a potential litigant
should pursue the possibility of private settlement.

3. *Eliminate revenge.*

One of the tests proposed litigation must pass, for those who desire to act in the Lord's way, is a test of motive. Is the contemplated litigation a good-faith, necessary attempt to settle a dispute and obtain justice, or is the proposed litigation an attempt to obtain revenge against an adversary?

Revenge is never a proper motive for a Christian. As the apostle Paul wrote to the Romans: "Dearly beloved, avenge not yourselves, but rather give place unto wrath: for it is written, Vengeance is mine; I will repay, saith the Lord." (Rom. 12:19.) The Book of Mormon has the same teaching: "Man shall not smite, neither shall he judge; for judgment is mine, saith the Lord, and vengeance is mine also, and I will repay." (Morm. 8:20.)

The prophet Moroni described the Nephites whom he led as "thirst[ing] after blood and revenge continually." They were "without principle, and past feeling." Seeing this, he said, "I fear lest the Spirit of the Lord hath ceased striving with them." (Moro. 9:5, 20, 4.)

The desire to use civil legal action to punish a defendant rather than to obtain restitution for a plaintiff is a familiar motive, but it is unworthy of Latter-day Saints. If the motive is revenge, a Saint will not initiate litigation, nor will he force another person to initiate litigation against him.

4. *Act to protect others.*

In contrast to the forbidden motive of revenge, there is another motive that may justify or even compel initiating litigation: to protect persons other than the parties to the immediate controversy. The test of this possible justification is whether the initiating party is acting primarily to further his or her own interests or primarily and genuinely to protect the interests of others.

If the behavior that has injured the plaintiff is a recurring pattern that seems likely to inflict serious injury on others in the future, the plaintiff's responsibility to those other persons may require protective action through criminal or civil proceedings. Those who may need to be confronted in this way include persons who are predators in sexual abuse or civil fraud. Other examples include professional persons who are involved in a course of conduct that is victimizing a succession of patients or clients, each of whom is unlikely to complain because of the potential embarrassment or expense entailed in forcing disclosure. Where there is a potential for serious future harm to others, a victim has more to consider than his or her own self-interest or obligation to forgive. A person who is positioned to stop a rogue elephant before it injures the other villagers has a duty to do so. A person in a position to take legal action of a preventive or corrective nature to protect potential future victims may have a duty to do so.

5. *Consider the effect of civil action upon those who are sued.*

Decisions involving litigation should always comply with the Savior's command: "All things whatsoever ye would that men should do to you, do ye even so to them." (Matt. 7:12.) The Golden Rule is not a popular deterrent against civil litigation, but it applies nonetheless.

About a decade ago, while I was serving on the Utah Supreme Court, I gave a talk at Brigham Young University on "Christian Settlement of Disputes." Afterwards, a thoughtful student wrote me a letter suggesting things a Latter-day Saint should consider before initiating litigation. In addition to private settlement and other principles already discussed here, he suggested this test:

Do we seek a level of recompense that is a question of

need or only one of desire? Is it the life of ourselves, our families—which surely we owe them—we seek, or luxury through the mistake of another? (Mormon 9:28.)

What will be the consequences of our action for those who have wronged us? Are we so important that we must receive what we have every right to have at the price of financial and perhaps spiritual ruin in bitterness for another person and his family? And what if that person's ruin means a similar fate for his employees and their families? Are we more important than all of them? The principle of forgiveness is based on the concept that we, like Christ, are literally willing to lay down our lives, ourselves, for other men. The love God requires of us is bounded neither by family ties nor even time. It is for all men. (Enos 1:12–18, 3 Ne. 5:13–14; Mormon 9:35–36.)[49]

The young man who wrote this letter had personal experience with this subject. He had already practiced what he preached.

These are things I have considered often. When I was a seventeen-year-old high school senior I was injured in a football game by a young man who ran halfway across the field to hit me five yards out of bounds and fully three seconds after the play was blown dead. Nine years later I was informed by another young man who attended the school that their football coach suggested each member of the team put a dollar in the pot and whoever hurt me badly enough to get me out of the game would get the money. It was a weekly practice for the team. . . .

It has occurred to me that I could own that football coach and perhaps the school district that hired and maintained him. But I simply do not believe my adolescent athletic aspirations were as important as the people I might vengefully destroy for shattering them. If the school was forced to pay for negligence, then everyone in the city would have to pay. I am not *that* important.

> Surely, none of us [is] important enough to justify de-
> stroying others. Of us it is required to forgive every man.
> (D&C 64:8–10.)[50]

The test of putting others' interests ahead of self-interest
is a rigorous one. It is inherent in the practice of consecration, which the Lord described as "every man seeking the
interest of his neighbor, and doing all things with an eye
single to the glory of God." (D&C 82:19.) It is the essence
of the example of our Lord and Savior, Jesus Christ, who
gave himself as a sacrifice for all of us.

The test of putting others' interests ahead of our own is
obviously a test grounded in the Lord's way, not the way of
the world. It is required by principles of right rather than
by rules of law.

In his powerful 1978 commencement address at Harvard
University, novelist Aleksandr Solzhenitsyn challenged the
people of "the West" to base their conduct on higher principles than "the letter of the law." He described "Western
society" as he saw it: "If one is right from a legal point of
view, nothing more is required, nobody may mention that
one could still not be entirely right, and urge self-restraint,
a willingness to renounce such legal rights, sacrifice and
selfless risk: it would sound simply absurd. One almost never
sees voluntary self-restraint. Everybody operates at the extreme limit of those legal frames."[51]

Solzhenitsyn concluded with this vivid description of
what I believe to be an eternal principle:

"I have spent all my life under a communist regime and
I will tell you that a society without any objective legal scale
is a terrible one indeed. But a society with no other scale
but the legal one is not quite worthy of man either. A society
which is based on the letter of the law and never reaches
any higher is taking very scarce advantage of the high level

of human possibilities. The letter of the law is too cold and formal to have a beneficial influence on society. Whenever the tissue of life is woven of legalistic relations, there is an atmosphere of moral mediocrity, paralyzing man's noblest impulses.

"And it will be simply impossible to stand through the trials of this threatening century with only the support of a legalistic structure."[52]

6. *Think of responsibilities ahead of rights.*

When we think of the effect of our actions upon others rather than simply what we can obtain for ourselves, we are approaching the decisions of life in terms of our responsibilities rather than our rights. President Vaclav Havel of Czechoslovakia included that truth in his address to the joint session of the United States Congress on February 21, 1990. He spoke about the kind of philosophical changes that must take place in the Western world if we are to achieve our objectives for peace and prosperity. He suggested that the Czechs' sad experience of the last half century contained a lesson they could offer to the West:

"The salvation of this human world lies nowhere else than in the human heart, in the human power to reflect, in human meekness and in human responsibility.

"Without a global revolution in the sphere of human consciousness, nothing will change for the better in the sphere of our being as humans, and the catastrophe toward which this world is headed, whether it be ecological, social, demographic, or a general breakdown of civilization, will be unavoidable. . . .

"Interests of all kinds: personal, selfish, state, national, group and, if you like, company interests still considerably outweigh genuinely common and global interests. We are still under the sway of the destructive and vain belief that man is the pinnacle of creation, and not just part of it, and that therefore everything is permitted. . . .

"In other words, we still don't know how to put morality ahead of politics, science and economics. We are still incapable of understanding *that the only genuine background of all actions—if they are to be moral—is responsibility.* Responsibility to something higher than my family, my country, my firm, my success. Responsibility to the order of Being, where all our actions are indelibly recorded and where, and only where, they will be properly judged." (Emphasis added.)

President Havel's eloquent plea for responsibility sounds a note not often heard in American public life. As a people we are preoccupied with rights—constitutional rights, civil rights, legal rights. But the financing and fulfillment of rights depends entirely on the acceptance and fulfillment of individual and group responsibilities. And, as Havel demonstrates, it is only by an appeal to something higher than self-interest or legal requirements that we can be persuaded to fulfill those responsibilities.

Responsibilities are closer to heaven than rights because responsibilities represent what we give, whereas rights represent what we seek to receive.[53] The Lord's way emphasizes responsibilities; the world's way emphasizes rights. One does not exclude the other, but the point of emphasis determines the outcome in many instances.

In short, a good Latter-day Saint can participate in litigation, but will do so only after focusing on his or her personal responsibilities (not just his or her rights): by practicing forgiveness, by pursuing private settlement, by disclaiming revenge, and by considering the effect of the proposed litigation on others.

NOTES

1. Letter to author, June 22, 1975.
2. Ibid.
3. Boyd K. Packer, "Balm of Gilead," *Ensign* 17 (November 1987): 16.
4. Warren E. Burger, "Isn't There a Better Way?" *American Bar Association Journal* 68 (March 1982): 275.
5. Bayless Manning, "Hyperlexis: Our National Disease," *Northwestern University Law Review* 71 (1977): 772.
6. Marc Galanter, "Reading the Landscape of Disputes," *U.C.L.A. Law Review* 31 (1983): 4–11.
7. Warren E. Burger, "The State of Justice," *American Bar Association Journal* 70 (April 1984): 66.
8. James E. Talmage, *Jesus the Christ* (Salt Lake City: Deseret Book, 1949), 235–36.
9. Bruce R. McConkie, *The Mortal Messiah* 2 (Salt Lake City: Deseret Book, 1980): 137, 141.
10. John W. Welch, *The Sermon at the Temple and the Sermon on the Mount* (Salt Lake City: Deseret Book, 1990).
11. A. H. J. Greenidge, *The Legal Procedure of Cicero's Time* (South Hackensack, New Jersey: Rothman Reprints, 1971), 259, 261–62, 273–74, 459, 470.
12. StB, III, 362, quoted in *The Anchor Bible*, 1 Corinthians, commentary by William F. Orr and James Arthur Walther (Garden City, New York: Doubleday, 1976), 196.
13. M. Elon, "Jewish Law Sources and Application," *Israel Law Review* 2 (1967): 524–25; also see Welch, *The Sermon at the Temple*, 54–56.
14. *Journal of Discourses* 6:319.
15. *Journal of Discourses* 3:241, 238.
16. Ibid., 238–39.
17. Edwin Brown Firmage and Richard Collin Mangrum, *Zion in the Courts* (Urbana and Chicago: University of Illinois Press, 1988), 373.
18. Ibid., 261.
19. Ibid., 278. See also 293–370.
20. Ibid., 264–71.
21. See, generally, James B. Allen and Glen M. Leonard, *The Story of the Latter-day Saints* (Salt Lake City: Deseret Book, 1976), 258–62.
22. See *Journal of Discourses* 20:105.
23. Ibid., 104–5.
24. Ibid., 104.
25. Ibid., 106.
26. Firmage and Mangrum, *Zion in the Courts*, 371–72.
27. *Messages of the First Presidency*, comp. James R. Clark, 4 (Salt Lake City: Bookcraft, 1970): 82.

28. Committee report, quoted in Firmage and Mangrum, *Zion in the Courts,* 343.

29. James E. Talmage, "Judiciary System of the Church of Jesus Christ of Latter-day Saints," *Improvement Era* 22 (April 1919): 498–99.

30. Anthony W. Ivins, "Right Relationship Between the Church and the State," *Improvement Era* 26 (June 1923): 680.

31. Ibid., 682.

32. Ibid., 685.

33. Ibid., 686.

34. Bruce R. McConkie, *Doctrinal New Testament Commentary* 2 (Salt Lake City: Bookcraft, 1970): 337.

35. Packer, "Balm of Gilead," 18.

36. Gordon B. Hinckley, "Of You It Is Required to Forgive," *Ensign* 21 (June 1991): 2, 4.

37. Letter to author, March 23, 1989.

38. Letter to author, April 13, 1989.

39. McConkie, *Doctrinal New Testament Commentary* 1:228.

40. *Journal of Discourses* 6:319.

41. Ibid., 14:82, 84.

42. Ibid., 19:53–54.

43. *Conference Report,* October 1916, 7–8.

44. Gordon B. Hinckley, "The Healing Power of Christ," *Ensign* 18 (November 1988): 54, 59.

45. Quoted in Burger, "Isn't There a Better Way?," 275.

46. Roger Fisher, "What About Negotiation as a Specialty?" *American Bar Association Journal* 69 (September 1983): 1221.

47. Packer, "Balm of Gilead," 16.

48. Letter to author, October 12, 1988.

49. Letter to author, August 31, 1983.

50. Ibid.

51. Aleksandr Solzhenitsyn, Commencement Address, *Harvard University Gazette,* June 8, 1978.

52. Ibid.

53. See, generally, Dallin H. Oaks, "Rights and Responsibilities," *Mercer Law Review* 36 (1985): 427–42.

CHAPTER 7

CRITICISM

Criticism is another subject on which the Lord's way stands in contrast to the way of the world. Some Latter-day Saints do not understand this contrast, which involves a complex interaction between agency and freedom on the one hand and charity and forbearance on the other. The contrast between the Lord's way and the world's way is most pronounced and the misunderstanding is most evident in the counsel that church members refrain from criticism of church leaders.

Criticism has several meanings. One is "the act of passing judgment as to the merits of anything."[1] This kind of criticism is inherent in the exercise of agency and freedom. In the political world, critical evaluation inevitably accompanies any knowledgeable exercise of the cherished freedoms of speech and of the press. In the private world, we have a right to expect critical evaluation of anything that is put into the marketplace or the public domain. Reviewers of books and music, sports writers, scholars, investment analysts, and

189

those who test products and services must be free to exercise their critical faculties and to inform the public accordingly. This kind of criticism is usually directed toward issues, and it is usually constructive. It has an appropriate role to play in relations among the Saints and in respect to church programs and leaders, although, as pointed out later, when applied to the Lord's servants and the Lord's work it should be done in the Lord's way.

Another meaning of criticism, the kind discussed in this chapter, is "the act of passing severe judgment; censure; fault-finding."[2] This kind of criticism is usually directed toward persons, and it is usually destructive. It is pervasive in our society. President Gordon B. Hinckley has said: "We live in a society that feeds on criticism. Faultfinding is the substance of columnists and commentators, and there is too much of this among our own people. It is so easy to find fault, and to resist doing so requires much of discipline."[3]

Faultfinding and Evil-Speaking

The kind of criticism described as faultfinding and evil-speaking is obviously un-Christian. The apostle Paul said, "Let all bitterness, and wrath, and anger, and clamour, and evil speaking, be put away from you." (Eph. 4:31.) He counseled the Saints to lay aside "all malice, and all guile, and hypocrisies, and envies, and all evil speakings." (1 Pet. 2:1.)

These commandments are repeated in modern revelation: "See that there is no iniquity in the Church, neither hardness with each other, neither lying, back biting, nor evil speaking." (D&C 20:54.) "Cease to find fault one with another." (D&C 88:124.) "Cease to speak evil one of another." (D&C 136:23.)

Speaking in the Salt Lake Tabernacle in 1879, Elder George Q. Cannon applied these scriptural principles in giving this specific instruction: "Tattle about one another; backbite, slander and speak evil of one another; are such things proper for Latter-day Saints? No. They should be banished from our society and from our households. Our children should be taught better. When they speak evil of any one they should be checked and told if they cannot say something good concerning their fellows, to say nothing."[4]

Elder George Albert Smith contrasted the two types of criticism identified at the beginning of this chapter: "There is a difference in criticism. If we can criticize constructively under the influence of the Spirit of the Lord, we may change beneficially and properly some of the things that are being done. But if we have the spirit of fault finding, of pointing out the weaknesses and failings of others in a destructive manner, that never comes as the result of the companionship of the Spirit of our Heavenly Father and is always harmful."[5]

More recently, President Gordon B. Hinckley voiced the same distinction and gave the same counsel: "I am not asking that all criticism be silenced. Growth comes of correction. Strength comes of repentance. Wise is the man who can acknowledge mistakes pointed out by others and change his course.

"What I am suggesting is that each of us turn from the negativism that so permeates our society and look for the remarkable good among those with whom we associate, that we speak of one another's virtues more than we speak of one another's faults."[6]

Elder Marvin J. Ashton applied this principle collectively as well as individually when he said, "No religion, group, or individual can prosper over an extended period of time with fault-finding as their foundation."[7]

These commandments and this counsel are given for a reason. The primary reason is to preserve the spiritual well-being of the potential critic, not to protect the person or persons who might be criticized. The apostle Paul advised the Saints to "grieve not the holy Spirit of God" (Eph. 4:30) by evil-speaking. Of faultfinders, President Brigham Young said, "The Spirit of God has no place in [such] persons."[8] We will lose the Spirit of the Lord if our attitude and our actions are faultfinding.

Criticism That Is True

Does the direction to avoid faultfinding and personal criticism apply only to statements that are false? Certainly not.

Since some criticism is true, counsel to forgo criticism and evil-speaking has been characterized as a degrading of the truth. Not so. To refrain from criticism (even criticism that is true) leaves the truth unimpaired. Such counsel simply urges that there are circumstances in which we should not share (especially not trumpet) what we consider to be the truth about other persons. As the writer of Ecclesiastes taught, "To every thing there is a season, and a time to every purpose under the heaven." Specifically, there is "a time to speak," and there is also "a time to keep silence." (Eccl. 3:1, 7.)

The counsel to suppress or mute certain kinds of criticism is based on the same principle the apostle Paul applied in counseling the Corinthian saints to abstain from eating meat offered as sacrifices to idols. In fact, he taught, an idol is nothing. But since some of the members are weak and might misunderstand, those who have this knowledge should "take heed lest by any means this liberty [knowledge] . . . become a stumblingblock to them that are weak." (1 Cor. 8:9.) A Protestant theologian, Krister Stendahl, concludes: "The gist of Paul's thought is that integrity is of no value in itself."[9]

The most important consideration is how we use the truth. When he treated this same subject in his letter to the Romans, Paul said, "If thy brother be grieved with thy meat, now walkest thou not charitably. Destroy not him with thy meat, for whom Christ died." (Rom. 14:15). Christians who have concern for others exercise care in how they use the truth. Such care does not degrade the truth; it ennobles the truth.

Truth surely exists as an absolute, but our *use* of truth should be disciplined by other values. For example, it is wrong to blackmail a person by threatening to reveal embarrassing facts unless money is paid, even if the facts are true. Doctors, lawyers, and other professionals are forbidden to reveal facts they have received in confidence, even though those facts are true. It is also wrong to make statements of fact out of an evil motive, even if the statements are true.

One who focuses on faults, though they be true, tears down a brother or a sister. The virtues of patience, brotherly kindness, mutual respect, loyalty, and good manners all rest to some degree on the principle that even though something is true, we are not necessarily justified in communicating it to any and all persons at any and all times.

Just as the gospel of Jesus Christ provides for the demands of justice to be superseded by the application of mercy (Alma 42), so should the *use* of truth be disciplined by the constraints of love. As Paul instructed the Ephesians, we will "grow up into" Christ by "speaking the truth in love." (Eph. 4:15.)

In a message titled "Truth—*and More,*" Elder Russell M. Nelson highlighted the contrast between the single-minded surgeon who coldly announces the truth about a terminal illness and the compassionate surgeon who mingles that message with assurances of love and support that help the patient and his family handle the truth. Truth is powerful and absolute in its existence, but its communication should usually be guided by companion principles. "Otherwise," Elder Nelson observed, "the sword of truth, cutting and sharp as a surgeon's scalpel, might not be governed by righteousness or by mercy, but might be misused carelessly to embarrass, debase, or deceive others. . . . Indeed, in some instances, the merciful companion to truth is *silence*. Some truths are best left unsaid."[10]

A church member wrote me to describe what he called "the anguish of one who makes the error of honest criticism." He said, "It does hurt, most painfully, both the speaker and the accused." This man, who had spoken ill of his stake president, wrote of his regret "that I was the instrument of such pain." He concluded: "Silence is a far better virtue at times than is bare truth."[11]

The use of truth should also be constrained by the principle of unity. One who focuses on faults fosters dissensions and divisions among fellow Saints in the body of Christ. Contention is displeasing to the Lord and drives away his Spirit. (See page 140.)

A plea to constrain the use of truth provides no justification for lying. The principles of love, unity, righteousness, and mercy do not condone falsehood. The Lord commanded, "Thou shalt not bear false witness" (Ex. 20:16), and he has not revoked that command. When truth is constrained by other virtues, the outcome is not falsehood but silence for a season. As the scriptures say, there is "a time to keep silence, and a time to speak." (Eccl. 3:7.)

Similarly, the counsel to avoid destructive personal criticism does not mean that Latter-day Saints have a duty to be docile or indifferent to defective policies, deficient practices, or wrongful conduct in government or in private organizations in which they have an interest. As is evident from the teachings of Elder George Albert Smith and President Gordon B. Hinckley quoted earlier, our religious philosophy poses no obstacle to constructive criticism of such conditions. The gospel message is a continuing constructive criticism of all that is wretched or sordid in society. But Christians, who are commanded to be charitable, should be "speaking the truth in love" (Eph. 4:15) and shunning personal attacks and shrill denunciations. Our public communications — even those that are protesting deficiencies — should be reasoned in content and positive in spirit.

Criticism of Church Leaders

Does the commandment to avoid faultfinding and evil-speaking apply to personal criticism of Church leaders? It does. The Prophet Joseph Smith warned: "It is an eternal principle that has existed with God from all Eternity that that man who rises up to condemn others, finding fault with the Church, saying that they are out of the way while he himself is righteous, then know assuredly that that man is in the high road to apostacy and if he does not repent will apostatize as God lives."[12]

Jude warned against those who "despise dominion, and speak evil of dignities" and who "speak evil of those things which they know not." He referred to "all their hard speeches which ungodly sinners have spoken" against the Lord, and called them "murmurers, complainers, walking after their own lusts." (Jude 1:8, 10, 15–16.) President David O. McKay said this about what he called "murmurers" and "faultfinders":

" 'Speak not against the authorities.' What does it mean? Be not a murmurer; that is what it means. It is one of the most poisonous things that can be introduced into the home

of a Latter-day Saint — this murmuring against presidents of
stakes, high councilors, Sunday School superintendents,
[etc.]. . . . Better stop murmuring and build. Remember that
one of the worst means of tearing down an individual is
slander. It is one of the most poisonous weapons that the
evil one uses. Backbiting and evil speaking throw us into
the class of malefactors rather than the class of benefactors."[13]

In our relations with all of our church leaders — local or
general, male or female — we should follow the apostle Paul's
direction: "Rebuke not an elder, but intreat him as a father."
(1 Tim. 5:1.)

These commandments and this counsel against speaking
evil of church leaders are not given to immunize or protect
leaders. The leaders I know are durable people. Local leaders earn their way in a world of unrestrained criticism, and
general officers made their way successfully in that world
before they received their current callings. They have no
personal need for protection; they seek no personal im-
munities from criticism — constructive or destructive. They
seek only to fulfill what they understand to be the responsibilities of their callings, to the Lord and to his people.

Three experiences recited in the Old Testament explain
why the children of God should refrain from criticizing those
whom the Lord has called.

On one occasion the whole congregation of the children
of Israel became dissatisfied and "murmured against Moses
and Aaron in the wilderness." "What are we, that ye murmur
against us?" Moses asked them. "The Lord heareth your
murmurings which ye murmur against him: and what are
we? your murmurings are not against us, but against the
Lord." (Ex. 16:2, 7–8.)

Similarly, when the children of Israel ignored the
prophet Samuel's inspired warnings and begged him to

anoint a king to rule over them, the Lord directed the prophet to do as they asked, explaining: "They have not rejected thee, but they have rejected me." (1 Sam. 8:7.)

Saul, the wicked king, was pursuing the young warrior David without cause, and seeking to take his life. While King Saul slept in the midst of his troops, David and one of his soldiers stealthily crept to his side. Declaring that God had delivered him into their hands, David's companion was about to kill Saul with his own spear. "Destroy him not," David ordered, "for who can stretch forth his hand against the Lord's anointed, and be guiltless?" (1 Sam. 26:9.)

In these three instances, the Bible teaches that murmuring or rejecting or acting against the Lord's servants amounts to taking that same action against the Lord himself. How could it be otherwise? The Lord acts through his servants. That is the pattern he has established to safeguard our agency in mortality. His servants are not perfect, which is another consequence of mortality. But if we act against them, we are working against the Lord and his cause and will soon find ourselves without the companionship of his Spirit.

There are other such teachings in ancient and modern scriptures. The prophet Isaiah denounced those who "make a man an offender for a word, and lay a snare for him that reproveth in the gate." (Isa. 29:21; see also 2 Ne. 27:32.) (Those who "reproved in the gate" in Isaiah's time were the religious leaders.) This modern revelation from the Doctrine and Covenants is to the same effect:

"Cursed are all those that shall lift up the heel against mine anointed, saith the Lord, and cry they have sinned when they have not sinned before me, saith the Lord, but have done that which was meet in mine eyes, and which I commanded them.

"But those who cry transgression do it because they are
the servants of sin, and are the children of disobedience
themselves. And those who swear falsely against my servants,
that they might bring them into bondage and death—wo
unto them; because they have offended my little ones they
shall be severed from the ordinances of mine house.

"Their basket shall not be full, their houses and their
barns shall perish, and they themselves shall be despised
by those that flattered them. They shall not have right to the
priesthood, nor their posterity after them from generation
to generation. It had been better for them that a millstone
had been hanged about their necks, and they drowned in
the depth of the sea." (D&C 121:16–22.)

These teachings identify a vital difference between criticism aimed at leaders chosen in the world's way and criticism aimed at leaders chosen in the Lord's way. It is one
thing to depreciate a person who exercises corporate power
or even government power. It is quite another thing to
criticize or depreciate a person for the performance of an
office to which he or she has been called of God.

Government or corporate officials, who are directly or
indirectly elected or appointed by majority vote, must expect
that their performance will be subject to critical and public
evaluations by their constituents. That is part of the process
of informing those who have the right and power of selection
or removal. The same is true of popularly elected officers
in professional, community, and other private organizations.
I suppose the same is true of religious leaders who are
selected by popular vote of members or their representative
bodies. Consistent with gospel standards, these evaluations,
though critical and public, should be constructive.

A different principle applies in The Church of Jesus Christ
of Latter-day Saints, where the selection of leaders is based

on revelation, subject to the sustaining vote of the membership. In our system of church government, evil-speaking or criticism of leaders by members is always negative. As President George F. Richards of the Council of the Twelve said in a conference address in April 1947: "When we say anything bad about the leaders of the Church, whether true or false, we tend to impair their influence and their usefulness and are thus working against the Lord and his cause."[14] This is why the Holy Ghost will not guide or confirm criticism of the Lord's anointed or of church leaders, local or general. This is why we are commanded and counseled to refrain from criticism of church leaders. It is for our own spiritual well-being.

Contrary to what some have said, the teachings against criticism of church leaders are not an assertion of infallibility, a claim of right to unchallenged wrongdoing, or a bid for blind obedience by church members. As discussed below, we *can* communicate our differences with church leaders. But it must be done in the Lord's way.

Some—even some Latter-day Saints—cannot accept this counsel. Observing this fact, an LDS scholar wrote me to suggest the reason: "that some people view the world in terms of ideologies that, in spite of their merits, are, in the last analysis, at odds with the teachings of the Restored Gospel."[15]

The Lord's command to avoid criticism, faultfinding, and evil-speaking will never be welcome in a society where controversy is a popular form of entertainment, where opposition is institutionalized, and where personal criticism is commonplace. Some Latter-day Saints do not understand and accept the reality that the institution of "loyal opposition," which serves a valuable purpose in a democracy governed by the majority, is a contradiction of terms when applied to a theocracy. Some also do not understand that faultfinding is spiritually destructive to those who engage in it, and that members who engage in personal criticism of church leaders isolate themselves from the Spirit of the Lord. There are ways to differ with church leaders, but they are the Lord's ways, not the world's ways.

What If We Differ with Church Leaders?

So what do we do if we feel that our Relief Society president or our bishop or a General Authority is in transgression or is pursuing a policy of which we disapprove? Is there no remedy? Are our critics correct when they charge that Latter-day Saints are sheep without a remedy against the whims of a heedless or even an evil shepherd?

There are remedies, but they are not the same remedies or procedures that are used with leaders in other organizations.

Our Father in Heaven has not compelled us to think the same way on every subject or procedure. As we seek to accomplish our life's purposes, we will inevitably have differences with those around us, including some we sustain as our leaders. The question is not *whether* we have such differences, but *how we manage them*. What the Lord has said on another subject is also true of the management of differences with his leaders: "It must needs be done in mine own way." (D&C 104:16.) We should conduct ourselves in such a way that our thoughts and our actions do not cause us to lose the companionship and guidance of the Spirit of the Lord.

The first principle in the gospel procedure for managing differences is to keep our personal differences private and not allow them to be a source of contention. (See pages 140–51.) In this we have worthy examples to follow. Every student of church history knows that there have been differences of opinion among church leaders since the Church was organized. Each of us has experienced such differences in our own work in the auxiliaries, quorums, wards, stakes, and missions of the Church. We know that such differences are discussed, but they are not discussed in public and they are not pursued in a spirit of contention. Counselors acquiesce in the decisions of their president. Teachers follow the direction of their presidency. Members are loyal to the counsel of their bishop. All of this is done quietly and loyally, even by members who would have adopted a different policy or pursued a different procedure if they had been in the position of authority.

Why aren't these differences discussed in public? Public debate — the means of resolving differences in a democratic government — is not appropriate in the government of the Church. We are all subject to the authority of the called and sustained servants of the Lord. They and we are all governed by the direction of the Spirit of the Lord, and that Spirit functions only in an atmosphere of unity. That is why personal differences about church doctrine, policy, or procedure need to be worked out privately and without contention. There is nothing inappropriate about private communications concerning such differences, provided they are carried on in a spirit of love.

There are at least five different procedures a member can follow in addressing differences with a leader — general or local, male or female.

1. The first of these procedures — and the most benign — is to overlook the difference. President Brigham Young described how he did this in a circumstance in which he felt "a want of confidence" in the Prophet Joseph's financial management. After entertaining such thoughts for a short

time, he saw that they could cause him to lose confidence in the Prophet and ultimately to question God as well. He concluded: "Though I admitted in my feelings and knew all the time that Joseph was a human being and subject to err, still it was none of my business to look after his faults. . . . He was called of God; God dictated him, and if He had a mind to leave him to himself and let him commit an error, that was no business of mine. . . . He was God's servant, and not mine."[16]

Elder Lorenzo Snow also observed some "imperfections" in Joseph Smith, but he elected to overlook them and even to draw strength from them: "I thanked God that He would put upon a man who had those imperfections the power and authority He placed upon him . . . for I knew that I myself had weakness, and I thought there was a chance for me."[17]

2. A second option is to reserve judgment and postpone any action on the difference. In many instances, the actions we are tempted to criticize may be based on confidences that preclude the leader from explaining his or her actions publicly. In such instances there is wisdom in a strategy of patience and trust.

3. The third procedure, which should be familiar to every student of the Bible, is to communicate our differences privately to the leader involved. The Savior taught: "If thy brother shall trespass against thee, go and tell him his fault between thee and him alone: if he shall hear thee, thou hast gained thy brother." (Matt. 18:15.)

This course of action may be pursued in a private meeting, if possible, or it may be done through a letter or other indirect communication. How many differences could be resolved if we would only communicate privately about them! Private communications would remove many ob-

stacles to individual growth and correction. Private communication of differences also removes the inference (present in some public criticism) that the critic is seeking
personal aggrandizement rather than public benefit. Some
differences would disappear when private communications
identified them as mere misunderstandings. Other differences would be postponed with an agreement to disagree
for the present.

4. A fourth option is to communicate with the church
officer who has the power to correct or release the person
thought to be in error or transgression. The Bible calls this
"tell[ing] it unto the church." (Matt. 18:17.) Modern scripture,
in the revelation we call "the law of the Church," describes
this procedure: "And if he or she confess not thou shalt
deliver him or her up unto the church, not to the members,
but to the elders. And it shall be done in a meeting, and
that not before the world." (D&C 42:89.)

Note the caution that this remedy is to be private—"not
before the world." This is not done in order to hide the
facts, but rather to enhance the opportunity for reform so
that any correction can serve as a basis to improve the life
of a brother or sister.

President John Taylor described these last two remedies
when he taught how we should sustain a leader:

"But supposing he should . . . be found lying or cheating,
or defrauding somebody; or stealing or anything else, or
even become impure in his habits, would you still sustain
him? It would be my duty then to talk with him as I would
with anybody else, and tell him that I had understood that
things were thus and so, and that under these circumstances
I could not sustain him; and if I found that I had been
misinformed I would withdraw the charge; but if not it would
then be my duty to see that justice was administered to him,

that he was brought before the proper tribunal to answer for the things he had done; and in the absence of that I would have no business to talk about him."[18]

Also speaking of what should happen when a church member is in transgression, Elder James E. Talmage related these principles to the contrasting duties of church members and church judges:

"The Lord hath declared that there must not be iniquity in his Church, and he has provided officers whose specific and specified duty is to hunt out iniquity, to run it down, so that every case may be dealt with, and the afflicted ones perchance, be saved. He has not told us to cover up sin in the Church. That is not the Lord's will, nor purpose nor plan. He has told us that we should avoid gossip and slander and all kinds of misrepresentation, and speaking ill against our brethren, whether we regard them in their official capacity as officers of the Church, general or local, or otherwise. I have no right to speak in condemnation of my brother, unless I do it in an official capacity, in the exercise of the authority of the Holy Priesthood, and then I should do it in love and with yearning for him."[19]

5. There is a fifth remedy: we can pray for the resolution of the problem. We should pray for the leader whom we think to be in error, asking the Lord to correct the circumstance if it needs correction. At the same time, we should pray for ourselves, asking the Lord to correct us if we are in error.

A person who approaches a difference with a church leader by praying about it keeps himself or herself in tune with the Spirit of the Lord. That person also goes directly to the One who can resolve the problem. It may be resolved by inspiration to the leader or by communication of added understanding, strength, or patience to the person who prays.

All five of the above are appropriate options for members who differ with their leaders. The preferred course depends upon the circumstances and the inspiration that will guide those who prayerfully seek. By following these procedures, members can work for correction of a leader or for change of a policy. Members who do so in the correct spirit will not grieve the Spirit of the Lord. They will not alienate themselves from their leaders or their brothers and sisters in the Church.

Despite the commandments and counsel I have reviewed, some members persistently and publicly criticize church leaders. What about them?

Throughout our history we have had members who have criticized the Church and its leaders. Church disciplinary action against such members has been rare or nonexistent. Persistent, public critics punish themselves. By deliberately separating themselves from those the Lord has called as leaders of his church (local or general), critics forfeit the guidance of the Spirit of the Lord. They drift from prayer, from the scriptures, from church activity, and from keeping the commandments. They inevitably lose spirituality and blessings. As the prophet Nephi observed, those who succumb to pride and "works of darkness" are on the way to spiritual destruction, "for the Spirit of the Lord will not always strive with man." (2 Ne. 26:10–11.)

Another consequence of the divine warning against criticizing leaders is addressed to those leaders themselves. It stresses their special responsibility in the exercise of their authority. In contrast to government and corporate officers, who have the power and privilege to be high-handed and authoritarian in the use of their powers, church leaders have strict limits on the way they can exercise their authority. The Lord has directed that the powers of heaven can be exercised only "upon the principles of righteousness"—that is, "by persuasion, by long-suffering, by gentleness and meekness, and by love unfeigned." (D&C 121:36, 41.) And this command is enforced:

"When we undertake to . . . gratify our pride, our vain ambition, or to exercise control or dominion or compulsion upon the souls of the children of men, in any degree of unrighteousness, behold, the heavens withdraw themselves; the Spirit of the Lord is grieved; and when it is withdrawn, Amen to the priesthood or the authority of that man." (D&C 121:37.)

Conclusion

Just as a church leader's source of authority is different from that of a government or corporate leader, so the procedure for correcting a church leader is different from the procedure used to correct leaders chosen by popular election. But this contrast is appropriate to the way in which our leaders are called and released. By following approved procedures, we can keep from alienating ourselves from the Spirit of the Lord.

Those who reject the authority of the scriptures or of latter-day prophets cannot be expected to agree with what is said here. Those who see freedom or truth as absolutely overriding principles in all human actions cannot be expected to be persuaded by the scriptures that teach that "knowledge puffeth up, but charity edifieth." (1 Cor. 8:1.) I urge those who are troubled by this counsel to consider it in terms of the teachings of the scriptures rather than in terms of their personal preferences or the canons of their particular profession.

Those who govern their thoughts and actions solely by the principles of liberalism or conservatism or intellectualism cannot be expected to agree with all of the teachings of the gospel of Jesus Christ. As for me, I find some wisdom in liberalism, some wisdom in conservatism, and much truth in intellectualism — but I find no salvation in any of them.

The role of a preacher or a practitioner of righteousness is not to be popular with the world or to be esteemed by any particular group, but to be right with God. Isaiah affirmed that fact when he condemned the rebellious "which say to the seers, See not; and to the prophets, Prophesy not unto us right things, speak unto us smooth things, prophesy deceits." (Isa. 30:10.) It is easy to preach freedom or truth. Praise for those subjects is usually safe and always popular. It is infinitely more difficult to preach how men and women should *use* freedom or truth. The preacher of that message may command respect, but he or she will not win popularity.

I conclude with a message of hope. When Isaiah condemned the critics of his day, he concluded with a prophecy. He said that in time the children of God would "fear the God of Israel" and "sanctify [his] name." Continuing, he declared, "They also that erred in spirit shall come to understanding, and they that murmured shall learn doctrine." (Isa. 29:23–24.) In that spirit I pray for the day when all of us will know God and keep his commandments. In that day, as Isaiah foretold, the "king shall reign in righteousness," and "the work of righteousness shall be peace; and the effect of righteousness quietness and assurance for ever." (Isa. 32:1, 17.).

NOTES

1. *Random House Dictionary,* unabridged edition, under the word "criticism."

2. Ibid.

3. Gordon B. Hinckley, "Five Million Members—A Milestone and Not a Summit," *Ensign* 12 (May 1982): 46.

4. George Q. Cannon, *Journal of Discourses* 20:290.

5. George Albert Smith, *Conference Report,* October 1934, 50.

6. Gordon B. Hinckley, "The Continuing Pursuit of Truth," *Ensign* 16 (April 1986): 4.

7. Marvin J. Ashton, *Be of Good Cheer* (Salt Lake City: Deseret Book, 1987), 9.

8. Brigham Young, *Journal of Discourses* 8:13.

9. Krister Stendahl, *Paul Among Jews and Gentiles and Other Essays* (Philadelphia: Fortress, 1976), 611.

10. Russell M. Nelson, "Truth—and More," *Ensign* 16 (January 1986): 70–71.

11. Letter to author, February 19, 1987.

12. Quoted from *The Words of Joseph Smith,* comp. and ed. Andrew W. Ehat and Lyndon W. Cook (Provo: Brigham Young University Religious Studies Center, 1990), 413.

13. David O. McKay, *Gospel Ideals* (Salt Lake City: Improvement Era, 1953), 143.

14. George F. Richards, *Conference Report,* April 1947, 24.

15. Letter to author, February 6, 1987.

16. Brigham Young, *Journal of Discourses* 4:297.

17. Lorenzo Snow, as quoted by Elder Neal A. Maxwell in "Out of Obscurity," *Ensign* 14 (November 1984): 10.

18. John Taylor, *Journal of Discourses* 21:208.

19. James E. Talmage, *Conference Report,* October 1920, 61–62.

CHAPTER 8

CHURCH DISCIPLINE

Mortals are governed by law. Some laws are established by God. Some are established by man. The content and enforcement of these two systems of law, sacred and secular, have some similarities and many differences. In this chapter we will examine some of those similarities and differences, comparing and contrasting the Lord's way and the world's way.

At some times in recorded history, sacred power and secular power have been joined in a single authority. Examples include the prophet-leader Moses in the Old Testament and the prophet-king Benjamin in the Book of Mormon. During other times, the secular authority and the sacred authority have been separated. Human laws have been given by a king or a representative assembly and administered by secular authorities, and God's laws have been given through a prophet or a priest and administered by religious authorities. In the Bible, this separation is illustrated by the contrasting authorities of the Israelite kings and prophets. The Book of Mormon describes how King Mosiah gave the prophet Alma authority over the Church (Mosiah 25:19; 26:8), but the king continued to rule in secular matters (Mosiah 27:1–3). In that divided jurisdiction, the king declined to judge persons who were brought before him for sin or iniquity, sending them to be judged by Alma, the high priest. (Mosiah 26:6–12.)

The Savior taught his Jewish followers that they should render unto Caesar the things that were Caesar's and unto God the things that were God's. (Matt. 22:21; Mark 12:17; Luke 20:25.) The apostle Peter taught the early Saints to submit themselves to civil authority. (1 Pet. 2:13–17.) These teachings recognize that the saints of that day were subject to two different authorities—the laws of man and the laws of God.

Whenever the laws of God are given and administered by one authority and the laws of man are given and administered by other authorities, some who are subject to these two different laws and authorities can become confused. Some may not understand which laws apply to a particular circumstance. Others may misunderstand which authorities administer a particular law. And some may not understand which procedure applies when a particular law has been broken. Such misunderstandings occur in our own day. Some Latter-day Saints are confused over the content, purposes, and procedures of the two kinds of laws that apply to them, the laws of God and the laws of man.

The divinely directed pattern in this dispensation is clear. It is one of dual jurisdiction. The children of God in every nation are subject to one authority that establishes and administers the laws of God and to another group of authorities who establish and administer the laws of man.

Modern revelations prescribe that dual system and instruct the faithful how to live within it. The Saints are directed to be "subject to the powers that be" and to keep what are called "the laws of the land" in addition to what are called "the laws of God" or "the laws of the Church." (D&C 58:21–23.) The official "declaration of belief" of The Church of Jesus Christ of Latter-day Saints, adopted in 1835 and published in the first edition of the Doctrine and Covenants, declares that "human laws [are] instituted for the express purpose of regulating our interests as individuals and nations, between man and man," and that "divine laws [are] given of heaven" to prescribe "rules on spiritual concerns, for faith and worship." Significantly, the scripture adds that "both [are] to be answered by man to his Maker." (D&C 134:6.)

The Laws of Man

The purpose of "human laws" (which I have chosen to call the laws of man) is to protect all citizens and to secure public peace and harmony. Rulers and magistrates are "placed for the protection of the innocent and the punishment of the guilty." (D&C 134:6–8.)

The laws of man seek to achieve their purposes through criminal laws and civil laws. Criminal laws punish (and sometimes seek to rehabilitate) one person who has harmed another. Civil laws resolve disputes between private parties by providing a means by which injured persons can obtain money or other compensation from those who have injured them. Civil laws also seek to prevent one person from committing future harm against another. All of these efforts tend to preserve peace and harmony by encouraging injured parties to forgo private retribution or revenge and look to the laws and civil authorities to punish their adversary, to obtain compensation for their losses, or to deter or prevent future wrongs.

The Church's official declaration of belief states that "crime should be punished . . . by the laws of that government in which the offense is committed." (D&C 134:8.) The civil authority should "punish guilt" and should also "restrain crime." (D&C 134:4.) To assist, "all men should step forward and use their ability in bringing offenders against good laws to punishment." (D&C 134:8.) Thus, in the 1831 revelation called "the law of the Church," the Lord directed the people of his church that if any persons among them shall kill or rob or steal or lie, they "shall be delivered up and dealt with according to the laws of the land." (D&C 42:79, 84–86.)

In addition, where man's laws and institutions provide remedies, members of the Church are directed to "appeal to the civil law for redress of all wrongs" involving personal abuse or property damage. (D&C 134:11.)

The Laws of God

The part of God's law that directs human behavior is called commandments. The procedures that encourage church members to keep the commandments and that specify the consequences when they fail to do so are now called church discipline.

In contrast to the laws of man, which are concerned with preserving the peace in mortality, the laws of God are concerned with promoting exaltation in eternity. Although there is some overlap between the two, these differing purposes dictate important differences in their content and procedures.

One of the most important differences between the laws of God and the laws of man is the fact that the content and procedures of the former are dictated or guided by revelation, while the latter take no account of this. The discussions of revelation in chapters 1 and 2 are, therefore, an essential foundation for the following consideration of contrasts between the content and the administration of these two systems of law.

One of the most obvious contrasts concerns penalties. It is, of course, clear that the Church, which administers the laws of God, has no authority to take away a transgressor's life or property or to inflict any physical punishment. The Church "can only excommunicate them from their society, and withdraw from them their fellowship." (D&C 134:10.) Thus, church discipline consists of giving cautions in a private interview, imposing a probation consisting of restrictions or requirements pertaining to the exercise of church membership, or withdrawing a member's fellowship or membership.

Since church discipline is very limited in the consequences it can assign, what is meant by the scriptural statement that "the murderer who deliberately killeth . . . shall die"? (2 Ne. 9:35; also see D&C 42:18–19.) This cannot be a direction for capital punishment, since the punishment of taking life is a consequence reserved to the laws of man. In context, what is said in these scriptures clearly concerns the *eternal significance* of deliberate homicide. God has forbidden this kind of shedding of blood "from the beginning of man." (Ether 8:19.) A deliberate murder is what the scriptures call "a sin unto death." (1 Jn. 5:16.) It deprives the murderer of eternal life (1 Jn. 3:15) because there is "no forgiveness" for this act (D&C 42:79). In other words, a person who deliberately kills another shall die *spiritually*.

Most of the other commandments and procedural directions in the scriptures also concern the laws of God, not the laws of man. If we overlook that fact, we can easily misinterpret the scriptures. Similarly, the content and pro-

cedures of the laws of man do not apply to the spiritual
activities of the Church, including church discipline. If we
overlook that fact, we can easily fall into serious distortions
in the administration of the laws of God.

Those who are experienced in administering the laws
of man, especially judges and lawyers, are particularly susceptible to the mistake of trying to apply criminal or civil
law principles to the administration of church discipline. I
experienced that mistake in an analogous circumstance.

During the university disruptions of the late 1960s, I
served as chairman of the disciplinary committee of the
University of Chicago. In 1969 our committee heard university charges against more than 150 students cited for
disruptive behavior in a seventeen-day seizure of the university administration building. Some were defended by law
students, who attempted to apply various criminal or civil
court procedures to the administration of university discipline. For example, one budding lawyer (then enrolled in
my criminal procedure class) argued that the university
could not discipline students involved in the disruption because the Bill of Rights of the United States Constitution
guaranteed that they could not be punished without being
formally charged by the indictment of a grand jury. It took
our committee almost a week of deliberations to sort out
which procedural rules were necessary to fundamental fairness and therefore applicable to university disciplinary proceedings (such as notice of the charges and an opportunity
to present a defense), and which legal (even constitutional)
procedures were not necessary to fundamental fairness and
therefore were not required as a part of private disciplinary
proceedings.

Church discipline is analogous. Some procedures familiar to civil and criminal proceedings do not apply in

church disciplinary councils. The administration of church discipline takes its own course, guided by the revelations of God. That is a most important fundamental fact to be remembered by all who participate in a church disciplinary council.

Another important contrast between church discipline and criminal proceedings is that these two different processes generally focus on different offenses. Thus, the revelation called the law of the Church gives various commandments and then directs that "if any man or woman shall commit adultery, he or she shall be tried before two elders of the church, or more." (D&C 42:80.) A similar direction is given as to persons who "do any manner of iniquity." (D&C 42:87.) However, as noted above, this same revelation directs that murderers, robbers, thieves, and liars should be turned over to the laws of the land. (D&C 42:79, 84–86.) Why the contrast?

The laws of man punish murder, robbery, theft, and lying. The public officials who enforce the laws against these crimes are relatively effective at determining who has violated them and how they should be punished. The acts of murder, robbery, theft, and lying also have consequences under the laws of God. However, when a church member is accused of these crimes under the laws of man, it is usually desirable for church discipline to await adjudication by the public authority. In this way church discipline does not prejudice the proceedings in a civil or criminal court, and those administering church discipline can benefit from the evidence gathered and the conclusions reached by the public authorities.

In contrast, the laws of man are not much concerned with adultery and other iniquity, or they treat these acts with far less seriousness than they are regarded under the laws of God. In that circumstance, it is desirable for adultery and other iniquities to be handled by church discipline, pursuant to the laws of God. For the same reason, an alleged crime that is also a serious transgression under the laws of God may warrant church discipline even if a civil court has dismissed the criminal charges for technical reasons.

Thus, although they partially overlap, the laws of God and the laws of man have separate purposes, separate coverage, and independent enforcement.

The Primary Purpose of Church Discipline

The laws of God seek to lead his children to exaltation (salvation). In furtherance of that objective, the paramount purpose of church discipline is to save souls. Church discipline encourages members to keep the commandments of God. Its mere existence, and especially the fact of its application in a particular case, stresses the seriousness and clarifies the meaning of the commandments of God. This is extremely important in an otherwise permissive society. Those who administer church discipline should use that occasion to stress the high standards of the gospel.

Where necessary, church discipline assists transgressors to repent by helping them to recognize and forsake sin, make restitution, and demonstrate their renewed commitment to keep the commandments. President Harold B. Lee explained: "The gospel is to save men, not to condemn them, but to save it is sometimes necessary to confront and to discipline as the Lord has directed us."[1]

The laws of God achieve their purposes through justice, mercy, and the atonement of Jesus Christ. Church discipline is concerned with all of these, but most particularly with mercy and the atonement.

In contrast, the laws of man focus on justice, have no

theory of mercy, and take no account of the atonement. When the criminal law has been violated, justice usually requires that a punishment be imposed. The symbol of justice includes a scales in balance and a weighmaster who is blindfolded to assure impartiality.

People generally feel that justice has been done when an offender receives what he deserves — when the punishment fits the crime. Thus, our church's declaration of belief states that "the commission of crime should be punished [under the laws of man] according to the nature of the offense." (D&C 134:8.) If a criminal has confessed and shows a remorseful attitude, this may have some effect on the amount of punishment (in the discretion of the judge), but it is not likely to be decisive. The paramount concern of human law is justice. As a lesser concern, some of the laws of man seek rehabilitation of the offender, a partial mirroring of the principle of mercy and the divine goal of salvation.

Justice, Mercy, and the Atonement

The laws of God are likewise concerned with *justice,* but they are also concerned with the mercy made possible because of the atonement. Church doctrine explains this.

The idea of justice as what one deserves is the fundamental premise of all scriptures that speak of men's being judged according to their works. The Savior told the Nephites that all men would stand before him to be "judged of their works, whether they be good or whether they be evil." (3 Ne. 27:14; also see Mosiah 15:26–27; Alma 41:3–4.) In his letter to the Romans, Paul described "the righteous judgment of God" in terms of "render[ing] to every man according to his deeds." (Rom. 2:5–6.) Our second Article of Faith affirms that "men will be punished for their own sins, and not for Adam's transgression."

According to eternal law, when a commandment is broken, a commensurate penalty must be imposed. "There is a law given, and a punishment affixed," the prophet Alma taught, and "justice claimeth the creature and executeth the law, and the law inflicteth the punishment." "For behold," he continued, "justice exerciseth all his demands." (Alma 42:22, 24.) The justice of God "divide[s] the wicked from the righteous." (1 Ne. 15:30.) By itself, justice is uncompromising. This is how mortals became subject to temporal and spiritual death.

The good news of the gospel is that because of the atonement of Jesus Christ, there is something called *mercy* for the penitent. Mercy signifies an advantage greater than is deserved. If justice is balance, then mercy is imbalance. If justice is just what one deserves, then mercy is *more* benefit than one deserves. Shakespeare had one of his characters declare this truth: "In the course of justice none of us should see salvation. We do pray for mercy."[2] And the eternal law of mercy allows someone else to pay the penalty, satisfying the law of justice in behalf of the penitent transgressor.

In its relationship to justice and mercy, *the atonement* is the means by which justice is served and mercy is extended. For this purpose, the Messiah "offereth himself a sacrifice for sin, to answer the ends of the law, unto all those who have a broken heart and a contrite spirit; and unto none else can the ends of the law be answered." (2 Ne. 2:7; see also Rom. 5:18–19.) In one of the greatest of all scriptural declarations, Alma explains that because of the atonement, "mercy claimeth the penitent, and mercy cometh because of the atonement." (Alma 42:23.)

Justice is served and mercy is extended by the suffering and shed blood of Jesus Christ. In this way "God himself atoneth for the sins of the world, to bring about the plan of mercy, to appease the demands of justice, that God might be a perfect, just God, and a merciful God also." (Alma 42:15.) As Elder Boyd K. Packer explains in his illuminating parable *The Mediator,* "Through Him mercy can be fully extended to each of us without offending the eternal law of justice."[3]

Repentance

1. *Necessity.* The benefits of the atonement are subject to the conditions prescribed by Him who paid the price. The conditions include repentance. The requirement of repentance is one of the principal contrasts between the laws of God and the laws of man.

God has told us through his prophets that "none but the truly penitent are saved" (Alma 42:24), and that only those who repent are forgiven (D&C 1:32; 58:42). Elder Bruce R. McConkie said it tersely: The Messiah brought "mercy to the repentant and justice to the unrepentant."[4] Alma taught that "the plan of redemption could not be brought about, only on conditions of repentance of men in this probationary state." (Alma 42:13; see also Hel. 5:11.) Amulek testified that "only unto him that has faith unto repentance is brought about the great and eternal plan of redemption." (Alma 34:16.) Finally, in this dispensation our Redeemer declared, "For behold, I, God, have suffered these things for all, that they might not suffer if they would repent; but if they would not repent they must suffer even as I." (D&C 19:16–17.)

These eternal truths, fundamental in the doctrine of our church, explain why church discipline is concerned with assisting a transgressor to repent. Repentance is essential to qualify for the mercy made possible through the atonement. As a result, evidence of repentance is the most important single factor in determining what church discipline is necessary to accomplish its principal purpose — to save the soul of the transgressor. This is a matter that calls for the spiritual discernment given to the Lord's judge. The redemptive function of church discipline and the revelation necessary for its implementation have no counterpart in the laws of man.

2. *Confession.* Under the laws of man, a confession only serves the function of strong evidence of guilt. It is not essential, because if there is other evidence an accused person can be found guilty without it.

Under the laws of God, a confession is absolutely essential, because there is no repentance without confession. "He that covereth his sins shall not prosper: but whoso confesseth and forsaketh them shall have mercy." (Prov. 28:13.) "If we confess our sins, he is faithful and just to forgive us our sins, and to cleanse us from all unrighteousness." (1 Jn. 1:9.) "By this ye may know if a man repenteth of his sins — behold, he will confess them and forsake them." (D&C 58:43; see also 61:2, 64:7.)

Repentance begins when we recognize that we have done wrong. We might call this "confession to self." This occurs, President Kimball said, when a person is willing "to convict himself of the transgression without soft-pedaling or minimizing the error, to be willing to face facts, meet the issue, and pay necessary penalties — and until the person is in this frame of mind he has not begun to repent."[5]

An acquaintance who had been guilty of serious transgressions described his feelings about this step: "There is a tremendous release when you can face up to your crimes and deceptions, and start living an honest life again." Taking this initial step gave him what he described as "a certain degree of peace in my life."[6]

The next step, for all our sins, is to confess them to the Lord in prayer.

In addition, when the sins are of a serious nature, they must be confessed to the priesthood leader designated by the Lord—the bishop. Elder Marion G. Romney described the sins that must be confessed to the bishop as those transgressions "of such a nature as would, unrepented of, put in jeopardy his right to membership or fellowship in the Church of Jesus Christ."[7] These last two confessions are what the Lord prescribed when he referred to "confessing thy sins unto thy brethren, and before the Lord." (D&C 59:12.)

3. *Restitution.* Restitution is also an essential ingredient of the repentance sought by church discipline. Transgressors must do all they can to restore what their transgression has taken from others. This includes confession to and seeking the forgiveness of those they have wronged. It also includes making the disclosures necessary to protect those who have been put in jeopardy by their wrongdoing. For example, they may need to alert persons to health or safety hazards they have created. As part of restitution, transgressors may also need to make disclosures to civil authorities and to accept the consequences. In contrast, while criminal courts will sometimes sentence a defendant to restore what he took from a victim, such restitution is, at best, an incidental concern of the punishment meted out by the laws of man.

4. *Suffering.* Suffering is probably the most misunderstood ingredient of repentance. This misunderstanding may result from the fact that there is a great gulf between the role of suffering under the laws of man and its role under the laws of God.

The laws of man inflict punishment to make a malefactor suffer for his crime. Punishment is a principal object of the laws of man. Criminal courts seek to make an offender "pay" for his wrongdoing.

Some have looked on church discipline in the same light. Bruce C. Hafen explains: "Some who carry the burden of serious sin also [mistakenly] believe they must somehow 'pay' for their mistakes through a Church disciplinary council, feeling that some high level of public shame will make adequate payment."[8]

The idea that a disciplinary council is supposed to punish a transgressor or make him suffer to pay for his wrongdoing misunderstands the purpose of church discipline and its relationship (and the relationship of suffering) to repentance, mercy, and the atonement.

Under the law and justice of God, sinners *are* punished. We believe that men will be punished for their own sins. (Article of Faith 2.) Through the prophet Isaiah, the Lord said he would "punish the inhabitants of the earth for their iniquity." (Isa. 26:21.) God's law could not exist "save there was a punishment." (Alma 42:17.) There is "a punishment affixed" for every sin. (Alma 42:18; also see Amos 3:1–2.) Amulek explained that "he that exercises no faith unto repentance is exposed to the whole law of the demands of justice." (Alma 34:16.) Justice requires that the *unrepentant* sinner suffer for his own sins. "If they would not repent," the Savior said, "they must suffer even as I." (D&C 19:17.)

What about *repentant* sinners? Are they punished? Must they suffer? Alma declared that "repentance could not come unto men except there were a punishment." (Alma 42:16.) The punishment that leads to repentance and the punishment that makes repentance possible must include suffering, but whose suffering is this, and what is the role of church discipline in it?

The suffering that impels a transgressor toward repentance is his or her own suffering. But the suffering that satisfies the demands of justice for the repentant transgressor is the suffering of our Savior and Redeemer. He suffered for the sins of all, "that they might not suffer if they would repent." (D&C 19:16.) In the great words of Isaiah, "He was wounded for our transgressions, he was bruised for our iniquities: the chastisement of our peace was upon him; and with his stripes we are healed." (Isa. 53:5.) If we will only repent, the Redeemer has paid the price for our sins. As Elder Packer explained, justice "can ask no more. It would not be just."[9]

Does this mean that there is no suffering for the repentant sinner? Because Christ suffered for our sins, some think that all a sinner must do is express sorrow for his sins and accept Christ as his Savior, and all the suffering is the Lord's. This is not so. President Spencer W. Kimball, who gave such comprehensive teachings on repentance and forgiveness, said that *personal* suffering "is a very important part of repentance." "Many people cannot repent until they have suffered much. . . . If a person hasn't suffered, he hasn't repented. . . . He has got to go through a change in his system whereby he suffers and then forgiveness is a possibility."[10]

As President Kimball explained, the repenting sinner must suffer for his sins, but this suffering has a different purpose than punishment or payment. Its purpose is *change*. The fruits of the transgressor's personal suffering are the broken heart and contrite spirit described in the scriptures. The Savior commanded, "Ye shall repent of your sins, and come unto me with a broken heart and a contrite spirit." (3 Ne. 12:19.) When the Savior did away with the sacrifices and burnt offerings of the law of Moses, he explained, "Ye shall offer for a sacrifice unto me a broken heart and a contrite spirit." (3 Ne. 9:20.) How appropriate that the new offering to remind sinners of the sacrifice and suffering of their Redeemer would be a broken heart and a contrite spirit, which could only be attained by the suffering of the penitent! Father Lehi explained that this personal condition was essential to qualify for the mercy of the atonement: "Behold he offereth himself a sacrifice for sin, to answer the ends of the law, unto all those who have a broken heart and a contrite spirit; and unto none else can the ends of the law be answered." (2 Ne. 2:7.)

What, then, is the role of church discipline, in contrast to the punishment that is the intended result of the judgment of a criminal court? In its primary purpose—to save the souls of transgressors—church discipline is intended to facilitate repentance. Personal suffering is inevitably part of that process. Sometimes, as in the discipline of disfellowshipment or excommunication, both punishment and suffering will be inflicted by the decision of the disciplinary council. But the infliction of punishment and personal suffering is not the purpose of a disciplinary council.

The objective of church discipline is to facilitate repentance, whose purpose is to qualify a transgressor for the mercy of God and the salvation made possible through the atonement of Jesus Christ. Consequently, church discipline is not an instrument of punishment but a catalyst for change. The purpose of the suffering that must occur as part of the process of repentance is not to *punish* the transgressor, but to *change* him. The broken heart and contrite spirit required to "answer the ends of the law" introduce the repentant transgressor to the change necessary to conform his life to the pattern prescribed by his Redeemer.

This discussion of the doctrinal basis for church discipline answers the transgressor's familiar questions and pleas: "Why must I repent? Why must I confess to my wife? Why must I confess to the bishop? Why must I make restitution? Why are you trying to punish me? Why must I suffer the

shame and inconvenience of church discipline?" Like wayward Corianton, some transgressors have difficulty understanding "the justice of God in the punishment of the sinner."
(Alma 42:1.) And they do not understand the conditions of
mercy. "Why must I suffer at all?" they ask. "Now that I have
said I am sorry, why can't you just give me mercy and forget
about this?"

Such questions have some force under the laws of man.
Under those laws, mercy can rob justice (as happens in the
case of a pardon or executive clemency).

In contrast, under the laws of God mercy cannot rob
justice. The sinner must repent or he must pay the full
penalty of suffering for his own sins. The object of God's
laws is to save the sinner, not simply to punish him, but
there is no exemption from the conditions a transgressor
must meet to qualify for the mercy necessary for salvation.
The repentant transgressor must be changed, and the
conditions of repentance, including confession and suffering, are essential to accomplish that change. To exempt a
transgressor from those conditions would deprive him of
the change necessary for his salvation. That would be neither
just nor merciful.

Change of Life

We often think of the results of repentance as simply
cleansing us from sin. That is an incomplete view of the
matter. A person who sins is like a tree that bends easily in
the wind. On a windy and rainy day the tree may bend so
deeply against the ground that the leaves become soiled
with mud, like sin. If we only focus on cleaning the leaves,
the weakness in the tree that allowed it to bend and soil its
leaves may remain. Merely cleansing the leaves does not
strengthen the tree. Similarly, a person who is merely sorry

to be soiled by sin will sin again in the next high wind. The susceptibility to repetition will continue until the tree has been strengthened.

When a person has gone through the process that results in what the scriptures call a broken heart and a contrite spirit, the Savior not only cleanses that person from sin. He also gives him or her new strength. The new strength we receive from the Savior is essential for us to realize the purpose of our cleansing from sin, which is to return to our Heavenly Father. To be admitted to his presence, we must be more than clean. We must also be changed from a weak person who has transgressed into a strong person with the spiritual stature to dwell in the presence of God. We must, as the scripture says, "becometh [as] a saint through the atonement of Christ the Lord." (Mosiah 3:19.) This is what the scripture means in its explanation that a person who has repented of sins will forsake them. (D&C 58:43.) Forsaking sins is more than resolving not to repeat them. Forsaking involves a fundamental change in the individual.

King Benjamin and Alma both speak of "a mighty change of heart." King Benjamin's congregation described that mighty change by saying that they had "no more disposition to do evil, but to do good continually." (Mosiah 5:2.) Alma illustrated that change of heart when he described a people who "awoke unto God," "put their trust in" him, and were "faithful until the end." He challenged others to "look forward with an eye of faith" to the time when we will "stand before God to be judged" according to our deeds. (Alma 5:7, 13, 15.) Persons who have had that change in their hearts have attained the strength and stature to dwell with God. That is what we call being saved.

That is the ultimate purpose of church discipline. And that is why church discipline uses rules and procedures different from those used to enforce the laws and obtain the justice of man.

Other Purposes of Church Discipline

While saving souls is the primary purpose of church discipline, there are two secondary purposes, both supportive of the primary purpose and each important in its own right: protecting the flock and preserving the good name and influence of the Church.

1. *The shepherd must act to protect the flock of God.* He must act to protect the innocent from the predator. As Alma taught: "For what shepherd is there among you having many sheep doth not watch over them, that the wolves enter not and devour his flock? And behold, if a wolf enter his flock doth he not drive him out? Yea, and at the last, if he can, he will destroy him. And now I say unto you that the good shepherd doth call after you; and if you will hearken unto his voice he will bring you into his fold, and ye are his sheep; and he commandeth you that ye suffer no ravenous wolf to enter among you, that ye may not be destroyed." (Alma 5:59–60.)

The threat to the innocent may be loss of life, bodily injury, or loss of property, such as by fraudulent practices. The innocent can also be threatened by the doctrinal deviances we call apostasy (discussed later in this chapter).

The shepherd has a responsibility to protect the flock against all of these threats. That responsibility may require him to deny a predator the fellowship of the Saints or even to sever his membership in the flock. As Jesus taught: "If he repent not he shall not be numbered among my people, that he may not destroy my people, for behold I know my sheep, and they are numbered." (3 Ne. 18:31; see also Mosiah 26:34–36.)

It is, of course, also true that the protection of innocent

persons (from physical and financial, but not spiritual, harm) is one of the objectives of the laws of man.

2. *The other secondary purpose of church discipline is to preserve the influence of the Church for good — its capacity to perform its mission to teach and influence people for righteousness.* Church discipline does this by safeguarding the purity, integrity, and good name of the Church. There are two parts to this effort, the first focusing on transgressions by members in general, and the second focusing primarily on the most visible and influential members, including officers and teachers.

The *first* application of this purpose of church discipline is the leader's responsibility to warn members of the flock against sin and to rebuke those who are in transgression. The scriptures contain many definitions of this responsibility. (For example, Mosiah 26:6; 1 Thes. 5:14; 1 Tim. 5:20; Titus 1:10–13.) They even state that the leader who fails to teach and admonish must bear the burden of sins himself. Thus, the prophet Jacob writes of magnifying one's office by "taking upon us the responsibility, answering the sins of the people upon our own heads if we did not teach them the word of God with all diligence; wherefore, by laboring with our might their blood might not come upon our garments; otherwise their blood would come upon our garments, and we would not be found spotless at the last day." (Jacob 1:19; also see 2 Ne. 9:44; D&C 68:25; 88:81–85; Ezek. 33:2–9.)

In a sermon given while he was president of the Council of the Twelve, President John Taylor warned: "I have heard of some Bishops who have been seeking to cover up the iniquities of men; I tell them, in the name of God, they will have to bear . . . that iniquity, and if any of you want to partake of the sins of men, or uphold them, you will have to bear them. Do you hear it, you Bishops and you Presidents? God will require it at your hands. You are not placed in position to tamper with the principles of righteousness, nor to cover up the infamies and corruptions of men."[11]

In an 1885 sermon, President George Q. Cannon condemned sexual immorality and then stressed the importance of leaders' confronting and correcting this and other transgressions by the rank-and-file members of the Church: "Now, such a condition of things if permitted to continue in our midst, unchecked, would be productive of the most terrible consequences. The Spirit of God would undoubtedly be so grieved that it would forsake not only those who are guilty of these acts, but it would withdraw itself from those who would suffer them to be done in our midst unchecked and unrebuked."[12] This teaching is rooted in the pervasive scriptural direction that the transgressor who fails to repent and forsake shall be cast out.

During the reign of King Mosiah, when dissenters and disbelievers deceived many and caused them to sin, "it became expedient that those who committed sin, that were in the church, should be admonished by the church." (Mosiah 26:6.) And the Lord instructed the prophet Alma, "Whosoever will not repent of his sins the same shall not be numbered among my people." (Mosiah 26:32; see also vs. 36.)

Similarly, the apostle Paul, on receiving reports that there were fornicators in the congregation of the Corinthians, reminded them "that a little leaven leaveneth the whole lump." "Purge out therefore the old leaven," he directed them, "that ye may be a new lump." (1 Cor. 5:6–7.) Repeating in more specific terms, the apostle instructed that the Corinthians not "keep company, if any man that is called a brother be a fornicator. . . . Therefore put away from among yourselves that wicked person." (1 Cor. 5:11, 13; see also 2 Thes. 3:6, 14; Titus 3:10.)

We have the same direction in this dispensation: "Him that repenteth not of his sins, and confesseth them not, ye shall bring before the church, and do with him as the scripture saith unto you, either by commandment or by revelation. And this ye shall do that God may be glorified — not because ye forgive not, having not compassion, but that ye may be justified in the eyes of the law, that ye may not offend him who is your lawgiver." (D&C 64:12–13; see also 20:80.) In short, "He that sinneth and repenteth not shall be cast out." (D&C 42:28; see also 42:75; 41:5.) Otherwise, we undermine the commandments (laws) and offend the lawgiver.

Second, the good name and influence of the Church are especially threatened by the transgressions of its most prominent members, including officers and teachers, since their transgressions are most likely to dilute the moral authority and teaching effectiveness of the Church. A transgression by a member in a prominent position could seriously detract from the Church's ability to teach correct principles, unless the Church takes public action to discipline the transgressor. In contrast, the church discipline required for the transgressions of a member who is not in the public eye, especially if those transgressions are not well known, can be dictated solely by what is needed to save the soul of the transgressor. This contrast, which assigns more serious and more public consequences to the transgressions of the more highly placed and prominent, is supported by the revelation that states, "Of him unto whom much is given much is required; and he who sins against the greater light shall receive the greater condemnation." (D&C 82:3.)

These concerns about the purity, integrity, and good name of the Church seem to be the basis for what the Savior taught his apostles at Capernaum. "If thy hand offend thee, cut it off," he taught, explaining that "it is better for thee to enter into life maimed, than having two hands to go into hell." (Mark 9:43). The *hand* seems to be a reference to the *rank-and-file members* of the Church. In his inspired translation, the Prophet Joseph Smith inserted an explanation of the intent of this passage: "or if thy *brother* offend thee *and confess not and forsake not,* he shall be cut off." (JST Mark 9:40; emphasis added.) As clarified, the direction is not to cut off every offender in the rank and file, but only those who do not confess and forsake.

In contrast, the next two examples, the *foot* and the *eye,* seem to refer to *leaders.* They are held to a higher standard. Because of their visible and influential position, they should be cut off for transgression without regard to whether they confess and forsake. The italicized portion is the text the Prophet Joseph Smith added in the inspired translation.

"And *again,* if thy foot offend thee, cut it off; *for he that is thy standard by whom thou walkest, if he become a transgressor, he shall be cut off.* It is better for thee, to enter halt into life, than having two feet to be cast into hell; into the fire that never shall be quenched. . . . And if thine eye *which seeth for thee, him that is appointed to watch over thee to show thee light, become a transgressor and* offend thee, pluck *him* out. It is better for thee to enter into the kingdom of God, with one eye, than having two eyes to be cast into hell fire." (JST Mark 9:42–43, 46–47.)

To cut off a leader or a member means to sever that person's membership, fellowship, or some of the person's privileges. In context, then, these scriptures direct the application of what we now call church discipline, and they call for more rigorous discipline for leaders.

This comparison of the different purposes of law enforcement and church discipline is not complete without an important caution. The principles and considerations to be followed by priesthood leaders are specified in the Church's *General Handbook of Instructions.* The examples discussed in this chapter are selected to illustrate relevant comparisons with the civil and criminal law and do not give the complete guide required for administration of church discipline. In matters of principle as well as procedure (discussed below), priesthood leaders must be guided by the *General Handbook of Instructions.*

Procedures of Church Discipline

The contrasts between the purposes of church discipline and the purposes of civil or criminal law enforcement also result in some differences in procedures. These are discussed here from the standpoint of church discipline.

Informal Discipline

Informal discipline includes (1) private counsel and caution and (2) informal probation. These measures are administered privately and confidentially by the bishop or stake president without any formalities such as notice or record-keeping and without any public notice of the action taken. Generally, even counselors to the bishop or stake president are unaware of the imposition of informal discipline. Civil or criminal court procedures have alternatives to formal adjudication (such as private settlement of civil disputes and various diversions of criminal complaints), but they have no procedures equivalent to the Church's informal discipline.

Formal Discipline

Formal discipline is administered by a ward or stake or mission disciplinary council (formerly called a church court) in an ecclesiastical proceeding that involves notice, presentation of evidence, opportunity for the member to be heard, and a decision formally reached, recorded, and communicated.

The principal similarities and differences between a disciplinary council and a civil or criminal court proceeding are discussed below. For example, the procedures of civil law are initiated by the complaint of a plaintiff, and the procedures of criminal law are set in motion by the action of a law enforcement officer. Similarly, the procedures of church discipline can be invoked by the complaint of a victim or by the action of a church leader. However, in contrast to the criminal law, there is no law enforcement officer in church discipline, and the church authority who initiates the action can act by the power of discernment (revelation) as well as by personal observation or formal evidence. A home teacher could even perform this function, since the revelations give him the duty "to watch over the church always, . . . and see that there is no iniquity in the church." (D&C 20:53–54.)

Judge and Other Participants

A disciplinary council is like a court in that both have a judge. In terms of organization, that is where the similarity ends. Unlike a civil or criminal court, a disciplinary council has no prosecutor, no defense attorney, and no jury.

The bishop (or stake or mission president) is the judge. A bishop is appointed "to be a judge in Israel." (D&C 107:72.) He is to judge "by the testimony of the just, . . . according to the laws of the kingdom which are given by the prophets of God." (D&C 58:18.) His counselors counsel with him, but he makes the decision.

In a stake disciplinary council, the stake presidency is assisted by twelve high councilors. Their role is easily misunderstood. Uninformed persons are tempted to liken the high council to a jury. In view of the not-well-understood instructions in section 102 of the Doctrine and Covenants, there is also a tendency to view individual high councilors as prosecutors or defenders. Neither of these comparisons is appropriate.

Members of the high council are present to "stand up in behalf of the accused, and prevent insult and injustice." (D&C 102:17.) In other words, they are to give added assurance that the evidence is examined in its true light and that the procedures and treatment of the accused are consistent with equity and justice. Their roles are illumination and persuasion, not advocacy or decision. They cannot dictate or veto the decision of the judge, although they can have the evidence reconsidered if they "discover an error in the decision." (D&C 102:20.)

Nonadversary System

In the Anglo-American legal system (with which most church members are familiar), wrongdoers are processed through what is called an adversary system. The accused and his defense attorney are adversary to the prosecutor — putting the prosecution "to its proof," as the saying goes, and opposing it at every step. That attitude and that procedure are effective for their assigned role in administering the laws of man, which aim at punishment, but they are completely at odds with the procedures specified for church discipline.

A disciplinary council is concerned with the welfare of the individual member and, if convinced that he is a transgressor, with the extent of his repentance. The paramount purpose of church discipline is to save the transgressor. In that setting, the recipient of church discipline should be submissive, not adversary. An attitude of adversariness is not an attitude of repentance. As Professors McConkie and Millet have noted, "When a person repents in the sincerity of his soul, he does all in his or her power to make amends; is eager to receive whatever judgment the Lord and his earthly servants feel should be meted out; and pays whatever price is necessary to return to full fellowship. The sinner in no way seeks to set the terms of the probation or to temper the justice or punishment required by the sin. His heart is an open book. There is no sham, no hypocrisy, no duplicity."[13]

Use of a Member's Confession

The nonadversary nature of church discipline proceedings is evident in another difference. In contrast to the rule in criminal cases, a confession cannot be used as evidence in a church disciplinary council unless the confessing transgressor consents. This rule vividly illustrates the bishop's or stake president's solemn duty to keep the content of a member's confession strictly confidential. Confidentiality encourages members to communicate freely with their bishops. Members' unrestrained and trusting communication with their bishops is essential in view of the vital role of confession in the process of repentance and forgiveness. In church discipline, then, the importance of a confession as evidence of the guilt of one transgressor is subordinated to the importance of confessions in the process of repentance of transgressors generally.

The requirement of consent before using a confession does not prevent disciplinary councils from fulfilling their primary purpose of saving the souls of transgressors. A repentant person will give consent. The lack of permission from an unrepentant transgressor does not prevent a disciplinary council from proceeding on the basis of other evidence. (Nor does it prevent the bishop from imposing informal discipline on the basis of the confession.) If no other evidence is available, so that the disciplinary council cannot proceed, the principal loser is the unrepentant transgressor. His refusal to consent stands in the way of his being helped by the action of a disciplinary council.

Deceiving the Judge

The same principle blunts the damage suffered if the transgressor succeeds in deceiving the church officer responsible to give church discipline.

Suppose a transgressor is treated more leniently than if he had not succeeded in his deception. What does it matter? The purpose of church discipline is not to put the scales of justice in balance by assessing a "penalty commensurate with the wrong." The purpose of church discipline is to aid the transgressor's repentance and to save his soul. If he feigns repentance and receives no discipline or if he receives excessively lenient discipline, he is the principal loser.

God, who knows the acts and the innermost thoughts and motives of us all, will be the final judge in the eternal process for which church discipline is only the mortal introduction. In church discipline, the mortal judge can forgive sins as a representative of the Church, but the only one who can absolve sins is God himself.[14] And God has declared that "none but the truly penitent are saved." (Alma 42:24.)

Sufficiency of Evidence

In common with a criminal or civil court, in a contested case (where the accused denies his guilt) a church disciplinary council acts on the basis of evidence. As President Joseph F. Smith declared on September 13, 1917: "If a man is accused we do not expect him to prove his innocence in the Church any more than he would be expected to prove his innocence under the laws of the land. We expect the evidence to be brought to prove his guilt beyond all question, if he is guilty; and when we receive that evidence we must deal with it according to righteous principles, exercising all the mercy and charity we can, looking always for the salvation of men and not for their destruction."[15]

If a person has committed transgression but denies it and is not disciplined by a disciplinary council because of insufficient evidence, that person is the principal loser. The law of mercy and the atoning sacrifice of Jesus Christ cannot operate for the benefit of one who has refused to acknowledge and confess his sins. Amulek explained the terrible consequences of postponing repentance to the end: "For behold, if ye have procrastinated the day of your repentance even until death, behold, ye have become subjected to the spirit of the devil, and he doth seal you his; therefore, the Spirit of the Lord hath withdrawn from you, and hath no place in you, and the devil hath all power over you; and this is the final state of the wicked." (Alma 34:35.)

For now, we can only hope that the transgressor's heart will change and he will repent and qualify for mercy. In the meanwhile, the cleansing process must wait, and the transgressor's salvation is in jeopardy.

If a criminal trial is begun in a court in the United States and it then appears that the prosecution has insufficient evidence to establish the charges, the only alternatives are to terminate the proceeding or to find the defendant not guilty. In either event, the defendant can never be prosecuted again for that offense because the Constitution forbids double jeopardy.

In contrast, because of the different procedures and objectives of church discipline, if the evidence presented in a disciplinary council is insufficient to justify formal church discipline but the presiding officer is convinced that the matter should be kept open instead of being concluded at that time, he can adjourn the council for a time to seek or await additional evidence.

Evidence in a Charge of Adultery

Where the charge is adultery and the accused person denies it, church disciplinary councils are subject to a unique and stringent burden of proof. The revelation known as the "law of the Church" directs:

"And if any man or woman shall commit adultery, he or she shall be tried before two elders of the church, or more, and every word shall be established against him or her by two witnesses of the church, and not of the enemy; but if there are more than two witnesses it is better.

"But he or she shall be condemned by the mouth of two witnesses; and the elders shall lay the case before the church, and the church shall lift up their hands against him or her, that they may be dealt with according to the law of God." (D&C 42:80–81.)

To illustrate the operation of this rule, suppose one church member confesses to adultery with another member and then becomes the accuser of that other person. Further, suppose the other person denies the act, and there is no other direct or strong circumstantial evidence or revelatory testimony that could provide the second witness required by this revelation.

Can the other person be given formal church discipline for adultery? No, *not yet.* The presiding officer has some latitude for informal discipline, but because of the lack of a second witness, the person accused of adultery receives no formal church discipline *for the moment.* The matter remains in the same state as other suspected but unproven transgressions.

Why are two witnesses (which means two separate sources of evidence) required for a charge of adultery and not for other serious transgressions? Perhaps this is because the sin of adultery is both serious and (usually) secret. It is the kind of transgression that is easy for a vindictive person to charge and very difficult for an innocent person to disprove. The requirement of two witnesses is an extraordinary protection for the innocent in a circumstance where protection is needed.

An additional reason is found in the fact that adultery is probably the most serious transgression that is commonly considered by a church disciplinary body. Other serious transgressions, such as murder or robbery, are usually examined first by criminal courts, which are subject to their own stringent rules of evidence. Thus, the revelation quoted above establishes a strict standard of proof for an accusation commonly treated by church discipline, an accusation that is both serious and subject to manipulation.

Concern for the Innocent

Church discipline is much more flexible than civil or criminal procedures in its capacity to adapt to the needs of innocent persons who would be affected by the proceedings. Laws and administrative pressures often force civil and criminal courts to act on rigid timetables and without regard to the interests of the innocent. Church discipline is more flexible in its operation and more comprehensive in its view. It can accommodate long delays, if needed for the good of the transgressor or his or her spouse or other family members or for the good of the innocent victim. It can consider the needs of such innocent persons in determining the discipline to impose or the extent to which it will be made public.

The Role of Revelation

A major contrast between civil or criminal courts and church disciplinary councils is the disciplinary council's reliance on revelation. This occurs in two ways. One is general and familiar and the other is specific and exceptional.

In general, the participants in a disciplinary council rely on revelation to guide them in performing functions that are comparable to those performed in civil or criminal courts — understanding and weighing the evidence in a contested case and determining the appropriate discipline to impose.

For example, the Doctrine and Covenants section prescribing the judicial procedures for high councils directs that "after the evidences are heard, the councilors, accuser and accused have spoken, the president shall give a decision according to the understanding which he shall have of the case." (D&C 102:19.) President Joseph F. Smith described the effect of that direction when he explained that the duty of the high council is "to find out the truth, the facts, and then judge according to the truth and the facts that are brought to their understanding."[16] These instructions seem to contemplate that the decision will be based upon the evidence before the council, evaluated, and applied with the aid of the inspiration that is sought in the performance of everything done by the authority of the holy priesthood.

In addition, revelation can provide other guidance in a disciplinary council, this being specific and exceptional.

The Lord commanded the early leaders of the Church to take action against unrepentant offenders. He also prescribed the procedure to be followed in these contested cases: "Him that repenteth not of his sins, and confess them not, ye shall bring before the church, and *do with him as the scripture saith unto you, either by commandment or by revelation.*" (D&C 64:12; emphasis added.)

To "do with [an unrepentant transgressor] as the scripture saith" is to follow the principles and procedures specified in the scriptures. In 1831, when this direction was given, the leaders of the Church had many scriptures explaining the principles of church discipline and the transgressions for which it should be imposed. These scriptural directions were found in the Bible, the Book of Mormon, and a modern revelation, the "law of the Church" (D&C 42), given just six months earlier. (The revelation prescribing the procedures for high councils, section 102, came several years later.)

The succeeding words of the verse quoted above explain *how* the scriptural directions are to be applied in church discipline: "either by commandment or by revelation." (D&C 64:12.)

To apply the scriptures by commandment means to follow their directions literally, according to their terms. This includes the familiar judicial function of receiving and weighing the evidence, as is done by a civil or criminal court. For example, in a revelation given just a month earlier, the bishop was identified as "a judge in Israel . . . to judge his people *by the testimony* of the just." (D&C 58:17–18; emphasis added.)

In contrast, to apply these scriptures "by revelation" (D&C 64:12) contemplates something more than following their literal terms and being limited to the evidence before the council. The subsequent revelation pertaining to high council procedures gives one illustration of the meaning of this direction: "In case of difficulty respecting doctrine or principle, if there is not a sufficiency written to make the case clear to the minds of the council, the president may inquire and obtain the mind of the Lord by revelation." (See D&C 102:23.)

This reference to a "difficulty respecting doctrine or principle" seems to limit this direction to revelations on the governing standards — such matters as what the commandments mean (that is, what they forbid). It does not seem to refer to a revelation that would show the guilt of a person who could not be proven guilty by the evidence before the council. This interpretation is confirmed by something President Joseph F. Smith said shortly after he became president of the Church. In a criminal trial for murder, a witness testified that he knew the accused was guilty because he had learned this by revelation. Responding to the ensuing public criticism that the Church approved this witness's testimony, President Smith declared: "Such evidence would not be permissible even in a Church court, where rules of evidence, though not so technical, are founded largely upon the same principles that govern the rules of evidence in a court of law."[17]

President Smith's statement disassociates the Church from a procedure in which a witness declares an accused person guilty on the basis of revelation. However, his statement does not deny that a witness could receive inspiration to assist him in his testimony, such as in recalling or expressing his evidence. And President Smith's statement surely does not rule out reliance on revelation to the presiding officer and members of a disciplinary council on the central question of the guilt or innocence of the accused person. We could not deny the efficacy of revelation on this subject without going contrary to the organization, purpose, and divine direction of the Church. But even as we affirm the appropriateness of revelation on this important subject, we must stress that in this circumstance revelation is subject to an important limitation that does not apply to the presiding officer's receiving and weighing evidence by conventional means or to his receiving revelation to clarify the meaning of a commandment.

When a disciplinary council acts upon evidence in a manner comparable to a civil or criminal court, the presiding officer is the judge and his decisions do not have to be sustained unanimously by the other members of the council. If one of the council members thinks there is an error in the decision, the case "shall have a re-hearing" (D&C 102:20), which I interpret to mean a reconsideration, not a rehearing of the evidence. But, it is provided, unless this reconsideration results in "any additional light" that would cause the decision to be altered, "the first decision shall stand, *the majority of the council having power to determine the same.*" (D&C 102:21–22; emphasis added.) Stated otherwise, when it comes to weighing evidence in a contested case, the outcome is determined by the presiding officer and a majority of the council.

I believe that it is otherwise when the decision is based on revelation rather than evidence. If a disciplinary council were to rely upon revelation to provide its finding of guilt, they could do so only in compliance with the procedure established for the action of priesthood councils generally: "Every decision made by either of these quorums must be by the unanimous voice of the same; that is, every member in each quorum must be agreed to its decisions, in order to make their decisions of the same power or validity one with the other." (D&C 107:27.) In other words, if the disciplinary council relies on revelation to provide any element of proof not present in the evidence before the council, all members of the council must be united as to that element.

Public or Private

Still another difference between the procedures of those councils or tribunals that enforce the laws of man and those that concern the laws of God is the extent of public exposure given to their actions.

The constitutions and laws of various states and nations guarantee a public trial for one who is accused of a crime. That is an important guarantee of fairness and justice for a criminal defendant. In contrast, most church discipline is confidential. To safeguard the privacy of the member and the process of repentance, the judge and all other participants are bound by the most solemn duties of confidentiality. When disciplinary action has been taken, the outcome (but not the details of the transgression) may need to be made known, but only to the extent necessary to serve the purposes of the discipline.

If the purpose of a particular discipline, such as excommunication or disfellowshipment, is to safeguard the good name and moral influence of the Church, the disciplinary action may need to be made public to accomplish its objective. Some announcement may also be necessary where the discipline is meant to protect the innocent. If the flock is to be protected against a predator, he may need to be publicly identified as such.

However, in the largest group of cases, where church discipline is motivated solely by a desire to save the soul of the transgressor, the disciplinary action is confidential except for private communication to persons who need to know. In general, a decision to place a person on probation is not announced to anyone. Decisions to excommunicate or disfellowship are announced in confidence to the local officers who need that information to perform their church duties.

These principles are dictated by revelation. The revelation referred to as "the law of the Church" states the basic principle of confidentiality: "If he or she confess not thou shalt deliver him or her up unto the church, not to the members, but to the elders. And it shall be done in a meeting, and that not before the world." (D&C 42:89.)

The revelation next states that persons who have "offend[ed] many . . . shall be chastened before many," and "if any one offend openly, he or she shall be rebuked openly, that he or she may be ashamed." (D&C 42:90–91.) In contrast, "If any shall offend in secret, he or she shall be rebuked in secret, that he or she may have opportunity to confess in secret to him or her whom he or she has offended, and to God, that the church may not speak reproachfully of him or her." (D&C 42:92.)

This revelation shows the interaction between two different purposes of punishment—protecting the good name and moral influence of the Church and facilitating repentance. When a serious sin is widely known or there were many victims—and especially when the transgressor is a person occupying a prominent position in the Church—the purpose of church discipline concerned with the good name and influence of the Church dictates that the church discipline be widely known. He who "offend[ed] openly . . . shall be rebuked openly." On the other hand, where a sin is not known widely, repentance and church discipline can be a private affair. He who "offend[ed] in secret . . . shall be rebuked in secret." Similarly, when persons have not confessed or repented, they are delivered up to a meeting of elders who act for the Church "and that not before the world." This shows the importance of confidentiality in church discipline that concerns ordinary members and only seeks to serve the purpose of saving the soul of the transgressor.

Apostasy

This discussion of differences between the laws of God and the laws of man would not be complete without considering the offense of apostasy. Some of the serious transgressions in church discipline, such as murder, robbery, and sexual abuse, are also serious crimes. In contrast, there are two serious transgressions that are not serious crimes in civil law: adultery (discussed above) and apostasy. Although it has some parallels in the secular crimes of treason, sedition, and the like, apostasy is unique to religious law. As defined and administered by The Church of Jesus Christ of Latter-day Saints, apostasy is basically an offense of teaching and/or practicing—not just believing—false doctrine.

The essential distinction between believing false doctrine and preaching it was defined in this instruction given by Elder George Q. Cannon:

"A friend . . . wished to know whether we . . . considered an honest difference of opinion between a member of the Church and the Authorities of the Church was apostasy. . . . We replied that we had not stated that an honest difference of opinion between a member of the Church and the Authorities constituted apostasy, for we could conceive of a man honestly differing in opinion from the Authorities of the Church and yet not be an apostate; but we could not conceive of a man publishing these differences of opinion and seeking by arguments, sophistry and special pleading to enforce them upon the people to produce division and strife and to place the acts and counsels of the Authorities of the Church, if possible, in a wrong light, and not be an apostate, for such conduct was apostasy as we understood the term."[18]

A half-century later, President Joseph F. Smith affirmed this distinction in an important article titled "Principles of Government in the Church." He said that a man who professes to be a member of The Church of Jesus Christ of Latter-day Saints, but "who ignores and repudiates the doctrine of the atonement, . . . is not worthy of membership in the Church.

"He may be considered harmless and of no great danger to others, particularly, as long as he keeps his mouth shut and does not advocate his pernicious doctrines, and be permitted to remain a member of the Church; but the moment you find him trying to poison the minds of somebody else — the innocent, the unsuspecting, the unwary — trying to sow the seeds of death and apostasy and unbelief and infidelity in the minds of innocent people, that moment it becomes the duty of the bishop of the ward where the man resides to take him up and try him."[19]

For purposes of church discipline, the Church currently defines apostasy as (1) repeatedly acting in clear, open, and deliberate public opposition to the Church or its leaders; (2) persisting in teaching as church doctrine information that is not church doctrine, after being corrected by one's bishop or higher authority; or (3) continuing to follow the teachings of apostate cults (such as those that advocate plural marriage) after being corrected by one's bishop or higher authority. Total inactivity in the Church or merely attending another church does not constitute apostasy.

Though very important to the doctrinal integrity of the Church and the protection of the flock of God, apostasy is a difficult transgression to correct by church discipline. Unlike the perpetrators of other transgressions, the apostate is almost always defiant and unrepentant. As a result, the disciplining of an apostate can turn out to be the very opposite of the helpful, ministering, and private event that is the model and primary purpose of church discipline. Unless administered with great care, a church disciplinary proceeding for apostasy is likely to assume some of the character of an adversary criminal proceeding. To prevent this, the church officers who are involved should be especially well informed on the differences between church discipline and criminal prosecutions. They should be careful to accomplish the purposes of church discipline, especially to protect the flock of God, without being drawn into the technicalities and punishment mentality of the criminal process.

Conclusion

In summary, the laws of man and the laws of God have different, though partially overlapping, purposes. The laws of man are concerned primarily with achieving justice — having the offender pay his debt to society. The laws of God are also concerned with justice, but they are part of the broader framework that includes mercy and the atonement of Jesus Christ. Hence, the principal purpose of church discipline is not to punish the transgressor, but to aid his repentance and save his soul. Consequently, the administration of church discipline focuses on the conditions that encourage the offender to repent and receive mercy through the atonement of Jesus Christ, and to achieve the change of life that will permit him to go on to exaltation.

This contrast is not well understood. Some members of the Church make the mistake of judging the appropriateness of church discipline on the basis of whether a transgressor received justice, evaluating justice in terms of whether he was punished in proportion to his transgression. Members who attempt that kind of evaluation misunderstand the laws of God and the purposes of church discipline. Others err in attempting to evaluate the justice or appropriateness of discipline without knowing the total facts, which are confidential in a church disciplinary proceeding and are usually known only to the bishop or stake president. Beyond that, even if the external facts were known, an outside observer cannot know the most important single fact bearing on what church discipline is needed: the extent of repentance of the transgressor.

The procedures of church discipline differ from the procedures of civil and criminal courts in ways that facilitate the different purposes of discipline in contrast to adjudication. All of this is consistent with the Lord's declaration that "it must needs be done" in the Lord's way. (D&C 104:16.)

NOTES

1. Harold B. Lee, Address to Regional Representatives Seminar, October 1, 1969, 11–12.

2. *The Merchant of Venice,* act 4, sc. 1.

3. Boyd K. Packer, *The Mediator* (Salt Lake City: Deseret Book, 1978), 21.

4. Bruce R. McConkie, *The Promised Messiah* (Salt Lake City: Deseret Book, 1981), 337.

5. *The Teachings of Spencer W. Kimball,* ed. Edward L. Kimball (Salt Lake City: Bookcraft, 1982), 86.

6. Letter to author, August 22, 1988.

7. Marion G. Romney, *Conference Report,* October 1955, 125.

8. Bruce C. Hafen, *The Broken Heart* (Salt Lake City: Deseret Book, 1989), 152.

9. Packer, *The Mediator,* 20.

10. *The Teachings of Spencer W. Kimball,* 88, 97, 99.

11. John Taylor, *Conference Report,* April 1880, 78.

12. George Q. Cannon, *Journal of Discourses* 26:139.

13. Joseph F. McConkie and Robert L. Millet, *Doctrinal Commentary on the Book of Mormon* 2 (Salt Lake City: Bookcraft, 1988): 300.

14. *The Teachings of Spencer W. Kimball,* 101.

15. James R. Clark, comp., *Messages of the First Presidency of The Church of Jesus Christ of Latter-day Saints* 5 (Salt Lake City: Bookcraft, 1971): 85.

16. Joseph Fielding Smith, *Gospel Doctrine* (Salt Lake City: Deseret Book, 1986), 181.

17. Ibid., 40.

18. George Q. Cannon, *Gospel Truth*, ed. Jerreld L. Newquist (Salt Lake City: Deseret Book Co., 1987), 493 (sermon delivered November 3, 1869).

19. Joseph F. Smith, in *Messages of the First Presidency* 5:83, and *Improvement Era*, November 1917, 7, 11.

INDEX

Absolutes, rejection of, 53

Actor who lectured BYU audience, 64

Adler, Mortimer J., on religion and science, 60–61, 62

Adversary techniques. *See* Contention

Adultery, 238–39

Agency, viii, 29

Alma, 28

Analogy of reasoning and methane, 57

Anderson, Richard Lloyd, 148

Apostasy, 246–48

Apostle, calling as, 6–7

Argument, warnings against, 148. *See also* Contention

Ashton, Marvin J.: on contention, 149–50; on fault-finding, 191–92

Ask, to receive revelation, 34

Athlete who refused to sue, letter from, 183–84

Atonement, 217–19, 222–24

Attorneys, invitation to speak to, 30

Basic Self-Reliance booklet, 130, 131

Benson, Ezra Taft: on contrast between Lord's way and world's way, 8; on proving truth of Book of Mormon, 91; on self-reliance and welfare, 119–20; on government assistance, 132–33

Bishop, role of: in welfare program, 112–13, 121, 122–23; and church discipline, 228–30, 232, 233

Blackmail, 193

Boasting of miracles and signs, 96–97

Book of Mormon: written by inspiration, 56; signs in, 83–85; gold plates taken away, 91; proving truth of, 91; teachings in, on caring for the poor, 103; teachings in, on contention, 141–42, 147; teachings in, on litigation, 160

Brigham Young University, 31–32, 64

251

Broken heart and contrite spirit, 224

Burger, Chief Justice Warren, 158

Callings, church: acceptance of, requires changes in ways of doing things, 5–7; shaping oneself to dimensions of, 7–8; may require change of attitude and thinking, 8

Cannon, George Q.; on viewing signs, 87–88; on testimony from within, 91; on proving gospel by miracles, 94; on avoiding contention, 144; on faultfinding, 190–91; on leader's responsibility for church discipline, 229; on apostasy, 246–47

Care for the poor: scriptural commandments to, 102–4; presupposes care for self and families, 103–4; government efforts to, 104–7; poverty programs to, 106; purposes of church welfare in, 108–10; spiritual is primary objective in, 110; Christ's teachings on, 110–11; goals of, stressed by prophets, 111–12; Church's program, principles of, 112–15; stresses self-reliance, 115; taxation to pay for, 133. *See also* Church welfare program

Casebook, error in, and revelation, 28

Change of heart, mighty, 226

Chicago, building stake center in, 27

Chicago, University of, disruptions at, 214

Chicago Bears, lawsuit against, 156

Christensen, Bruce L., 48–49

Church, practices of, are different from world's, 4–5

Church discipline: and man's laws, jurisdictions of, 210–16; purpose of, 216–17; and repentance, 219–25; and confession, 220–21; and suffering, 221–23; punishment as part of, 222; and atonement, 222–24; facilitates repentance, 224; results in change of heart, 226; protects the innocent, 227, 245–46; to preserve influence of Church for good, 228–32; leader's responsibility in, 228–30; and transgressions of prominent leaders, 230–31; outlined in *General Handbook of Instructions*, 232; procedures of, 232; informal, 232; formal, 232–33; stake disciplinary council, participants and procedures in, 233–39; uses nonadversary system, 234–35; role of judge in, 236; evidence in, 236–38; courts, compared with civil courts, 237–38; in dealing with adultery, 238–39; concern of, for the innocent, 239; role of revelation in, 240–43; and unrepentant offenders, 240–41; evidence in, 242–43; privacy in, 244; on occasion, made public, 244–45; and apostasy, 246–48; and procedures in civil and criminal courts, 248–49. *See also* Laws

Church leaders, criticizing. *See* Criticism

Church welfare program: purposes and objectives of, 108–9; is temporal and spiritual, 109–10; spiritual is preeminent over temporal in, 111; is gospel in action, 112; administration of, 112–14; provides temporary assistance, 114; and helping those who help themselves, 121;

contrasted with government assistance, 122–24; danger of dependence on, 124; changes in methods of administering, 124–25; storehouses, bishop's, 125–26, 126–27; welfare projects, 126; sent relief to Europe after World War II, 126–27; recent changes in, 127–31; new emphasis on prevention, 131; and government assistance, changes in, 132–33; challenges for, 134. See also Care for the poor

Clark, J. Reuben: on bishop's role in church welfare, 113

Comfort, function of revelation, 24

Commandments: keeping, to receive revelation, 34–35; promises for keeping, 98

Communication about things of God, 18

Condemnation, seeking of signs can lead to, 84–86

Confession, as part of repentance, 220–21

Confirmation, as function of revelation, 28

Consecration, 184

Conservatism in approach to welfare, 120

Contention: meaning of, 138; in classroom, using adversary technique, 139; in debate, Joseph Smith corrected, 139–40; George Q. Cannon comments on, 140–41; scriptural teachings against, 141–47; on manner of baptism in Book of Mormon times, 141–42; Savior forbade all manner of, 142; teachings on, in Sermon on the Mount, 142–44; teachings on, in Sermon on the Plain, 144; teachings of apostle Paul concerning, 144–47; James

warned against, 147; Book of Mormon prophets warned against, 147; warnings against, in early restored church, 147–48; warnings against, from modern writers, prophets, 148–51; avoiding, example of church leaders in, 150. See also Litigation

Conversion by signs, 87–88

Courts, church: in pioneer times, 164–65; role of, defined by various General Authorities, 166–68. See also Discipline, church; Litigation

Courts, civil, principles governing use of, 169. See also Church discipline; Litigation

Cowdery, Oliver, 23, 28, 65, 68

Crackerjack, lawsuit concerning, 156

Criticism: meanings of, 189–90; faultfinding and evil-speaking, 190–92; that is true, 192–95; Paul's counsel on, 193–94; and honesty, cautions on use of, 194; constructive, 194–95; of church leaders, 195–96; and murmuring, 196; examples of, from scriptures, 196–98; of government and corporate officials, 198; in theocracy, 200; and resolving differences with leaders, 200–206; and keeping differences private, 200–201; consequences of, 205–6; response of, by leaders, 205–6

Debate, "Great Medieval," 48

Deception of Satan, how to avoid, 68

"Declaration of belief" of Church, 155, 212

Defense of scriptural truths, 92

Disciplinary council. See Church discipline

Discipline, church. *See* Church
   discipline
Discussions, gospel, 57
Dishes, washing, author's
   experience in, 3–4
Disputations. *See* Contention;
   Litigation
Disputes, settlement of, 182
DNA, 93
Doolittle, Alfred P., 121

Ends justify means, belief that, vii,
   ix
Eternal life, objective of, viii
Evidence in church disciplinary
   councils, 242–43
Evil-speaking. *See* Criticism
Experts and expertise, 64
Eyring, Henry, 89

Faith: and revelation, learning by,
   19–22; requirement for
   receiving revelation, 33; and
   science, 61–64; to develop, is
   purpose of life, 91
Fast offering, 121
Faultfinding. *See* Criticism
Faust, James E., on church
   government, 10; on revelation,
   19–20
Fisher, Ben C., 53
Fisher, Roger, 179
Forgiveness, 170–75; letters on,
   173–74; commandment on, 175–
   76. *See also* Contention

General Handbook of Instructions,
   232
G.I. Bill, 117
Gifts, spiritual, 66
God: knowledge about, 18;
   learning about, through faith,
   19; wisdom of, 20; learning the
   things of, 55–56, 73
Goethe, 48

Good works, 35
Goodman, John, on U.S. welfare
   system, 105
Government: church, is not
   democratic, 10; efforts of, to
   care for the poor, 104–7; civil,
   welfare programs, 117–19;
   assistance, basic principles
   concerning, 132–33

Hafen, Bruce C., 91
Harris, Martin, 147–48
Havel, Vaclav, quotation from, 185–
   86
High council, role of, in
   disciplinary council, 234, 240
Hinckley, Gordon B.: on revelation,
   19; on writing church history,
   71; on church welfare program,
   128; on forgiveness, 172–73; on
   litigation, 178–79; on criticism,
   190, 191
Holy Ghost, 26
Homestead Act, 117
Humility as requirement for
   receiving revelation, 33–34
Hunter, Howard W.: on rejecting
   reality of miracles and signs, 99;
   on welfare booklet, 130

Impel to action, function of
   revelation, 30–32
Inform, function of revelation, 26
Inspiration, 29–30, 66
Intellect or reason, 50
Intellectual approach to religion,
   100
Intelligence and knowledge, 43
Intuition, 46
Ivins, Anthony W., on civil and
   church courts, 167–68

Jesus Christ: taught that disciple's
   ways should be different from
   world's, 9–11; and woman at

well, 13–14; miracles performed by, 78–81; miracles of, as signs to unbeliever, 80; teachings of, concerning contention, 141–44
Journals and symposia, 57–58
Justice and mercy, 193, 217–19, 225

Kimball, Spencer W.: on spirituality and prophets, 52; on seeking signs, 86; on helping the poor, 106–7, 112; on six principles of welfare program, 111–12; on changes in welfare administration, 125; on suffering of repenting sinner, 223
Kipling, Rudyard, poem by, 12
Knowledge: about God, 18; sacred, and reason, 18–19; and intelligence, 43; secular, 46–47, 58; through revelation, those who reject, 53; meaning of Joseph Smith's statement on, 72–73; when acquired by means of signs, 85. See also Learning; Reason; Revelation

Laws of God and of man, jurisdictions of, 209–14, 239. See also Church discipline; Litigation
Lawmakers who compromise, 10
Lawyer, British, who became "expert" on U.S. law, 64
"Lest We Forget," 12
Leader's Guide to Welfare, 131, 133–34
Leaders, criticism of. See Criticism
Learning: commandment to seek, 16; by reason and revelation, 17; by study and reason, 17–19; sacred, pursuit of, 58; the things of God, 73. See also Reason; Revelation
Lee, Harold B.: on revelation, 23–24; on teaching by the Spirit, 39;

on mysteries of God, 41–42; on knowledge, 45–46; on how to measure learning, 71; on changing methods in welfare, 128; on purpose of gospel, 216
Lewis, C. S., 122
Limitations, human, God is not subject to, 4
Lincoln, Abraham, 179
Litigation: letter from BYU student concerning, 153–54; two extreme positions on, 155–56; when to use courts for, 155–56, 169; attitude of no religious restraints on, 156; frivolous cases, 156; amount of, increases in, 157–58; costs of, 158; by Church leaders, 159–60; some instructions concerning, are temporary, 160; apostle Paul's counsel on, 161–62; methods of, in New Testament times, 162; in pioneer days, 164–65; statements of General Authorities on, 166–68; church's current position on, 169; principles governing use of courts for, 169–85; and forgiveness, 170–75; revelation given to early Saints on, 170–71; settle privately, if possible, 175–81; spiritual reasons for settling, 179–80; and revenge, 181; to protect others, 181–82; effects of, on those who are sued, 182–85; athlete who refused to sue, letter from, 180–81; responsibilities and rights, 185–88
Lord's ways: and man's ways, vii–ix, 2, 8; scriptures on, 2–3; are higher than man's ways, 3; and power, 11; in story of woman at well, 13–14; regarding reason and revelation, 72–74; in

developing faith, 91; regarding
signs and science, 97–100; of
caring for the poor, 107–108,
112; contrasted with
government welfare, 122–24;
regarding litigation, 184, 186;
regarding criticism, 198, 199,
207
Lucifer. *See* Satan

Man's ways. *See* Lord's ways
Matthews, Robert J., on secular vs.
spiritual truth, 61–62, 63
Maxwell, Neal A.: on the Lord's
ways, 3; on faith and
submissiveness, 58; on faith and
scriptural truth, 92
McConkie, Bruce R.: on faith and
revelation, 22; on agency and
inspiration, 29; on studying
scriptures, 35–36; on teaching
by the Spirit, 39–40; on proving
spiritual verities, 56; on avoiding
contention, 149, 151; on
litigation, 159, 168, 175
McConkie, Joseph F.: on religion
and science, 90; on evidences
and testimony, 92; on
repentance, 235
McKay, David O., on faultfinding
and murmuring, 196
McMullin, Keith B., 130–31, 134
Meekness, 9
Mercy and justice, 193, 217–19, 225
Millet, Robert L.: on mysteries of
God, 42–43; on evidences and
testimony, 92; on repentance,
235
Miracles: not used to prove
religious truth, 78; gospel not
dependent on, 94; quotation on
Mormon belief in, 99–100. *See
also* Signs
Mission president, leadership
meeting of, 1–2

Monson, Thomas S., on changes in
caring for poor, 128–29
Mortality, purpose of, vii–viii
My Fair Lady, 121
Mysteries of God, 41–43

Nelson, Russell M.: on caring for
the poor, 102; on contention,
148–49, 150–51; on truth, 193–
94
Nephi and Laban, 31
Nibley, Hugh: on reason vs.
revelation, 47–48; on merger of
religion and philosophy, 49–50;
on miracles, 86; on proving by
scientific methods, 93; on
extremes in religious things,
100

Olsen, Chasty, author's
grandmother, 31

Packer, Boyd K.: on reason and
revelation, 51; on inspiration,
66; on objective history, 71; on
litigation, 156–57, 179; on
forgiveness, 172
Page, Hiram, 68
Patriarch, experience of, with
forgiveness, 180
Paul, apostle, teaching of,
concerning contention, 144–47
Plural marriage, revelations on, 70
Popular acclaim, 9
Power, exercise of, 10–11
Prayer: answers to, 26; sometimes
there are no answers to, 36–38;
and choosing between equally
acceptable alternatives, 37; and
trivial matters, 37–38; when
unknown reasons affect choice,
38; to resolve problems with
church leaders, 204–5;
confession through, in
repenting, 220–21

Priesthood quorums and church welfare, 113

Proof in spiritual things, 97–98

Prophecy as function of revelation, 24

Prophets called from among unlettered, 52

Protecting others, motive for litigation, 181–82

Protestants who asked about religious experiences of Mormons, 96–97

Providing in the Lord's Way, A Leader's Guide to Welfare, 131–32

Pseudoreligions, 104

Punishment and church discipline, 222–23

Radio transmitter, analogy of, 65

Rationality, 46, 49

Ratzinger, Joseph Cardinal, on theology and science, 89–90

Read, Leonard E., 143

Reason: definition of, 16–17; must yield to revelation, 22; and revelation, methods of learning, 45–47; without revelation, to understand gospel, 51; is "god" of intellectuals, 53; and journals, symposia, etc., 57–58; is not coequal with revelation, 58–60; cannot be used to prove existence of God, 59–60; primacy of, in learning some subjects, 60–61; is not alternative to revelation, 65; and study, in finding truth, 65; and revelation, sequence of, 66; authenticates revelation, 67–70; limits on, 70–72; outranked by revelation, 71–72

Reasoning: powers of, 17; mortal, secondary to revelations, 21; likening, to oxygen and methane, 57

Reconciliation in relationships, 143

Rees-Mogg, William, 120

Relief Society, role of, in church welfare, 113–14

Religion: and rational science, 50; Mortimer J. Adler's definition of, 61; and scientific methods, 89; and superstition, 100

Repentance, 35; and church discipline, 219–20, 240–41; and confession, 220; through prayer, 220–21; and restitution, 221; and suffering, 221–23; and atonement, 222–24; and justice and mercy, 225; results in life changes, 225–26. *See also* Church discipline

Responsibilities and rights, 185–86

Restitution as part of repentance, 221

Restraint, function of revelation, 26–28

Revelation: definition of, 16–17; and faith, learning by, 19–22; warnings of, in learning of God, 21; trusting in, 21; forms and functions of, 22–32; and inspiration, 23; is available to all, 23–24; and testimony, 24; and prophecy, 24; comforts, 24–25; uplifts, 25–26; informs, 26; and restraint, 26–28; confirms, 28–30; impels to action, 30–32; requirements for receiving, 33–36; when not received, 36–38; fruits of, 38–41; and mysteries of God, 41–43; and reason, methods of learning, 45–47; vs. reason, history of, 47–51; those who reject, 54; and reason, relationships between, 58; and reason, correspondence concerning, 59–60; primacy of, in learning some subjects, 60–61; and learning, not mutually exclusive, 64; in acquiring sacred knowledge, 64–65; and reason, sequence of, 66–67; is authenticated by reason, 67–70; true, edifies recipient, 67–68; true, is consistent with position of recipient, 68–69; for church, comes through prophets, 68–69; who may receive, 69; true, is consistent with gospel principles, 69–70; checking authenticity of, 70; outranks reason, 71–72; learning by, 73; comes by the Holy Spirit, 74; and church disciplinary councils, 240

Revenge: revelation on, 171; not proper motive for litigation, 181

Richards, George F., 199

Richards, Stephen L, 178

Rigdon, Sidney, 26, 74

Rights and responsibilities, 185–86

Rockne, Knute, 115

Romney, Marion G.: on duty to help the poor, 110, 120–21; on importance of self-reliance, 118–19; on confession of sins, 221

Saint Augustine, 50

Salvation, plan of, vii–ix

Sandberg, Carl, 115

Satan: premortal plan of, vii–ix; deceptions of, 68; would like to corrupt self-reliance, 122

Scholars who proclaim from own learning, 55

Science: and faith, 60–64; and signs, 77; evidences of, and faith, 88–93; methods of, 88–89; cannot disprove religious truth, 91, 92; modern discoveries in, 92–93;

Screwtape Letters, 122

Scripture reading, requirement for receiving revelation, 35–36

Self-reliance: teachings on, 115–20;

is subject to confusion, 122; Satan would like to corrupt, 122

Self-interests vs. others' interests, 184

Semester system, 31–32

Sequential relationship of reason and revelation, 64–66

Shepherd protecting flock, analogy of, 227

Signs: definitions of, 77n; in Bible, 78–82; in restored church, 82–83; in Book of Mormon, 83–84; impose burdens, 84–86; seeking of, can lead to condemnation, 84; not evidences of truth, 86; conversion by, 87–88; role of, 94–97; to strengthen faith, 94; sharing of, 95–97. See also Miracles

Smith, George Albert, on criticism, 191

Smith, Joseph, 2, 4, 10, 22, 26, 34, 68, 70; example of, in studying Bible, 18; was called by revelation, 21; was comforted through revelation, 24–25; was appointed to receive revelation for Church, 68–69; on gaining knowledge, 72–73; receives revelation on three degrees of glory, 74; on personal manifestations, 96; corrected elders debating sacred subject, 139–40

Smith, Joseph F.: revelation of, 34; on charity and self-reliance, 116–17; on church courts, 166, 240; on settling differences with others, 177–78; on evidence in court proceedings, 236–37, 242; on apostasy, 247

Snow, Lorenzo: on revelation, 23; on "imperfections" in Joseph Smith, 202

Social security, 117–18

Solzhenitsyn, Aleksandr, 49, 184–85

Speech invitation, author nearly declines, 30

Spiritual gifts, 66, 95

Stake center, location of, author restrained on, 27

Stake president, 29–30, 232, 233–34

Storehouses, bishop's, 125–26, 127, 129

Study and reason, learning by, 17–19

Suffering as part of repentance, 221–23

Supernatural excluded by rationality, 49

Superstition is servant of signs, 100

Symposia, dangers in, 57–58

Talmage, James E.: on revelation, 23; on litigation, 159; on church courts, 167; on transgression of a member, 204

Tanner, Obert C., 50–51

Taxes to support government programs, 133

Taylor, John, 39; on settling differences among Saints, 165–66; on settling controversies, 177; on sustaining a leader, 203–4; on bishops and church discipline, 228–29

Teachers who do not follow assigned topic, 8

Teaching: by the Spirit, 39–40; using adversary techniques in, 139

Temples not built "after manner of world," 10

Testimony, 24

Time, God's, is different from man's, 4

Tithing, 98

Truth and criticism, 192–95

Truths, scriptural, defense of, 92

Uplift, function of revelation, 25–26

Vineyard, parable of, 5

Visions, 26

Ways, Lord's, vs. man's ways. See Lord's ways

Weaver, Richard M., 48

Welfare program, church. See Care for the poor; Church welfare program

Welfare projects, 126, 127, 129

Well, woman at, 13–14

Whitmer, David, 21

Woodruff, Wilford, 31, 70

Woodson, Robert L., on government welfare, 105, 106

Work: and self-reliance, 116–20; relationship of, to civil government, 117–18; and receiving public assistance, 119–20

World: customs of, 4; ways of, and accepting church callings, 5–6; scholars who seek acclaim of, 55. See also Lord's ways

Worldly possessions, 10

Wright, H. Curtis, 50

Young, Brigham, 33, 46, 70, 108; on self-reliance, 116; criticisms of lawyers by, 163; denounced use of civil courts, 163–64; on settling disputes, 176–77; on resolving differences with Joseph Smith, 202

Zion, redemption of, parable concerning, 5